D1566874

Highpockets

The Man, The Marine, The Legend

An Autobiography
Of
Major General Raymond Murray

Arranged, Researched
and
Written by

Zona Gayle Murray

Highpockets

Published/Printed by Direct2Press.com in the USA

First Edition

ISBN 978-0-578-03549-9

DEDICATION

To the Murray Family
&
the Band of Brothers,

Heroes....Everyone

Contents:

Reflections:

Lt. Gen., Victor (Brute) Krulak

I first met Ray in San Diego when he was assigned to the 6th Marine Regiment Naval Academy;   rooming with another single Marine who had been his classmate at Texas A&M.

He was married in 1937 and nine days later sailed for duty in China. He was first in Shanghai, then later was assigned to Peiping. Evelyn joined him a year later and they started their family. They returned to San Diego in 1940, and was there a short time before his orders were to Iceland.

I had been following his career and was not surprised when he was given a command in the Pacific. His performance there was outstanding. While he was commanding a combat service group in Hawaii, he was promoted to Lieutenant Colonel.

In 1949 the 5th Marines were assigned to me and Ray became my executive officer. At the time the 5th was under strength, had old equipment, no combat readiness; it made it necessary for us to train hard; this we did in the hills of Southern California. We didn't see our families for days at a time. Our job was to get the job done and have combat ready Marines. He was a very good executive, and in the midst of the training, war broke out in Korea. Part of the regiment was put aboard ship to Korea and assigned to Ray.

The wives were well acquainted, always willing to help each other, and took turns watching each others children. Evelyn was a charming, well adjusted woman, with the average amount of daily frustrations. She was very capable, a strong personality, and when Ray left for Korea, managed the home, the children and her prayers.

He did the impossible in Korea; with military strategy that was to go down in history. Fighting under impossible conditions, weather that dropped to 50 degrees below zero, surrounded and outnumbered at times to 200 to one. He broke through, he brought out his men, as he said, " There was no other way" fight or nothing, leading his regiment with Bob Taplett, they made their way out.

I knew he would do a fine job. I had forecasted he would be a success, and would continue to be one.

Foreword:

"How often, (but not often enough) we gather in hall and chamber, in chapel, mosque and synagogue, near the ocean, or by Flanders Field, to remember once more with the best words we can summon, terrible yet wonderful truth.

It is this: We stand where we stand because of military might. We are where we are because hundreds of thousands of Americans, millions, said yes when called to the colors over painful centuries of this nation's birth.

We live where we live because of the military, a cold word, because our fathers, brothers, sons and uncles said, "Sure, give me a gun and dress me up right, this is worth fighting for"

Women, too, not just in these public years but early on, put a lie to the notion that there existed a weaker sex, and went to war. All....all.... Fought private terrors and found certain joy, and died as the facts would have it.

Every man and woman created, protected and preserved the impudent, the unlikely, the dear place they knew as home, the United States of America. As often as we gather, it is never often enough. Revere them, honor them, call them grand, proclaim them heroic. All true. But most important, for this assembly and all others in glade and glen from Atlantic to Pacific: Remember them.

The above was written for Major General Raymond Murray, a legendary Marine, a man revered long after he left the Corps (if a Marine ever Leaves) and a stellar friend who died on Veterans Day 2004.

His history is well known and has been recorded many times; it will be sung for centuries if the universe has any order at all. But keep this much in mind: Murray was the hero of the Chosin Reservoir in Korea, where he saved thousands of Marines' lives by leading a fearful, bloody trek to safety.

He was an Oceanside man for many years, was Ray Murray,

one of the great tough guys of U.S. military history. Who became gentle as a wink"

(Arthur's note: This was written by John Van Doorn an Ernie Pyle award winner, as a war co-respondent, and friend of Major General Raymond Murray).

Authors notes:

What follows is the life of an incredible man. His role as a father, husband, active member in his community, and thirty three years in the Marine Corps.

How does one write about another person and capture the true nature of his character? Maybe, as we go through his life, we will then have an understanding of the substance of this man.. We wonder what makes a leader a hero. They seem to stand head and shoulders, no matter the physical height, above everyone else. When they walk in a room, there is a feeling this person is special.

His military records are in history books, available to everyone. But what about the humility, compassion, and the responsibility of caring for his fellow man? When we see this, along with super intelligence and the ability to overcome impossible odds, we have greatness, my friends.

Rather than being a story of certain events, it covers a full life. To capture this, I've gathered others recollections, used existing letters, and stressed some events to bring feeling as well as pointing out the tragedies of war. Conversations as I remember them, not word-for-word, but compiled to support a non-fiction documentary. I pray I've told them in a manner with respect for the feelings of all concerned.

A quiet man, but rest assured it was with quiet strength. He had an aversion to limelight, was always approachable. A combat no nonsense leader, there was never any doubt who was in command. I have been asked by the survivors of the Chosin Reservoir to: "Tell it as it was" The heavy fighting of the "Break Out" was from Yudam-ni at the Chosin to Hagaru-ri. After they reached Hagaru-ri, they knew they had a chance for survival. Those 79 hours, covering fourteen miles in sub-zero temperature, our two Regiments were half strength, surrounded by 120,000 sometimes 300,000 Chinese, they brought out their wounded; with their Colonel in the rear guard not leaving until everyone of his men were on their way. It took someone who had been in tough situations before, using every bit of knowledge he had to bring his men through this. They often said " although his six foot three presence was impressive, it was the substance of the man that made him the hero they referred to as "Highpockets"

This work of non-fiction is not an exact account, as I'm certain it will be told by other people in many different ways.

It is an overview of three wars, not to be considered a history, but from memory and a viewpoint of a commander. We will leave the history to the historians, who have covered our military and have researched every battle, and every war.

God Bless Them.   Zona Murray.

Command Levels of Marines:

Fire Team: Four enlisted men led by a Corporal.
Squad: A dozen enlisted men led by a Sergeant.
Platoon: About three dozen men led by a Lieutenant.
Company: Two hundred fifty men led by a Captain.
Battalion: A thousand men led by a lieutenant Colonel.
Regiment: About three thousand men led by a Colonel.
Brigade: Two or more regiments led by a Brigadier General.
Division: Twenty thousand men led by a Major General.

Regimental and battalion commanders have staff sections.
To assist their units, the have:
                    Medical: Doctors and Corpsmen.
                    Logistics
                    Communications

Marine Divisions: Are divided into three rifle units, with:
                    Artillery, combat support, tanks, medical,
                    amphibious tractors.

The 5th, about which, we are writing had three rifle battalions.
1st, 2nd and 3rd.

Acknowledgements:

It takes enormous support from many people, and the kindness of sharing their recollections, to make a book of this type possible.

To Name a few:

First: The Chosin Few survivors of the Reservoir. Each remembering something new each month we meet for dinner.

Excerpts from the oral interview with the Marine Museum. Jack Buck, Brig. Gen. Craig's Aide in Korea, now with the Marine Museum, San Diego.

Lt. Gen. Victor (Brute) Krulak, who contributed "Reflections"

Navy Doctors, courtesy of Jan Herman, and the Department of Navy, Bureau of Medicine and Surgery. Washington, D.C.

G.G. Downing 111, Parris Island, who gave permission to use excerpts from his fathers research of Quarters One and history of the first military forte on American soil.

John Van Doorn, who wrote the foreword.

France Conoley, a long time friend, who knew both Eve and Ray.

Elizabeth Osborne, editing and getting pictures ready for the book.

Mrs. Ronald (Alice) Rankin, from Coeur D Alene, Idaho, who sent the work being done on a Veterans Memorial Plaza, and the Congressional Record.

Helen McClure, the General's sister, and Mrs. Donald Murray, his brother's wife, who gave permission to print letters they had saved.

For reading the rough draft and still gave me the courage to carry on, when many times I considered, just putting it aside: My patient editor, Janet Wellington.

Maj. Gen and Mrs. James McMonagle

Terry and Bonnie Newman

Lt. Gen.Victor Krulak

Patricia and Tom Del Ruth

Father Michel Gagnon

Tom Morrow

Litzi and Jack Buck

Jo and Frank Whitton

The Soroptimist International of Oceanside/Carlsbad.

Gloria Lane, of the Women's International Center in San Diego.

My special thanks to Sylvia and John Van Doorn (I often thought if I could write as he does this would have been much easier.)

The gentle persuasion of David Straus and Laura and Bill Gall.

Technical problems: Solved by a very patient, retired military engineer, Larry Hall.

I thank each and every one, without their help and encouragement, this book would not have been possible.

Chapter One

Early Years

There are reasons it is fitting. In my stocking feet, I stand six feet three inches; most of the time erect, and at one hundred and eighty five pounds, have been referred to as raw boned. My pockets are somewhere near the chest level of most of the troops in my command.

Never heard the name mentioned to my face, but I've heard undertones and several times caught a muffled voice referring to me as Highpockets; believe it was tacked on in Iceland, coming from the radio squad. One of the men was working hard at becoming a writer and had a way of identifying each Marine with a name suitable to his physical appearance or his mannerisms. Hearing some of the descriptions, I began to think, I might be one of the lucky ones. Highpockets faired better than most, so I decided to stay cool and pretend not to hear it. If pet names bonded the men as brothers, so be it. There would be tough times ahead.

As I write of my life and three wars, more space will be given to the so-called "Forgotten War." A war in Korea: by far the most violent, fought under the most deplorable conditions imaginable, with greater loss in fewer days than any war in history. To have this war forgotten is to dishonor the brave men who fought and died there. So long as there are survivors, each will have a story to tell. As the pages unfold, you will hear mine. The high command must be careful and not ignore reliable sources of intelligence, careful it not result in a tragic loss of men, officers and equipment.

We were in a trap at the Chosin Reservoir, outnumbered, sometimes a hundred to one; the other enemy was the temperature, at times dropping to fifty below zero. The only way out was to rely on the unbreakable spirit of the Marines. They would not be defeated; they would not leave their wounded behind, or their dead; and they vowed some would make it out and live to tell their story.

I stand on their shoulders, any recognition I've received is owed totally to them. It was a privilege to lead them and I thank God for the honor. They were to accomplish the impossible and perform feats that made history; it is about them this story must be told.

There is always a possibility of war, and war is beyond the

comprehension of anyone who hasn't been there. Many stories have been told, everyone has his or her own. This will be mine, from a command position, covering areas and thoughts related to me, from the troops, sometimes positive and sometimes with justifiable anger. We are hoping our story will tell you what war does to a man. There seems to be scant coverage of what a commander personally feels when his troops are in the midst of a battle. I can assure you he is thinking of his men, how to overcome impossible battle conditions, the objectives to be taken, and knowing at times, you, yourself, may not make it. Making certain you have a qualified person, trained ready to take over. How human you feel at the loss of any man and making certain your wounded know you will do everything to take them with you, or you wont go. To find a moment to think about home and time to write.

The Marine Corps has been a large part of my life. I can't imagine a career in any other field. I spent thirty three years in this service, many as a field commander and soon became aware the strength is based in men working as a team, using weapons and machines, rather than weapons and machines using Marines. The fighting men, the riflemen are all parts of the battle. Today the private must have the initiative we required of the non-commissioned officers in the past. We are absolutely convinced battles are won by human brains, muscles and guts. A Marine must be able to cut the mustard in whatever situation he finds himself.

Some Marines are so young, sent to us from boot camp, haven't a full beard, but already the esprit de corps is present. When put into a do or die position, with an enemy of whom they have no quarrel, praying the cause and reasons for being there are worth dying for . The loyalty and bonding we observe as we see these young recruits shaping into Marines, with no fear for themselves, only fear they might suffer the agony of losing a buddy. These are the Marines I'm writing about who will accomplish feats that will make history.

The Marine Corps has been the same since 1776. To perform duties as the President directs. The Amphibious Task Force, of which I was part, finds its base in the sea, a vast area where no one pays rent, no over flight rights are required and no one's permission is necessary to operate. We select our area of operation. This is effectively and economically from its sea base. We lose ourselves in the vastness of the ocean, and make our attacks initially from the ships; our own aircraft may operate from carriers along with Navy squadrons, we do not require large airfields for these attacks.

Battles must be recalled from memory, time is limited on the front lines for note taking, but acts of bravery, almost beyond what a mind can grasp, stays in our memory forever, therefore will be seen from a different perspective. A personalized story is the experience of the person writing it.

2

I warn you, there isn't anything pretty about war. This is my story and no one can be absolutely accurate in recall, but, fortunately I am gifted with a good memory, a few notes, a scrapbook of pictures and a good wife I trust will use these to put into print.

It is also an autobiography so it will cover other years of my life. I managed a family life compatible with my service. I've loved been loved, fathered children, enjoyed years of retirement, and finally scored my age in golf. Personal events in my life are mine. I will write them as I prefer.

I'm getting ahead of my story. Didn't reach this height overnight and my life didn't begin when they started calling me Highpockets. I'm carrying the battle scars from three wars, and prodding from several sources to write something about it. This will start where life always starts. At the beginning.

We have experiences at different times in our lives, many stay indelible in our memories; perhaps not in detail, and may be altered to fit the time and place. It may be also altered to protect the privacy of individuals who are no longer with us. My family I'm certain, will each tell their story in their own way. I've tried to capture the essence of our lives and avoided details to protect the privacy of the people I love.

Friends and family describe us differently; the best thing we can do in self defense is to leave a few of our own words. I will attempt this but expect there will be a time when my memory will pause for a rest, so this will be told as events occur to me and not in any correct order.

I was born in Los Angeles, California. I was the first child of Alice and Tom Murray; the year was 1913, my birthday January 30. Los Angeles still had many orange groves and small farms, with neighborhood homes typically built before the turn of the century. In 1913, these homes were considered fairly new. Some were made of wood with long front porches and some made of stucco. Usually they had two bedrooms and, if uptown, an inside bath (further out of town a means was provided outside). The bath itself was a galvanized tub set up with warm water, most often in the kitchen. The style of the home was referred to as a bungalow, with two narrow cement strips to one side that served as a driveway to a one-car garage. It took a good driver to get down that narrow passage safely to the garage. I can't vouch for the driver's skill because in 1913, I wasn't too observant.

I can tell you about the wood frame homes with the long front porches, and their cement floors with railings on three sides, perfect for learning how to skate. If we were clumsy or if we were just learning and fell, we could grab one of the railings to keep our injuries to a minimum. I can also tell you about the Red Car It was a streetcar that went the entire length of Los Angeles. If a family lived within the areas it served, you could go all the way to the beach, using your head by asking for a transfer, and even taking side trips, all for a nickel or ten cents. We could play baseball in the

Tom Murray

Alice Murray

Six months old

At two years

quiet streets, walk to school, help the orange grove farmers pick their fruit for a small wage or some free oranges. No one locked their doors and there always was a plate of fresh baked cookies on the dining room table, for me, my siblings, or any straggler who happened to follow us home.

My father, Tom, was an administrator with the Boy Scouts. We had a vagabond life, moving every two years. During this time, the family grew. My brothers Don and Jack were born and three sisters were to arrive later: Helen, Marion, and Margie. My parents raised five of the children; we lost one, our three-year-old Margie, in an automobile accident. My mother was driving and I don't think she ever recovered from the loss.

We moved to Phoenix in 1920, Galveston, Texas in 1921, and then back to Redondo Beach. It seemed we were always moving, as the next assignment was Galveston, Texas in 1927. We went by train, the best way of travel then, and at every stopover, there would be rallies with any Boy Scout group we could get together. There would be singing, campfires, popcorn- always what appealed to anyone interested in scouting.

From Galveston, it was back to Alhambra for my first two years of high school, then to Harlingen, Texas. The family settled long enough for me to graduate from Harlingen High School. The school was everything a student could ask for. At least it was for me. I had the lead in the senior play, scored three touchdowns in three minutes, and was enough of a football hero to have one of the prettiest girls in school as my girlfriend. Her name was Margie. The high school yearbook has a way of socking it to you, their way of keeping one humble. I don't know how, but they tied "Romeo" to my lead in Pirates of Penzanze. Then after that glowing compliment, a prediction stated that if I ever made it in life, I would have to play baseball. So much for being a football hero.

I graduated from Harlingen in 1930, and then went to work in a citrus nursery the summer between high school and college. My job was to use insecticides throughout a rather large nursery to exterminate ants and scale which attacked the young trees; other jobs around the nursery filled out my day. My employer was a graduate of Texas A&M College and encouraged me to continue my education. He also stressed that being a state college the tuition was free. Being an honor student and somewhat good at football, this opened an opportunity for college. That fall I was enrolled as a student. Playing football as a freshman didn't often happen, and the principle physical hazing was a paddling on the behind with a shaved off baseball bat. It was a matter of pride, they told us, to go home for Christmas with your behind black and blue, just to show how tough you were. (We didn't think this proved anything, weren't we freshmen and doing as well as some of the upper classmen?) I lettered three years in football and also worked coaching football, played basketball and was part of the squad, but I didn't letter.

The college had good programs. Upper classmen who were good in a subject were assigned by the company commander to lower classmen who weren't getting good grades. It was a bit of military training and a way of teaching you to be responsible for how well the people under you did. Haven't checked if they are still doing it, but it would be good training today.

I took a liberal arts course, majoring in English Literature with a minor in History and Education. My intent was to eventually become a school superintendent. I took the standard ROTC courses that included History, Tactics, Weapons Instruction, and Close Order Drill. During my second year, the family moved back to Norco, California. It was not long after that, my father wrote that he wanted me to come home, work in a gas station, and help support the family. I answered his letter by saying I would be more help to the family if I stayed in school. Of course, there was no help from home. Those were tough financial years and there were no scholarships at Texas A&M, but the college had two ROTC programs, a Basic and an Advanced. They helped the advanced student by finding part-time work, and if on the football team and our grades were up, additional jobs to help. This was still the Depression, money was short and sometimes even the basic needs were not met. There was a time when money was so short I was without socks. One of the teachers noticed and gave me three pair. I washed and darned them (my mother had taught me how to take care of my clothes). Surprising how long clothes will last with good care. I needed money and I wanted to stay in school, so the program they worked out for me: assisting the coach, coaching football and finding odd jobs put me through to graduation. A summer camp, normally between junior and senior years, was mandatory. I attended camp at an Army installation near San Antonio. My recollection is that the camp lasted a couple of weeks and the instruction included live firing of small arms and small unit tactics. All of my instructors were either Army officers or enlisted men. All I believe were WWI veterans. It was understood that the advanced ROTC honor students would be offered a commission in the Army. However, we were between wars and the Depression was still not over, so all the commissions were used. All that was open were reserve commissions.

About a month before I graduated from college, the senior military officer at the school, an Army Colonel, called me into his office and asked me how I would like to be a Marine Officer. I replied, "I don't know. What is a Marine?" He explained that it was a small, but elite military organization that was, in 1935, expanding its officer corps, and was commissioning one hundred ROTC graduates from 52 colleges throughout the United States. Texas A&M was to provide the names of three principles and three alternates, and he was offering me the opportunity to apply for one of the principle appointments. The requirement to be selected was to be an honor graduate of

7

the school and to pass a physical examination.

When I graduated, I was given a reserve commission in the Army, my only choice, however, as I explained. Because I'd been offered the opportunity to apply for a commission in the Marine Corps, I took the physical examination. It was about a month after I graduated that I was notified I had passed the physical examination, and was accepted into the Marine Corps. I then resigned my reserve commission in the Army.

I decided to accept the Marine Corps offer because I felt that war in Europe was probably inevitable, considering the way Hitler was acting, and if war was starting in Europe, we would undoubtedly get into it too, and I might as well be as well trained as possible when it happened. Also, helping me in that decision was the financial aspect. My best prospect for a job upon graduation was as a teacher-coach in some high school at perhaps $90.00 per month, for nine months of the year, whereas the Marine Corps would pay $125.00 per month for twelve months. I planned to leave the service as soon as the war was over, or as soon as it appeared there would be no war, and to resume my aim at becoming a school administrator. Needless to say, I never looked back after I found out what the Marine Corps was all about. The commission I received was as a 2nd Lieutenant, USMC.

Three of the principles - of which I was one; the other two were Bruno Hockmuth and Joe McHaney -were given commission and we were ordered to the Navy Yard, Philadelphia, to attend the Marine Corps Basic School, a nine-month course where all newly commissioned Marine Lieutenants had to attend. At the time I was commissioned, all the 2nd Lieutenants were granted their commissions for a two-year probationary period before the commission became permanent. During that time, we were prohibited from getting married.

Off to Philadelphia for Basic School. We felt so proud of ourselves, something to behold out in the open world, coming from four years in an all-male college without any money to spend; now we had more money than we had ever had in our lives. We studied, but we also enjoyed ourselves. Our only problem was that all the women looked good. Years later, we thanked the Marines for making the rule that officers could not get married for two years. We could have made some bad choices.

When training finished, our orders were to report to San Diego. In San Diego, I reported to the 1st Battalion 6th Marines, ready to give my best and work hard at being a good officer. Instead, my football experience seemed to interest the commander more than my desire to be a good officer. So I played football. We had a good team and made quite a showing for the Marines.

Again, we dated and since we were officers, we were a little over self confident, in the nicest of all uniforms in the military, and we felt this

High School

Last look at Kyle
Stadium where I
playod football.
Texas A&M

On our way to San Diego to report for duty.

had to give us an edge. but not always. I tried for four weeks to get a date with this young lady before she finally consented to go to a party with me. We had a few drinks and since I was new at it, didn't realize how fast liquor could hit me. I managed to drive, but the woozier I got the slower I drove, hugging the curb at five miles per hour. When I finally got the young lady home, being a gentleman, I got out of the car to help her. I fell flat on the sidewalk, barely missing taking her with me. You guessed it, she had had it with me; can't remember her name, and I'm certain she has forgotten mine. A rough way to learn a lesson but it was one I never forgot.

San Diego is a beautiful city, with much to do. We could go dancing (the big band era was in full swing), a beautiful bay for sailing, and good movies. There was plenty to do. I took my time dating as I hadn't recovered from my encounter with the sidewalk. But I was young, and soon my roommate came in and announced he had met two nice girls and it would be nice if we could double date. He remembered their names as being France and Evelyn. I like the name France so said I would date her and he could date Evelyn. As it happened, Tex liked France, and I knew the minute I saw Evelyn Roseman, she was the girl I was going to marry. She was the daughter of a retired naval officer and San Diego had been their home for some time.

I called her Eve. It seemed appropriate. She was a tiny girl, about five foot one, pretty, and certainly aware of the pitfalls of military life. She could do almost anything, a very capable girl who could entertain, knit, sew, an excellent cook, and best of all, a lot of fun. How could I be so lucky? We dated and waited for the curfew on marriage to expire. Finally, on 20 August 1937, we were married. We had just nine days, nine days, as my orders came to leave for China.

During the nine days we were together twenty- four hours a day, making the most of every minute, building memories we would hold dear until we would be together again. Eve tried to be brave, but at times I would catch her fighting back tears. Then a smile would break through because she wanted this time together to be a happy time, but I'm sure she too caught me during many of my sad moments. Being brought up as a Navy daughter, seeing her father leave so many times, she mentioned she should have been conditioned. This time it was different, this was her husband leaving. She assured me she would write every day and live with her mother until we knew what our next orders would be.

I would be assigned to an anti-aircraft unit, to report and sail on a cruiser from San Diego.

Departure day, as most days are in San Diego, was bright and beautiful. The only visible moisture was when we would catch each other unaware and tears were rolling down our cheeks. We had arrived early; we didn't want any everyday distractions, just wanted to be with each other for every precious moment we had.

Time to leave. Eve walked me to the gangplank, took off her scarf and pointed to a spot on the deck where she wanted me to stand. She said she would be waving her scarf until I was out of sight. Ten minutes out to sea, the horizon appeared much too quickly, the scarf Eve was waving was no longer visible. Now with the 2d Marine Brigade, I was on my way to China.

CHINA; 1937-1940

I was assigned to a unit and sailed on the cruiser Marblehead from San Diego. It took us three weeks, with one stop-over in Honolulu, to reach Shanghai.

As a young officer I was particularly thrilled being assigned duty in China. It was still a very mysterious place, where not too many Americans had been. I'd always heard about the inscrutable Chinese and now was my chance to see and get to know these interesting people: In 1937, the Japanese invaded China and they captured a good portion of north China, including Peiping, and they also landed in the vicinity of Shanghai, but were met with opposition by the Chinese Army.

My unit was sent to Shanghai to join with other military organizations to protect American and foreigners living in the settlement. In 1937, Shanghai and a few other cities in China contained a large area of the city totally controlled by foreign governments. The Chinese had no rights in any of these areas. After the Opium War between England and China, China was forced to grant territorial rights to a number of European countries and America. This meant these countries had total control of specified areas in a number of Chinese cities, among which were Shanghai and Peiping. In Shanghai, for example, the British administered the International Settlement, which was most of the rest of the city. The Chinese had no rights in either of these areas.

Shanghai, when I arrived, was overrun with refugees from surrounding areas. There were thousands of people from the countryside living in the streets of the city, trying to escape from the war. The city administration had set up rice delivery points at several spots throughout the area to feed this great number of refugees. The refugees brought cholera with them. We would see bodies wrapped in mats along the streets each day waiting to be picked up by trucks. It was a problem beyond resolution, even though everything possible was being done to try to help.

At this time, September of 1937, as I recall, the Provisional Marine Brigade, located at the Marine Corps Base, San Diego, was ordered to Shanghai to help protect the International Settlement from attack by the

Japanese. We could not have held off the Chinese if they had decided they really wanted to take the city, but we were sort of a trigger. If they attacked us it meant war with the United States.

We were billeted in a partially finished building on Bubbling Well Road. Our living conditions weren't the greatest but neither were they bad. We had the run of the city, and when we weren't on duty, we would go to one of the several night clubs, conveniently open all night.

For the whole four months I was in Shanghai, the war was going on just outside the limits of the International Settlement, and a group of us used to, when we were off duty, go to the top of a four-story flour mill on the bank of the Soochow Creek, which formed a boundary between the settlement and the Chinese part of the city. We would watch the war going on across the creek. Soochow Creek was about seventy yards wide, so you can see how close we were to the fighting. While we were watching from this position, settled comfortably on the roof, with a beer and a bowl of peanuts, we would take sides from this lofty position and bring our own strategies on how each side could better fight their battles.

This duty was known as temporary duty. In other words, as soon as the emergency was over, the unit would return to San Diego. However, in January 1938, I was given permanent change of station orders to report to the American Embassy in Peiping for duty with the permanent Embassy Guard, a Guard five hundred strong. Since I had been married only nine days when I sailed to Shanghai, I naturally was upset to receive these orders. Dependents were being sent home from Peiping when the Japanese invasion started, so here I was at a new permanent duty station without my bride and no way of knowing when I would next see her.

Initially I lived with seven other officers in an apartment over the Peiping Post Office. We lived two to a room and each had a Number One boy who took care of our clothes and saw to it we had a bottle of beer and a bowl of peanuts waiting for us when we came home from work. As I recall, we had one cook for the entire group, who cooked some great meals.

The Guard was stationed in Peiping to protect the American Embassy and the Americans living in the area. The Embassy and our living quarters were located in an area known as the Legation Quarter, which was a walled section of the city. Peiping, in those days, had a high thick wall around the city. Within the city, was a walled Forbidden City, where the former Emperors of China lived, and several walled sections divided the city into several other distinct parts. Great gates at various spots along the walls allowed traffic to move from one part of the city to the other. I understand all these walls have been torn down. This is a shame because they gave the city so much of its character.

21 August:
Finally one day, after our first anniversary, my bride arrived in

13

Tientsin, where I had gone to meet her. We boarded the train and returned to Peiping where I had rented a house in the Russian Embassy compound. Practically all the personnel from the various Embassies, including our own, had moved with the Chinese government from Peiping to Hankow, to Nanking and finally to Chungking. We were still friendly with Russia and this was a nice house available in the compound.

Life in Peiping, in those days was like a fairy tale. It was before WWII and colonialism still existed. Peiping, unlike Shanghai, was normally administered by the Chinese, except for the Legation Quarter which was administered by the British; however, because of the extraterritorial rights; foreigners were not beholden to Chinese law. Though the Japanese had invaded north China and taken control of the city before I arrived there, foreigners were still treated the same way they had been treated before.

We rented our home on the Embassy ground for twenty-five dollars a month. We had a Number One boy, who ran the household, a coolie who helped the Number One boy, a cook, a coolie, who helped the cook, a wash amah who did the washing, and a private rickshaw boy, with a brand new rickshaw for Eve. All this cost me thirty dollars a month. Later, when Bill was born, we had a baby amah and another five dollars a month was added. To save face, a baby amah was a must; it was definitely a loss of face if we didn't. The only problem, the baby amah was in complete charge. She not only breast fed the baby, (better to immunize the child against health problems in the area) but was so much in charge it was difficult to squeeze in any time to bond with the baby. We decided if this were the custom, even though we would be leaving soon, we needed to go along. This gave Eve time to shop, and so long as she stayed in the compound, time to enjoy the culture and, outings with her friends. They had formed a bridge group, a book club, and with social events shared with husbands, it made an interesting life.

Our life was pleasant, a little close at times, trying to fit a staff of six in our small quarters. We had arrived without too many household effects and it was to our credit to have a Number One boy, who was able to borrow from all the other Number One boys, anything we needed for parties. It wasn't unusual to see some of our best dishes or best linens at a party in someone else's home.

Our workday was from 7:30 in the morning until 3:30 in the afternoon. When I came home from work we would usually go to the Peiping Club where I would play tennis for an hour or so, and then come home and take a nap. We would have dinner around 8:30 and, if invited to someone's home, dress for dinner. I would wear a tuxedo and Eve would wear an evening dress. If anyone decided to have a picnic, it was simple; we just told Number One boy how many we were having and where it was to be. He and the other Number One boys had it all set up when we arrived. What a great way to live.

Eve in China

Our home in the Russian Compound

While I was there I learned to speak Chinese and I would go to the various shops and bargain with the proprietor over something he had that I wanted. I don't think they really wanted anyone to pay full price, the fun was in the bartering. Eve and I were able to bring home some beautiful Chinese pieces I've given our children to enjoy.

While we were in Peiping we were able to go to the Great Wall and it was quite a sight, unbelievable what they were able to do in building a wall over mountainous terrain. Their desire for peace and their way of keeping invaders out was touching.

In addition to American Embassy Guards, there were British Embassy Guards, Italian and French Embassy Guards, and Japanese Embassy Guards. All Guard units were about the same size, and with the same mission. After the war started in Europe, the commander of the American Guard, who was the senior officer of all the guard units, arranged for the men of different guard units, who had countries fighting in Europe, to go on liberty on odd nights, so there wouldn't be any fighting among them. It was almost like a dream, for despite the fact the British, French, Italian and Japanese all lived within the walls of the Legation Quarters, we never had a serious incident.

The United States had been in Shanghai and Peiping for many years as part of a foreign contingent. Our unit went to Shanghai in 1937 on the initiative of the United States. Chaing Kai-shek had nothing to do with it. We did not fight during the entire course of the Sino-Japanese War until Pearl Harbor. Marines were pulled out of both Shanghai and Peiping and sent to the Philippines, where they participated in the battle there.

Being able to live pre-war during a peaceful time in China was a rare privilege and I am grateful I was given the opportunity to visit a great country I had long wanted to see. I'm also grateful China no longer has to suffer the indignity of colonialism. It is a shame they must live under what they have to live under now. Repressive, yes, but it is their country and not another country controlling it.

NEWS ARRIVED:

27 June, 1940: Orders delivered:
You will stand detached from your present station and duties on 3, **July 1940 and proceed as directed in base orders:**
Two first class tickets: Tangku, China to Kobe Japan.
Via: S.S. Tyozyo, Maru….No charge for infant.
Two Minimum first class tickets and one infant fare:
Kobe, Japan to San Francisco: Via President Coolidge.
We were happy to be on our way home and have a chance to show off our beautiful baby. The baby had a different idea of happiness and he

began to let us know it. We hadn't had a chance to bond with him and at four months he had a mind of his own.

He protested loudly. Getting nourishment from a foreign object he didn't recognize, he wanted to snuggle to the warm breast of his Amah. Onboard ship he told us a bit of what he thought of this new arrangement and we too, began to wonder if ever again we would be able to enjoy what we had grown accustomed to as the "good life" The shock was to come sooner than we expected. When I asked the steward if he would please warm the baby's bottle, he replied "do it yourself." That was a humbler if there ever was one.

My orders were first to report to Quantico, Virginia. They were then modified to the Marine Corps Base in San Diego. We rented a home in San Diego. Bill finally felt we qualified as parents and we settled in, enjoyed family and friends, warmed bottles, changed diapers, all the cozy touches families enjoy. It lasted six months. Have now reached the rank of Major, with it came orders to sail to Iceland as a company commander.

Iceland: Land of Fire and Ice

By April 1940, Germany had occupied Denmark. This put them in a position that the next move would be Iceland. Germany had taken over most of Europe and the people were in a state of enslavement. Great Britain was standing alone as most of Europe was lost, with only Switzerland and Portugal managing to stand neutral. It was necessary for England to keep the sea lanes open or their supply lines would be cut off. Convoys from Australia and New Zealand, via the Suez Canal and the Red Sea, were in danger of aircraft attacks and a sea infested with submarines. Supplies from the United States and Canada needed to come through the same waters. The northern route, although safer, was longer, and the more time at sea the greater the danger. By occupying Iceland, Germany would have control of the southern route and would cut off Allied supplies to Great Britain. It would also give them weather stations. Their stations in Greenland had not been the easiest to maintain and the operations were inadequate. Iceland was very coveted for this reason.

The British had declared their independence from Denmark and occupied Iceland on May 9, 1940, but their chances of holding Iceland were slim. They were in fear of defeat and only help from the West would save it. The other concern was that if England had to defend her other possessions, the English troops in Iceland would need to be withdrawn. The rumor was there was some agreement between the United States and Great Britain regarding the defense of Iceland, but the United States was neutral and made no comment. There was also a rumor that Iceland might be incorporated into the Monroe Doctrine Area, but Washington did not encourage this rumor. Whatever the negotiations, although neutral, we were committed to a war strength Brigade to defend Iceland. As Commander of the 2nd Battalion of the 1st Provisional Brigade, we set sail on May 21, 1941, very much in doubt of our destination. The ship I sailed on was the Heywood, capable of 15 to 20 knots. We sailed down and around the Panama Canal, changed directions around Cuba and came up the coast to Charleston, South Carolina, where we docked, took on supplies, and had a day or two on shore. I know Tommy Thompson and I went ashore twice, but most of the time we stayed close to the ship. Rumor kicked in again that we were on our way to French Martinique; their government seemed controlled and very much leaning toward sympathy with Germany, and they also had knowledge of the locations of submarines. It seemed, as time went on, Martinique was not to be our destination. We set sail again and the next rumor was Newfoundland, where we stopped for two days, started studying maps, and began to speculate that we would be a defending force for a large military installation. This was not to be and we set sail again on July 1. Six days later we got our first glance of a rocky island we would call home for the next eight months.

A total of 23 vessels, including battleships New York and Arkansas, docked at Reykjavik. The docking facilities were less than desirable. Rain and mud flats slowed down progress and shallow water made it necessary to use small boats and launches to move supplies to the beaches. It took four days to unload 1,500 tons of supplies, fighting the tide that inundated the supplies and beaches. The equipment needed to get to camps, and some were several miles away. Then pressure was put to get settled as the long days of summer gave the Germans visibility that could be to their advantage, plotting ways to parachute an air strike.

Brigade Headquarters were set up at Camp Lumley, near Alafors, the command placed under Brigadier General John Marston. The force at that time totaled 4,095 men, with supplies for ninety days brought with us, and we joined there with 25,000 men. The entire Brigade was placed along the coastline, so any attempt to move forces any distance in impossible weather was out of the question. Groupings of small forces were ready to defend the island, ready to immediately engage in whatever emergency was close at hand. The rest of the troops were billeted in ten camps, with the 5th Defense Battalion near the city of Reykjavik for aircraft defense, and the 6th Marines a mobile unit to be used at any point needed along the road to the Naval Base. The airfield had been top priority, with most of the men assigned to its readiness. But with winter in sight, we needed to come up with some type of warm quarters. The English Niessen Hut seemed to fit the need; it had a metal frame shaped in the manner of the Quonset hut, came in three sections, and could be assembled in a few hours. The roof and sides were corrugated metal supported by steel ribs and it could house sixteen men. The need to make it warm, windproof, and waterproof soon became apparent. We did this by piling rocks and dirt up four feet around the sides and bringing in a potbellied stove for heat.

11 October:

Found time to open mail. Always read first were my letters from Eve, then one from my little sister, Helen. I had to answer that one so she would continue to write.

11, October: Iceland

Dear Helen,

Here is your recalcitrant brother finally writing to you. I've started two letters before this one and never got them finished for one reason or other. I know that this is a heck of a way to treat one's sister and a very nice sister at that, but actually I have written to almost no one but Eve since I've been here. Am I forgiven? Please.

Eve has (incidentally, isn't she the nicest person you've ever known?) probably told you about Iceland and how I live and stuff, but I'll repeat just a little to make sure you've got the dope. Iceland is a pile of rocks, all volcanic with bog-like ground around the edges of it. It is uninhabited in the interior, that part of the island being generally nothing but solid rock. Many small glaciers and hot springs are found at various parts of the island, and in some cases the hot water is piped through houses to furnish steam, or rather hot water heat.

The weather is primarily rainy and cold, although during the latter part of July and early part of August the days were warm enough to go without overcoats. The island itself is not covered by ice and snow, but there are several glaciers and snowfields in the higher ground of the interior. I took a long trip one Sunday, shortly after we arrived, and went to the foot of one of the glaciers and it was very cold and dismal looking.

I live in what is known as a Niessen Hut, a long semi-cylindrical affair, with three other officers. We have divided the place with partitions, so we each have room to ourselves, and in the center of the hut, a living room. My room was just completed yesterday and I feel pretty ritzy today. The walls are painted white with green and brown trim and look something like a child's bedroom. We are very comfortable and are beginning to eat better than we have been. How are you making out with your nursing? Eve tells me you are on a diet and taking thyroid pills. You had better keep me informed of your progress as I fully expect when I come home five or six years from now I will find you sylph like.

What do you think of Bill now? From what I hear he must be slightly larger than a small ox. I certainly miss him.

Well, Helen, I'll try and write oftener, but I promise nothing. You write to me anyway, when you find time. Tell your friends to stay away from Iceland.

Your brother,
Ray

The food was deplorable and it affected morale to the lowest point; it was dehydrated, supplemented by smelly mutton and fish. Breakfast, lunch, and dinner got old soon on this steady diet. Sheep testicles are a delicate hors d'oeuvre and were enjoyed by the Marines until they discovered their source. Then their interest turned to the candy supply and they hit that heavily. The cost of living is high as everything is imported. Their products are cattle, sheep, hay, and fishing. Of course they eat more lamb and fish than most people, and crops are cultured to grow two or three crops per year, as heavy rainfall and long hours of summer make it possible.

We were here because German troops occupied Denmark, and the Danes could not defend the island.   But Britain could not last defending Iceland. Our problem was that we were supposed to be neutral, and we stood out like a red flag, in contrast to the spit and polish of the British. It was a condition that needed to be corrected, and the solution was that we would wear British Forces 79th Polar Bear Shoulder Patches, hoping this would confuse the Germans.

The British camp was called Baldurshaggi, and there was a song composed about it that had to be sung every night. I've forgotten most of the words, intentionally. It took some time for the British to get used to the Marines looking British, but in time they did become respectful and even saluted our officers. The canteens of the British camps and the YMCA of the Navy were really the only sources of recreation we had. The city did not have theaters or hotels large enough to accommodate their own people, and when there was an influx of 25,000 more troops, there was no way we could lean on their facilities. So we stayed pretty much with the British for recreation, and there was a good feeling between British and Americans. We visited back and forth, especially when different food or a good supply of liquor was on hand. We appreciated the fact that there was no language barrier as was the condition with the Icelanders.

During this time, Winston Churchill visited Iceland. We lined up the troops for his reviewing and it seemed like the line went on forever. We had to stand at attention, look straight forward, and we thought he would never get to the end of the line. We really wanted a good look at him and I think he knew it. He stood on a platform later and said a few words about his meeting with President Roosevelt in Argentina and complimented us on the fine work we were doing. I must say he looked just like his pictures, a bulldog persona that gave the impression that he was the right man for the job and was well able to handle any situation. It was a thrill to be in the presence of this man, who could move mountains with his gift of words and later inspired England. When at their lowest point in the war, bombed out and at a point when everything looked bleak, this booming voice brought the country back together with his famous speech about it being: "This our Finest Hour." Yes, he was, and well deserved to be, "Man of the Century." We were trained to be assault troops and here we were at an outpost with time on our hands, knowing the beauty of the Northern Lights, but filled with the boredom of waiting for something more important. We were restless and speculating, but combat ready in a place where it was forever light or forever dark, depending on the season. We hung blankets over windows to block out some of the light so we could get some rest. Never being able to tell the time of day or night did not make us happy campers. Even the well adjusted, I know, got restless. We trained hard both seasons. My answer to the boredom and having them combat ready involved working long hours and getting them tired enough to cut down on some of the complaining, so at the end of the day they were looking towards some serious rest. There was always plenty of water for showers as Iceland is made up of large glaciers next to steaming hot springs. The natural hot water is piped from the hot springs throughout the island for hot tap water. The warm current from the Gulf Stream keeps the island from being as cold as most areas in the far north.

Iceland has an interesting history; the Vikings settled it in about 870 and it went through several bouts of control with Norway and Denmark and finally gained independence. Most of the people live near the coast in villages and small towns. With Celtic and Nordic backgrounds, they are generally tall, blue-eyed, blond and beautiful. They seemed to be very independent people, very much into relationships, and with many single mothers, which seemed to be the accepted lifestyle, but only with the islanders. In 1941, single relationships without marriage were difficult even for Marines to understand, even with the intent on keeping their race pure. You could tell this because there was no fraternizing with the troops. We would go to one of the local recreation areas where there was dancing and if we asked one of the ladies to dance, she would dance, but not say a word. We never knew if they could speak English or not. The man would return her to her table and that was the extent of any contact we had with the local ladies. Early in August, a small group of Army Air Force arrived and went into quarters near the airfield. Then larger groups began to arrive making the force so large that Major General Bonesteel became the commanding General, with Brigadier General Marston reporting under his command; then the Marine Corps Brigade became part of the Army. Their systems of discipline and administration were different, but in time it did meld. The Marines were a bit put out with the Army; with them came sheets, pillowcases, and blankets that had not been part of the Marine supplies. We had made do with a canvas cot, a thin pad for a mattress and a makeshift blanket. My quarters were a bit different, with our private rooms, and we had blankets from home that made it seem a little better. No sheets, though.

11 November, 1941: Iceland

Dear Helen,

I received your letter yesterday and was glad to get it. It was such a nice letter, a sensible letter because you are such a nice, sensible girl. And let me tell you, that while you might get tired of being a nice, sensible girl all the time, I don't think you will ever regret being one. Today is Armistice Day.

Strange isn't it, that we celebrate the ending of one war while in the midst of another. History has proven, though, that while wars may last a long time, they don't go on forever. That is one consolation, isn't it? We don't know when we will be home but we strongly suspect it won't be until next spring. I don't think much about it because when I do I lose heart. If I weren't so happy with Eve I'd be sorry I love her so much, so loving her like I do makes me miss her terribly. I certainly miss her and Bill (isn't he something?), the little rascal. It isn't fair that I have to miss him at this particular time, but, at that, I'm not as bad off as a lot of people I know who haven't seen their families for a much longer time. I want him to have a sister but think I'm going to wait until the war is over before taking care of that. I want to watch one of my children, at least, grow up. Eve sent me some pictures of Bill the other day and he is so darned cute. I carry them in my wallet so I can look at them every once in a while. He certainly has a swagger hasn't he?

I was glad to hear that Dad is doing so well. He is a pretty good fellow at that, I guess, and while there are a lot of things he does that we don't like, we've got to hand it to him for starting all over again at 48, or whatever age it was when he started again. By the way, Helen, I asked Mother to send me the birth dates of all our family but she just won't write, so will you do me a favor and gather them for me?

Eve sent me two of the nicest blankets and they just arrived today. I can hardly wait to try them out. It must be time to eat, Helen, so bye for now. Write again soon, please.

> *Lots of love to my little sister,*
> *Ray*

It's winter again and pitch dark most of the time. We will be doing more classroom training and sent a detachment to Hill Vatensonday to guard the radio station. The troops were more restless when we heard that the 8th Marines were sent to Samoa, the 2nd Marine Regiment and a Battalion of the 10th set sail for the Pacific from San Diego, while we, the 6th, tried to control our thoughts, visualizing that we were being saved for heavier action.

We were eager to get into the fighting because of the humiliation suffered at the hands of the Japanese when Colonel Reginald Ridgely surrendered at Corregidor. We are the best damn Regiment in the Marines, why couldn't we get some action? Rumor in November was that the Brigade would withdraw and return to the United States.

About the time the troops really started complaining that the women were difficult and unapproachable and the whiskey could kill you, no warmth in either, Pearl Harbor was bombed. Now we had Pearl Harbor as well as Corregidor that we must make Japan atone for; a Pacific war would be fought, President Franklin Roosevelt declared war on Japan. We had been complaining about not having action, now it seems imminent.

7 January, 1942:

I was assigned to a British Force Tactical School and finished in time to join the Brigade on January 31, on our way back home. We were heavily supported by war vessels and had every assurance that we would arrive safely in New York. We were given furloughs, and those from the West Coast returned to Camp Pendleton for additional training and our orders to the next objective.

Upper-class housing in Iceland

Our visit with Winston Churchill

NEW ZEALAND

North Island.

AUKLAND ©

Bay of Plenty

Hawke Bay

Tasman Bay

WELLINGTON

Cape Palliser

Chapter Two

New Zealand

From April 1942 until October 1942 I enjoyed home and family in San Diego. Then my orders were to New Zealand. We landed near Wellington, in one of the most beautiful countries in the world and certainly the friendliest. Unlike Iceland, where none of the natives would invite us to join in their local gatherings, New Zealand actually reached out and embraced us. They invited Marines into their homes and shared what little they had.

Conditioning and practicing was our goal. These troops had to be battle ready. We were an amphibious force, well trained in the basics, now we needed to test endurance. The troops must be able to survive under any condition. I scheduled thirty-mile hikes, not popular and I must admit was as rough on me as they were on the troops. It was difficult for me to conceal the cramps in my legs and the blisters on my feet and stay ahead of the hikers. We needed to build strong legs and the ability to carry heavy backpacks. My next concern was, could they swim? Two strong volunteer swimmers, who had competed in high school swimming events and were still strong swimmers, saved the day. They were out there every day testing the ones we selected who might be our reconnaissance swimmers, and with these strong swimmers they built up a strong swimming team.

While we practiced playing war, the local people spent their days watching us charge up the beaches, fall on our stomachs, crawl with our rifles and grenades, and try to out maneuver the other half of the troops as our enemy.

Sometimes, I wondered if the combat ready troops forgot everything I taught them. Then they would come through and perform as professionals. By December we are ready for our next orders and embarked, for what I felt must be somewhere in the Pacific. . There were so many islands now occupied by the Japanese, it was any-one's guess.

We didn't know if we would be assigned to the Solomons, the Marianas or the Marshalls. The Japanese seemed to be completely in control of the Pacific. Some of the area we were studying, definitely was jungle. Not a desirable place to visit, much less a choice location for battle. Our orders came through; we would be at sea before we would know which island we were going to defend.

Occupied by the Japanese since July 1942
Captured by the Allies February 1943

Guadalcanal

The Allies, more concerned about stopping Hitler, made Europe the heaviest objective. The Japanese, during these eight months, were mopping up the Pacific Islands. Some of the Japanese fleet had been damaged but they were still strong and needed to be reckoned with. Their aircraft and warships had some of the best trained pilots and navy personnel in the world. What was deadly were the suicide missions flown by the Kamikaze pilots. They would dive into any objective, be blown apart, with no concern for their own lives, just determined to get their mission accomplished. Add this to excellent military training and the result was lethal.

The Solomons are a double row of mountainous, volcanic islands flanked by small atolls to the north, east and south. A scattered archipelago in the Southwest Pacific Ocean, there are eight main islands and many small ones. The southern group includes Guadalcanal, 92 miles long and 33 miles wide, with razor sharp peaks some 8,000 feet high. The rest is jungle and a difficult battle area.

The Northern Solomons were under the protection of Germany, later under the control of the League of Nations. Great Britain, the protectorate of the Southern Solomons had passed the control to Australia.. Gualalcanal was the largest of the British Solomon Islands, ten degrees below the equator and 1,000 miles east of northern Australia. Washington was worried about the enemy cutting off supplies from the United States, not only to Australia but also to New Zealand. Guadalcanal and Tulagi were being carefully watched. Tulagi, twenty miles across from Sealark Channel, was a Japanese seaplane base, and if taken, would be a prime objective for an airfield for the Allies and first on the list of battle order.

We were in big trouble trying to hold the island; the Japanese sank five Allied cruisers. The Navy, thinking the rest of the ships were needed elsewhere and fearful of losing any more warships, orders them to leave with most of the Marines' supplies. MacArthur wrote them off saying, "The Marines are doomed." They have nothing to fight with. This is not understandable. You must take care of the troops on the ground. When a country doesn't do that, they should re-examine who is really fighting the war. If they don't have the right equipment, healthy food, and well trained leaders, they are not prepared. They should not be placed in situations where the odds are, they will not come out alive. And to make an announcement that the Marines are doomed, proved he underestimated the Marines.

The island itself is a tropical rain forest of banyan trees, under-surface twisted vines, home to slimy creatures of every description; beautiful, but danger lurking in every direction. Where the undergrowth was a rotting, stinking bog it was the big contributor of jungle rot. The Marines had been isolated for four months, without supplies, eating anything they could find. They were sick with malaria and running sores. Jungle rot had taken its toll. This was the news we were getting when we sailed from Wellington, New Zealand in December 1942, when we thought we were being sent to Wake Island. We were escorted by the carrier Wasp and were two days at sea when we learned our destination was to be Guadalcanal, the first American offensive in the Pacific. We would be replacing Marines who were bone weary and emaciated with malaria. They had been fighting in bare feet, desperately protecting Henderson Field, which had to be held or the island was lost. General Vandergrift gave orders that it was necessary for survival, but if they lost it they would go into the hills and fight a guerrilla war. The General was without supplies, always hoping some were on their way, but was constantly getting messages, that the ships he needed were needed elsewhere, as the Navy could not support the Marines.

President Roosevelt's son, James, was a Marine. He alerts his father of the conditions on the island, the President intervened and supplies and food were on their way, including thousands of pairs of shoes. Admiral Halsey took over the fleet, and the fight became deadly; 65 ships were sunk: 30 were ours and the rest were Japanese. These hunks of iron and steel are somewhere in a watery grave between Tulagi and Guadalcanal.

We were there several days when we were ordered to attack along the coast. Our reconnaissance observed no extensive defense along the beaches. The 1st Battalion on the right flank on the beaches and the 2nd Battalion on the left. My battalion was back inland and didn't have the advantage of any kind of breeze, and climbing hills in steaming temperatures was rough. I had a thousand men to worry about, some dropping in the heat. The responsibility was heavy. We were getting bloodied in our first combat, and I stressed the responsibility we owed each other and also the individual challenges. Can we take it? Will we break? This was where our training must come in. Before it had been field maneuvers, this was the real thing. And there were some real Marines out there fighting, ones I could use as role models for the young group in my battalion.

Jim Crowe, was part of the force. I had known him for years and we had been in China together. He, in these years, was a very dramatic and

27

colorful person. We could always spot him by his mustache; I never measured it but word around was it was eight inches long from port to starboard and he twirled it to a thin upward curl at the end. He was also a fighter and a good one. On January 15, 1943, Jim Crowe, armed with his shotgun, followed by his gunnery sergeant and three Marines pushed into the jungle and took out two 77 mm guns and twelve or fourteen Japanese He was given the Army Bronze Star.

Another notable Marine was Merrit A. Edson. "Red Mike" Lt. Col. Edson lead his first Raider Battalion on Tulagi's South Coast. They waded through waist deep water to Tulagis' 600-foot-wide Blue Beach. They were cut bloody in the coral. Edson reached the island, held it and earned his second Navy Cross, fourteen years after earning his first on the CoCo River. Chesty Puller was Edson's executive officer and he was to become the most decorated Marine of all time.

These were Marines under the command of General Vandergrift. The quality of the force was the best our country had, fighting under the worst conditions, without supplies. They had held the island and the airfield that depended on the survival of the five battalions.

I am in awe of the quality of the commanders, holding the island under impossible conditions. I'm wondering if a combat beginner will survive, thrown in with these legends of the corps. Still addressed as Major, with my first combat command, as a battalion commander with the responsibility of over one thousand troops weighing heavily on my shoulders. Will I make the right decisions, will my training as an officer suffice? We were really getting bloodied, rounds were coming at us from all directions, I'm wondering will the next one hit its target? Will I break, will I hold up, in truth be able to stay and do my job? Whatever comes forward to make any kind of sense in these conditions, there is a point when training kicks in. I knew I must be professional, this was not a parade ground practice. I had my orders, the orders were to command.!

The steaming heat was a breeding ground for malaria and it didn't take long to take its toll; it was necessary for every officer to keep their troops on their feet, we could let the ones who were in the worst condition rest at night while the more able stood watch. There wasn't much rest for the rest of us, going for days at a time, sweating most of our weight off, sleeping on our feet for a few minutes when the firing would ease. Then the screeching, screaming birds would often warn us of impending danger. A startling, piercing cry sounding like a mortally wounded soul, would bring anyone back to attention, drawing rifles and ready to fight.

Enemy was everywhere and the losses were heavy, worried about the injured, and the corpsmen were on overload; we also had the dead to bring in as this stinking jungle would be the worst place in the world to leave a buddy. I asked for volunteers, a dozen Marines stepped forward, among them, my radio man, Leon Uris. Going through the jungle he was trying to keep his equipment above his head, but the slime is slippery, and he fell. I'm hearing words coming from him I won't repeat here. His equipment must be in the sludge. We started falling in where the injured needed to be evacuated, and we carried out our dead. Somehow we dodged the rounds and held on for a week.

Uris is working on his radio, getting some response and I'm ordering to try a little harder. " Uris, get that damn radio going, we are going to need help." Leon answers, " I'm doing my damnedest, Highpockets." I turned to him and asked " What did you say?" He answered, " I'm doing my best, sir" No, I'm telling him. "I meant the rest of it." He answered, "Oh, you mean Highpockets?" " Yes, that is what I mean." I'd never heard anyone actually call me Highpockets to my face. He wouldn't shut up, and added," it's only with affection, sir." I needed to turn my head so he couldn't see me smile. So, I issued an order. " Leon, in the field I'm Ray, at the command post I'm Major Murray, please have the men understand that. Now get the radio going"

With an island ninety miles long we needed full strength if we were going to win. A composite was formed of Army, Marines, including the 6th Marines and the Army's infantry regiment, with artillery from the 10th Marines, all under command of General Alexander Vandergrift's 1st Marines, were all part of the CAM Division. I do remember passing Point Cruz at the conclusion of this operation. By January 16, we had fought five days and gained just 1500 yards; we finally broke through and started our advance towards Cape Esperance. We took part in the fight of Kokubona and the advance to the Poha River, attacking the right side of the river. We kept pushing the enemy north, to where we pushed them off the island; 17,000 Japanese escaped, gone.

I personally was in Guadalcanal a very few weeks, six at the most. From the administrative landing somewhere in the vicinity of Henderson Field to Cape Esperance, I made it through my first combat command, jungle heat, slime, bugs and mire. Came through a bit bloodied with jungle scratches, insect bites, but most of the blood on my uniform was from a brave buddy who wouldn't or couldn't make it back on his own.
The latest I've heard is I am nominated for Lt. Colonel and it might come about in 1943, but I'm still a major, and commanding a battalion a rank above my grade.

Guadalcanal was on its way to being secure, with, this wonderful battalion; we held, we made it. And my first combat command awarded me my first Silver Star with a citation: "For conspicuous gallantry and intrepidity in action against Japanese forces while serving as commanding officer of the Marine Battalion on Guadalcanal"

We left February 19, the worst of the fighting was over and we were on our way back to New Zealand where, for the first time since 1941, all the units were under the same command.

Guadalcanal took its toll on our forces:

1598 officers and men were killed 1152 were Marines
4700 were wounded 2800 were Marines
25,000 Japanese retreated, and the battle of Guadalcanal was over.

This was the turning point of the Pacific War. The Japanese never advanced further than they already had in the Pacific.

New Zealand

Now back to New Zealand where all the units of the Marines were united under one command. When we returned, it was February, the weather was warm, the cots were clean, and now the long period of getting the battalion battle ready again. Very few were able to answer role call; the dysentery, hepatitis, and the effects from malnutrition had knocked the socks off the 2nd Battalion, 6th Marines. The hospitals and rehab centers were filled, battling the high fevers from malaria and dysentery. A few weeks of good care and healthy food, they began to feel better. Now they are starting to walk the three miles to catch a train and go into town for a movie or attend whatever would be going on at a service club. This was my clue to start work again. Our days began early, with, long hikes to condition the men who had been recovering from bouts of malaria. Those who had been carried onboard at Guadalcanal, suffering from this draining, debilitating disease, were slowly getting back in condition. We trained for eight months, heavy amphibious training and body building exercises. Forces came in to replace the casualties and the Division lineup underwent changes. The command passed to General Julian C. Smith and his chief of staff was "Red Mike Edson," the previous Raider at Guadacanal, with enough background to command the respect of us all.

Another debilitating problem kicked in, in the form of yellow jaundice. It is a reaction to atabrine, given to combat malaria. A high fever; whites of eyes, fingernails and urine all turned yellow, and it seemed no one was immune. Some were sicker from the prevention than they would have been with malaria. Both had pulled from the strength of the troops.

Six months into the rehabilitation we are wondering if we still have a regiment in fighting condition. We scheduled all three battalions for a hike, forty miles up the coast to Foxton. Through the years I've been reminded innumerable times about the Foxton hike.. Heard that I've been described as a fire breathing, gung ho commander who pushed his troops to unbelievable exhaustion. Most of the troops, eighteen, or nineteen-year-olds were pissed off to a point about the length of the hike, and wanted to see if the "Old Man" (I'm thirty years old) could stay out in front. Pushed they did, and did a good job of it. Damned near killed me, but I managed to let them know I wouldn't make them do anything I wouldn't do myself; and we completed our hike forty miles up and forty miles back. The other two battalions were trucked back and had to suffer the jeers from the 2nd. It took a week to heal the blisters and get the kinks out, but as I looked over these men I knew I had a fighting force again.

We were at a place called Peakakariki and came back for training at MacKays Crossing. In the hills, battalion schools were conducted and firing areas were provided for all the weapon training. Our amphibious training was extensive. Seemed it never ended, practicing loading and landing plans. Then, for four days we went aboard the "Feland" to put our training into practice. We did everything but go ashore. Finally in Wellington Bay we headed for the beach. All this training was adding up to expectations of being ordered to somewhere in the Pacific.

The first of November we rehearsed some more landing exercises, and the line of command went into effect. Marines three battalions were assigned to: One to Maurice Holmes, and 1st Battalion would be commanded by Willie Jones and the 2nd Battalion of the 6th would be mine.

We rehearsed at Efate and had been told we were going to an atoll but we weren't told where. There had been aerial photographs taken, of all things, the heads (outdoor toilets.) were on stilts near the beaches. By counting these it could be determined how many people were on the island. Then we were off to sea again. The destination was the New Hebrides, with a code name "Helen," a.k.a. Tarawa. This was to be our first assault on a strongly defended atoll and considered a tough one, the largest Pacific operation to date. And I would be commanding the 2nd Battalion of the 6th Marines as a Lieutenant Colonel.

It was sad leaving beautiful New Zealand and the friends we had made there. Some of the Marines had fallen in love with the beautiful women and asked permission to marry. This not only entailed mountains of paper work but left behind some very unhappy local suitors. The marriages turned out surprisingly well; have heard from several of the Marines who returned to make New Zealand their second home.

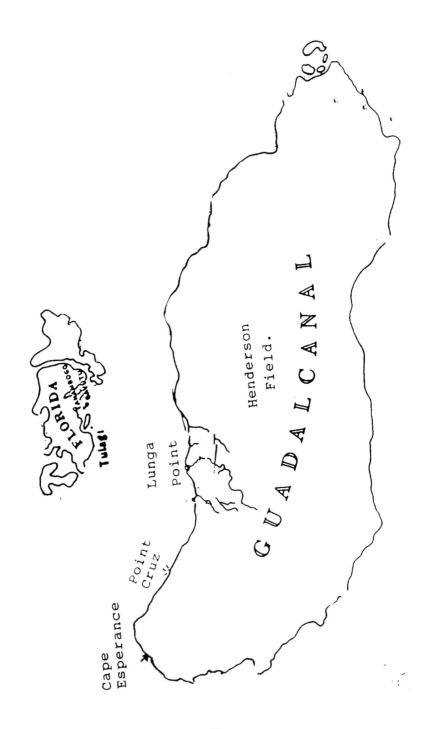

FLORIDA

Tulagi

Cape
Esperance

Point
Cruz

Lunga
Point

Henderson
Field.

GUADALCANAL

Chapter Three

Tarawa

We were at sea the day we learned our next destination would be in the New Hebrides, on an atoll with the code name "Helen," a.k.a. Tarawa, It was thought the landing should have been put off for at least three weeks until we were better prepared and had better knowledge of the tides, but when it was discovered the Japanese had stockpiled three thousand mines and didn't have the time to plant them, we knew this landing date would save lives.

A survey by air had taken a count of the latrines that were spaced along the beach. By counting them, we had a fairly accurate guess of how many people were on the island. This was worked out by David Shoup, and he didn't miss the mark too far when he came up with a number of four thousand. The tides were the big concern; there are high tides and neap tides, but a different tide, was imminent. Major Frank Holland, who had lived on the island for many years, had kept from getting bored by studying the tides for the British Government; cautioned the commanders about this dodging tide he could see coming and could not sanction a landing at that time. He warned it might hang the crafts on the reefs.

The General assigned to the command was Major General Julian Smith, a distinguished marksman and a former rifle team coach. As a teacher he had been one of the best, and it had been proven many times with his combat ready troops who had been in his training school. He was soft spoken, well respected, of high moral fiber, and the Marines would follow him. He was from the Chesapeake area and well aware of high tides and neap tides, a talented planner and an excellent leader. He was concerned enough with Major Holland's report to report this to Major General Holland Smith. General Smith issued a statement that if he didn't get some additional LVTs, the invasion would not go on. Some were sent from New Zealand, but we were still at about half of what was needed.

Smith's chief of staff was Colonel Merrit Edson, who had proven himself as commander of the 1st Raider Battalion at Tulagi and the recipient of the second Navy Cross and Medal of Honor for heroism at "Edson's

Ridge" on Guadalcanal. He rounded out his command with Colonel David Shoup, who sailed from New Zealand as a Lt. Col., and by the time he reached Tarawa he had been spot promoted to Colonel. He would be the only one of the three commanders to receive the Medal of Honor for Tarawa. Later in 1959, President Eisenhower selected a commandant and his selection was David Shoup. All three men were seasoned Marines and well aware of the conditions and fighting ahead.

This was the first American assault on a strongly defended atoll and was to become the epic battle of the entire Pacific. Two days after Pearl Harbor the Japanese landed on Tarawa, took it from the British, fortified it into a fortress, and boasted, " It will take a million Americans one hundred years to take this island." The island was just two and a half miles long and eight hundred yards wide, a mere speck in a forever ocean. It had a primitive airport and its value was: It was within bombing strike of the Marshall's. Betio, located on the southwest tip of Tarawa; near the entrance of the lagoon, a thousand yard pier over the reef due north was to be the first target.

.   There were three landing beaches that would sustain an amphibious landing, each six hundred yards apart. Red Beach 1 was on the northern tip, Red Beach 2, the pier, Red Beach 3 from the pier eastward. An amphibious assault is from the sea, and it must work as it is impossible to retreat, and consideration must always be considered as a miscalculation could be disastrous. Sometimes, just an hour can make a difference on whether it is successful. Co-ordination, getting ships loaded correctly to support moving equipment, and men heavily laden must go down rope ladders into crafts and must be battle ready when they reach the beach. We had been put through all this training and marched long distances carrying equipment and we, the 6th, were well known for our physical fitness. The heavy packs were part of the conditioning and gave us the edge we would need in combat.

From the Betio pier the Japanese could pour a flanking fire into the Marine assault troops. The Navy thought they had it well in hand with their air support and there would not be much left to do after they finished. Three hundred Navy planes made strikes every day, and dropped ten tons of bombs on Betio and twice as many on the beaches. But something was different. All the strikes and bombs weren't doing it. The Japanese had tunneled underground and into bunkers with six feet of concrete and massive amounts of coconut tree wood covering the concrete, making it almost impossible to penetrate. They had not been touched by the bombs. We knew then the heavy fighting would be done in open combat.

It was important to take Betio, as it was the largest of the sixteen atolls in the Pacific (if only a speck) lying along the equator. It was surrounded by a barrier reef with only a few inches of water, making it impossible to land any craft. Then the terrible tragedy of Tarawa began. The troops who were not in amphibious crafts would need to wade 400 yards towards the shore. The Japanese had dug potholes and strung barbed wire through them, and the men, weighted down with heavy weapons, stepped into these potholes. With the weight of the heavy packs, caught in the barbed wire, it made it impossible for them to surface. Some stepped off boats, went in over their heads and drowned. All this and fighting the gunfire; so many men were lost before they could fire a shot.

The survivors salvaged a few weapons and some dynamite. The officers and non-commissioned officers had been the first fallen. Colonel Shoup took a leg injury from a shell burst, and continued giving commands to the landing commanders for two and a half days and remained in charge of the fighting at Betio. His leg later became infected and he was replaced by his executive officer.

The 6th was in reserve, so we didn't make the assault landing. Jim Crowe made the landing and we almost lost him. We did go ashore, at least my battalion went ashore, not as a regiment but as a separate battalion; mine was the last one. We came ashore on Green Beach with orders to move up behind the 1st Battalion. Major Michael Ryan created us a safe landing, and brought our rubber boats in boats we named the condom fleet, through the choppy waters and floating bodies so thick he attached the rubber boats to Higgins' boats to get through. He did an excellent job; a low key person, he was soft spoken, never asking for any recognition. His only comment: " We are all doing our jobs the best way we know how." With this he brought us in without the carnage that took place on Red Beach. My understanding was we were supposed to back up the 1st Battalion on Green Beach but our orders came to proceed to Bairiki, to block the back door where the enemy was escaping, leaving from the eastern end of Betio, wading across to Bairiki.

We landed without opposition, then a machine gun crew opened fire on our boats. Air power saved the island. The few Japanese manning the guns were sitting behind large drums of gasoline, and strafing bullets ignited the drums and destroyed the entire crew. We forced the Japanese to fall back and cleared the island; then we were ordered back to Betio for a final cleanup of the rest of the islands.

I needed a local person who knew the island and could speak some English to answer questions and asked Dave Shoup if we could find a guide. A seventeen year old boy, who had attended Catholic school where the nuns taught English, spoke up. He was a native, possible Micronesian, spoke good English and joined our battalion and did a good job. He went to a great deal of trouble, forty years later, trying to find me, and described his job as being a seventeen year old spy who, if we didn't win the war, would be a young boy without a head. At the end of the chapter I will include some of the correspondence, and how far the Marine Corps Generals went to honor him. He sent pictures of General Kelley with me, and a picture of a naval officer. Yes, he was the one.

The islands are close together and at low tide it is possible to walk or wade from one to the other. The natives were very cooperative. They had been used badly by the Japanese, to build bunkers, clear brush and cut down their beloved coconut trees, so they were willing to help us, always telling the same story: "The Japanese are fleeing, they are just ahead of you." Many times they gave us an exact count. We started our cleanup through the islands, dirty, dusty, thirsty, dry mouthed, not even enough moisture to wet our lips, afraid to drink the water as it might be poisoned. We turned a corner and out of the blue came two English nuns, in full habit, waiting for us with water to drink. They and a priest had chosen to stay on after the occupation as part of the Sacred Heart Mission. Some more nuns showed up and asked if they could be of some help. They had all been teachers, and nurses, on the islands and were well trained in survival methods. We really welcomed their help as they relieved the corpsmen for additional rifle duty. The priest went to the limit to help, counseling, working with the nuns and the corpsmen and always made certain we had fresh water to drink . We traveled 45 miles, crossed 25 islands. One island had been a leper colony, evacuated some years back.

Mosquitoes were big and plentiful. Hands bitten would swell twice their size, eyes would puff closed, faces so lopsided we hardly recognized each other. And George company was being cut to pieces. They were enclosed in heavy brush that extended fifty yards in each direction, and we had to get to them before nightfall, as they were running out of ammunition. As I went into the brush I hear my orderly, Zutz, scream " Colonel! Watch out he has a knife." As a Japanese came from nowhere, with a knife aimed at the center of my back, my little orderly hit him with all his weight and pushed him off center; he missed his target. The knife cut through the fleshy part of my upper left arm. With my good arm I hit him and we grappled in the dirt until I could reach my 45 and let him have it with the butt, knocking him out cold and turned him over as a prisoner. The good nuns patched me up and we went on with the war. Thanks to Zutz, I was still in command.

We chased the Japanese through the islands, then tried to rest for the night. It wouldn't be. All hell broke loose, and as we moved forward we were in for some heavy fighting, much of it done by direct combat, eye to eye, bayonet to bayonet. The Marine losses were heavy; 32 dead and 59 wounded. Japanese casualties 175.

We knew we would be in for some heavy fighting as we pushed the Japanese to the last island, Naa, so we called for air support. The Navy pounded the island for twenty minutes. There weren't any Japanese left on the island. That finished, it was time to return to Eita and re-organize. Our orders were to stay and clean up the carnage. The rest of the Marines were on their way back to Hawaii.

We contacted and destroyed the enemy on Cora Island. Japanese casualties 423, wounded none. American casualties 98, wounded 213.

Tarawa was secured.

Everyone bathed. We needed to stay clothed at all times; it wasn't only the mosquitoes this time, but the flies who carried dengue fever. Navy Seabces came in and performed miracles. An airstrip appeared almost immediately, and the airfield was named Hawkins, for one of the heroes of Tarawa. Another one was built to bring in supplies.

They also started scraping out an area where we could have clean food. Some started to appear, and we had juices, vegetables, meat, and even ice cream. Tents were built and we had a real cot to sleep on. They seemed capable of doing anything. A generator appeared for electricity, areas were screened where we could get away from the flies and the heat. We had stayed behind as a ground defense for the Navy, with 90 mm guns, anti-aircraft guns and searchlights, but we never seemed able to bring down a Japanese plane.

We had one personal tragedy. A lieutenant went completely insane to a point where he was getting dangerous, raving and fighting like a tiger. The doctor said the fever had destroyed his mind and we had to conscript him away from the rest of the men. War is hell.

8, January, 1944:

We have been here forty-nine days. The first major battle the Japanese said would take one hundred years, was over in seventy-six hours. We, the 6th had been assigned the cleanup and had stayed on. Liberty Ship, S.S. Prince George was in the harbor, and had arrived at 0800 and was scheduled to leave at 1530. I was so sick with dengue fever. I had a fever reaching 104, and really hoped to die so I could be out of my misery. Every bone ached. I know now why they call it bone breaking, but it also acts like pneumonia, every breath I took I thought would be my last one. I began to sympathize with the poor lieutenant. I told Dick Nutting, my executive, "get the troops onboard if you can. I don't care if you leave me here or there, just do whatever you can." The first thing he did was put me on a stretcher and got me into sick bay, where I agonized while Dick put the gear and troops onboard. It was a ship going back to Hawaii and it would take twelve days to get there. Long time when I felt as bad as I did. It was hot, so most of the time I slept on deck. Wet and shaking with fever, I finally began feeling better, hoping to make it to Hawaii and not be buried at sea. Fevers have a way of bringing on a little drama, and being buried at sea wasn't to my liking.

Tarawa represented the first successful landing in modern history against a well defended atoll. It also proved amphibious assault was sound and Naval gunfire alone could not reduce a fortified target. It also gave us control of the Gilbert Islands and paved the way for the invasion of the Marshalls and the Marianas. When we look at our toll: one half of the force of Marines were killed or drowned before reaching the beach, the 125 amtracs, 75 were destroyed. The Japanese casualties were 4000, only 17 surrendered, I came to the conclusion, " if you do your job and the battalion does theirs, and you don't get killed, you get a silver star." I got my second star for Tarawa.

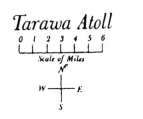

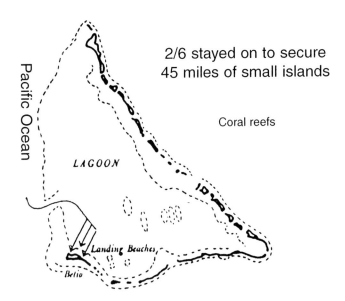

The first Atoll, the smallest with greatest loss of lives

Six foot concrete bunkers.
A tough assignment for the Navy guns.

Japanese guns aimed at us.

Another type of Japanese bunker.

Lookout Tower

My radio man, Leon Uris, who had enlisted just after Pearl Harbor, was a teenager who left school before he graduated. He learned to love the corps, and had been with me through Iceland, New Zealand, Guadalcanal and Tarawa and was very much a part of the 6th Battalion. He was there in the middle of the action. Because of an illness, he returned to San Francisco, and was there for the duration of the war. A few years later I was returning from Hawaii and was standing on the Marin side of the Golden Gate Bridge when I noticed a familiar figure. I walked over and said hello. "Uris aren't you? Did you ever write that war story you said you were going to write about the Pacific War?" He said he had been working on a newspaper in San Francisco and had written a manuscript titled "Battle Cry," and mentioned I would recognize the hero. It was fiction but related to our experience in the Pacific War. He had had rejections but he now had a publisher. (The story was later published and made into a film.) We kept in contact through the years and became very good friends.

I would be remiss in my writing if I did not relate some of the correspondence with my seventeen year old " Spy," Tony. These letters were received 40 years after Tarawa.

Forty years after the Tarawa battle a letter was received in Washington asking if a Colonel by the name of Murray could be located. The letter was from Toanimatang Teraoi, the young man I preferred to call "Tony," as I couldn't pronounce his name. His letter stated he had worked with me as a spy during the Tarawa conflict and would like to locate his friend. The letter was received by Russell J. Surber dated 23 November 1982, forwarded on to:

Brig. Gen. E. H. Simmons, USMC (Ret.)
Director of Marine Corps History and Museums
Headquarters, USMC, Washington, D.C.

The General's reply: **6 June 1983**

A letter was received from:
EMBASSY OF THE UNITED STATES
SUVA, FIJI
6 May 1983

To the Commander Donald Farber, USN
CINPAC Representative South West Pacific
American Embassy Suva

Stating:
Enclosed the correspondence of Mr. Toanimatang Teraoi, a citizen of Kiribati, regarding his services to the U.S. Armed Forces during the

41

invasion and capture of Tarawa during WW II. I would appreciate your assistance in forwarding Mr. Teraoi's letters to the appropriate United States Military Command for consideration and review.

It was signed:
Russell J. Surber
Charge d'Affaires A.I.

Enclosure:

Mr. Toanimatang Teraoi
Kawakawa, Onomaru Village
Butaritari Island
Northern District
Republic of Kiribati
Central Pacific

6 June 1983

Dear Mr. Teraoi,
        Commander D. J. Farber of the American Embassy at Suva has sent me your very interesting statement of 23 November 1982 in which you describe your assistance to the U.S. Marines during the course of the Tarawa campaign.
        The "American Colonel named Murray" to whom you refer is almost certainly Raymond L. Murray. At the time of the battle he was a lieutenant colonel and in command of the 2nd Battalion 6th Marines, which landed east and north of Betio. He is now retired, a major general living in Southern California. Because of the U.S. Privacy Act I cannot give you his address, but I have written him a letter enclosing your statement and I am certain you will be hearing from him directly.
With best personal wishes,

Sincerely,

It was signed by:
E. H. Simmons
Brigadier General
U.S. Marine Corps, (Ret.)
Director of Marine Corps History and Museums

15 June 1983

Brigadier General E. H. Simmons USMC (Ret.)
Director of Marine Corps History and Museums
Headquarters, USMC, Washington, D.C.

Dear Ed,

How interesting to receive a communication relating events of 40 years ago! And how remarkable that "Tony" should remember those events in such detail.

The story is true. I recall most of the details clearly after reading his story. I don't recall who was in the bunker (foxhole) with us but it probably was the division C/S and maybe Dave Shoup. I don't recall slapping Tony, but I do remember his trying to leave the dugout when the bombs were dropping and I remember grabbing him and telling him it was safer inside than out.

We were talking about 2/6 making a sweep of the rest of the atoll to clean out the rest of the Japanese. After the conference we returned to the island next to Betio where 2/6 had landed a day or so earlier to prevent any Japanese from leaving Betio, and began our move down the atoll.

Tony's figures as to the number and location of Japanese and Koreans was almost on the nose. We counted almost 160 bodies after our battle on the last island.

I hope you can arrange it so PX can sign a letter of appreciation to Tony. It wouldn't cost anything and would mean a great deal to him.

I have written to Tony and will enclose a copy of the handwritten letter I sent him.

All my best to you and forgive my typing: I'm without a secretary.
Sincerely,
R. L. Murray

Enclosure: Copy of handwritten letter to Mr. Teraoi

August 1983

Mr. Teraoi,

Major General Raymond L. Murray, now retired, who led the 2nd Battalion, 6th Marines, during the Battle of Tarawa, has told me of your courageous assistance to his unit during its drive to capture the northern islands of the atoll.

As we approach the 40th anniversary of that great battle, I want to commend you for your service to the United States and its Marine Corps. I assure you that, we as Marines, are grateful for what you did to help us gain victory.

On behalf of all United States Marines, I salute you!

Respectfully,
P. X. KELLEY
General, U. S. Marine Corps
Commandant of the Marine Corps

Mr. Toanimatang Teraoi
  Kawakawa Onomaru Village
    Butaritari Island
      Northern District
        Republic of Kiribata
          CENTRAL PACIFIC

Copy to: Mgen Raymond L. Murray, USMC (Ret.)

15 September 1983

Dear General Murray,

    General Kelley thought you would be interested in the enclosed follow-on correspondence.

Sincerely,
E. H. Simmons
Brigadier General, U. S. Marine Corps (Ret.)
Director of marine Corps History and Museums

Enclosure: Ltr to Ben Simmons from Russell Surber
       Dtd 23Aug83

Major General Raymond L. Murray, USMC (Ret.)
    Oceanside, California 92054

      Land & Survey Office
      P.O. Box 7
      Bairiki, Tarawa
      Republic of Kiribati
      Central Pacific

10 November 1983

E. H. Simmons
Brigadier General
U.S. Marine Corps (Ret.)
Director of Marine Corps History and Museums

Dear Sir,

> *I have the honor to reply to your letter dated on 6, June 1983. And to let you know with happiness that Major General Raymond Murray, is the friend I have been looking for. He has written me admitting my statement and said he would forward it to the Marine Commandant's office. This has been dispatched, knowing this by the Commandant's letter to me, General P. X. Kelley, acknowledging the receipt of my statement. He mentioned in his letter that "As the American People approach the 40th anniversary of the great battle, he wants to commend me for my service to the United States and its Marine Corps."*

> *I know without your help, my friend Raymond Murray could not be found. Thank you very much for all you have done for me. Will you send me a picture of yourself, I will hang it on my wall so I can remember who helped me find my friend.*

> *May I say again, thank you for your help and may God's blessing be with you and your staff whenever or wherever you may be.*

> *With my best personal wishes,*

Sincerely
Toanimatang Teraoi

7 December 1983

Dear General Murray

> *I think you will be interest in this heart-warming letter received from Mr. Toanimatang Teraoi.*

> *The whole sequence of events is the subject of my Director's Page in the forthcoming issue of FORTITUDINE.*

> *With best personal wishes to you for the holiday season.*

> > *Sincerely,*
> > *E. H. SIMMONS*
> > *Brigadier General, U. S. Marine Corps (Ret.)*
> > *Director of marine Corps History and Museums*

Major General Raymond L. Murray, USMC (Ret.)

Oceanside, California 92054

Land & Survey Office
P.O. Box 7
Bairiki, Tarawa
Republic of Kiribati
Central Pacific

4 October 1983

Dear Sir,
I have received your letter dated June 15,1983 and I am pleased to know you are still alive after the war. First I would like to apologize for the long delay in replying and this was caused by a sudden receipt of a letter from ("Big Red"). I guess you know a man with such a name. I was shocked by the content which read, "Dear Tony, you little fart. What the hell are you trying to do, get me before the Goddamned Court Martial?" After reading this letter I was downhearted as I thought it might be you with a nickname of Big Red and got angry with me by the content of my recent statement which may have been badly worded and may have led you to trouble. Therefore, I thought it would be wise to write to Big Red apologizing and ask him to let me know of my mistake as I did not mean to take anybody to a Court Martial with my statement. I have received a reply and it read, "Dear Friend, Please let me apologize for leading you to believe I was angry with you. It was a joke written in poor taste. I did not mean it that way but I can see you took me seriously and I am sorry."
Now I am happy to learn that Big Red was not you but a different person. I've placed him as the foreman who killed the Japanese Commander and took his medal.
Let me thank the Lord for his loving care of you and your battalion when you first left for the war until your successful return to America. Despite the wide ocean that separated us it cannot erase away the memories of our intersection in Tarawa which haunted me through the years of my life. I still remember your return from Naa and your battalion camped at Diana site and I recall having a ride with you in your jeep to your camp and this was the first time I saw you in a clean uniform, also the last day to meet before you left for an unknown destination. Will you tell me a brief story of your successful return, Please.
May I wish you and your family the best of luck and success in your

future and let God's speed always be with you everywhere you go.
Regards,
Toanimatang Teraoi (Tony)

DEPARTMENT OF THE NAVY
HEADQUARTERS UNITED STATES MARINE CORPS
WASHINGTON D.C. 20380

Hd

29 Nov 1984

Major General Raymond L. Murray, USMC (Ret.)
1504 Laurel Road
Oceanside, California 92054

Dear Ray,
    Thank you very much for sending me a copy of Toanimatang Teraoi's letter of 4 October.
    It is a humbling experience to read his letter. I don't know who "Big Red" might be, but I am shocked and horrified that he would send such a letter to Tony.
    With all best wishes to you,

Sincerely,
E. H. SIMMONS
Brigadier General, U. S. Marine Corps (Ret.)
Director of marine Corps History and Museums

    Land & Survey Office
    P.O. Box 7
    Bairiki, Tarawa
    Republic of Kiribati
    Central Pacific

17 July 1985

Dear Murray,
    I was glad to receive your letter 2 December 1984. Thank you for expressing your very shocked feelings about the letter written by Big Red. Please forgive me in being so late in replying. This was caused mostly by the pressure of work invasion, followed by three months admission to the hospital

for hepatitis. Anyway I'm fine now and think it is time to drop a line from Kiribati.

Sorry to hear you were wounded during the landing on Saipan in the Marianas. I am happy you are still alive.

You asked how I learned to speak and write English so well. I was born 16 October 1926, and when I was eight, went to boarding school where there were 70 students collected from all the islands. The school was called King George V. In 1940 the Japanese destroyed the school and put us all to work as laborers.

After the war I worked with the American soldiers cleaning up the area, doing laundry, burying the dead. This ended in 1944. 1945-47 I worked in the Residents Commissioner's office as a messenger and mechanical driver. Off and on through the years I've worked as a stevedore, tally clerk also in the Administration Department of Betio, code and decode clerk, and at the present, at the Land and Survey Division. This should bring you up to date, I've been married twice and have two children.

When you have time, please send me information about your family, your health, what you have done since you retired.

I promise I will write sooner next time. God be with you in all you do.

Sincerely,
Toanimatang Teraoi (Tony)

Bairiki, Tarawa
Republic of Miribati
Central Pacific

13 April 1987

Mrs. Sherry Smeltzer,

My name is Rurete T. Teraoi, I am Tony's son. I'm glad to hear from my father that he had received a letter from you.

We are only two in our family, me and an elder sister, but we have different mothers. I was born in 1959. I am married and we have three children, a girl and two boys. Their ages are nine, seven and four.

Sherry, I have bad news for you and I would appreciate it you would tell your father, and the rest of your family. My father, Toanimatang Teraoi, died last month on the 21st of March. He died of diabetes illness. Before he died he asked me to answer all the letters he received before he died. I'm not so good in English Language but I try for my father's sake.

I'm on leave now but I work as a seaman on the German vessel and have been in many parts of the world. We have a Marine training school here

48

in Kiribati and I passed my test after one year. I feel I am lucky.

*Give my regards to your husband and children and the rest of the
General's family. May God bless us all.*

Sincerely,
Rurete, Teraoi

22 June 1987

Dear General Murray,

What a poignant ending to the Tony saga!

*The faith those islanders had in us makes me feel very humble and
in many ways unworthy. I am not sure we have done so well by the world
since 1945.*

We will take note of Tony's passing in FORTITUDINE.

With all best wishes.

Sincerely,
E. H. SIMMONS
Brigadier General, U. S. Marine Corps (Ret.)
Director of marine Corps History and Museum

Tony, forty years later,
identified himself as my seventeen year old spy

Major General Raymond L. Murray, USMC (Ret)
Oceanside, California 92054

Leon Uris:

"Just as the battle of Belleau Wood stopped the great German onslaught on Paris in World War One, so did the bravery at Tarawa shatter Japanese illusions.

On that terrible day in November of 1943, what kept them coming through chest high water, their only armor, was the thickness of their dungarees? Faith in the Corps, faith in each other and love of their country. Each man said to himself, silently," I am a Marine."

And they are Marines, every one of them. They were the finest ever seen."

Retired Commander inspired author Uris

Retired Maj. Gen. Ray Murray said he remembers many men in his World War II Marine battalion saying they were going to write a book about their experience. So he wasn't too surprised when he received an unpublished manuscript one day in 1953.

"I thought it was interesting, but I didn't think it would sell very well," he said. "I didn't think anyone outside of our battalion would be interested."

The writing battalion member was Leon Uris, and the book was "Battle Cry," a bestseller that launched Uris' career and became a 1955 movie staring Van Heflin in the role modeled after Murray.

Murray's character was the battalion leader in the book, and while he recognizes some of himself, he said it definitely was not him. At one point, Van Heflin confronts a general and demands that he send his men into battle, something Murray said a lieutenant colonel would never do.

"The events he described in the book did take place," Murray said, except for the exchange between the general and his character.

Uris kills off the commander in the book. In real life, Murray went on to serve in Korea, was base commander of Camp Pendleton from 1960-'62 and was deputy corps commander in Vietnam, making him second in command of all the Marines at war.

"I didn't really get to know him well until after the war," Murray said of Uris.

The two reunited by chance in San Francisco after the war and have remained in touch since. Uris went on to write the best-sellers "Exodus," "The Haj" and "Trinity."

Murray said Uris lives in New York and is working on a new book about a Marine unit in the 1850s.

"He thinks it's going to be one of his best," Murray said.

— **Staff writer Gary Warth**

50

Hawaii

January 1944:

Before I left Tarawa I received a letter from Eve saying how worried she was about Michael. He had had a difficult time all winter with bronchitis and she was afraid it was getting worse. I was strapped down with this dengue fever and was concerned that if I flew home it would be an added burden to Eve and certainly something I should not be exposing to a baby. She had written often about him, trying to make me part of his baby life, as she had been three months pregnant when I left in October, and when he was born in April, I was not able to come home. When we arrived in Hawaii, 20 January, I was able to get on my feet, but it seems the recovery from dengue fever takes forever; it took three months before the fever finally left. During this time I continued to work with the troops, as they also had health battles of their own.

On 20, January, I had received a call from Eve; this precious little boy had died. His short life was from April 11, 1943 to January 21, 1944. When I was well enough to travel and arrived home, all arrangements had been taken care of, and my precious baby was gone without my ever seeing him.

I flew back to Hawaii, where a camp had been ready for us: clean beds, good food, a place to recuperate from ailments. We were a sorry crew; everyone brought something back with them. In time we gained our strength back, trained hard on the Parker ranch; the biggest ranch on the island, with room for everyone and every training program. The camp was located between two volcanic mountains, near the city of Hilo. As we were feeling better the training became strenuous and heavy; concentrating on amphibious landings on Maui. We were getting ready, our bodies toughened, for combat again when the news that the chiefs of staff in Washington had agreed to back Admiral Minitz's plan (in opposition to MacArthur's) to strike at Japan by way of Central Pacific: Saipan, 1200 miles from Tokyo. This was to be our next objective and the date was set for 15 June, 1944. We were to make the combat landing.

Saipan

15 June 1944:

Isles de los landrones

"Thieves Island"

a.k.a. Saipan.

Saipan is an island, 15 miles long and 4 miles wide, with a very rich history. It had been a pirate's hideout and a very dangerous place to happen upon when Magellan discovered the Mariana Islands and named them for the queen of Spain. The queen turned the island of Saipan into a Jesuit retreat and a Seminary base. The pirates lost their hideout.

By the Second World War, the Japanese were firmly entrenched in the Mariana Islands. It was the Marine objective to dislodge them from all the islands. We had secured Guadalcanal by February 1943 and Tarawa by January 1944, and we were looking towards Saipan as an airbase that would be within striking air miles of Japan.

We had been training for months at Camp Tarawa in Hawaii. Most of the training was in land rehearsal and without a clue of where we would be going next, but we knew from the extensive training it would be a tough objective; then we were told we would make the combat landing in Saipan. Saipan, just twelve hundred miles by air from Japan, had been mentioned as it would provide the airport we needed for a direct shot. Saipan is the objective and D day is set for 15 June, 1944.

As we approached the island, we could see a long skinny land area with a mountain range down the middle. A towering peak we identified as Mount Tapotchau, appeared to rise about fifteen hundred feet. A jagged reef surrounded the island, and in some areas extends out as far as 1800 yards from the shore.

The only approach could be with amtracs. We had learned a harsh lesson at Tarawa by not having enough amtracs, also by not having a demolition under-water surveillance to bring up information as to what was hidden in the reefs. We needed a clear passage.

The Navy pilots put an end to the Japanese air cover by what they called the "Marine Turkey Shoot" and brought down 402 Japanese planes in one day. Our battleships had been firing for two days on Japanese ships, sunk four of them, and we did not anticipate trouble here. We were to see how wrong we were.

15 June 1944 at 0542,

Vice Admiral Richmond Turner ordered: "Land the landing force." We were in LVTs and took our positions, displaying flags, designating which beach we were to control. The admiral delayed the "H" hour from 0830 to 0840 to give us time to get in position. The 2/6, my unit, was scheduled to land at Red Beach 1, but we had been pushed off course by a northerly tide and landed 400 yards north of our designation. We were the first assault wave in amphibian tractors. We had 75 mm guns firing rapidly. Our light gunboats fired rockets. 2/6 as well as 3/6 were the assault battalions, and by 0900 we were on shore but the smoke was heavy from a sugar mill fire at Charan-Kanoa and the trees on Tapotchau; it was impossible to see through the close fire. To this point the ships' guns and the strafing of bombs had finished the work they were going to do. Now it was up to the rifleman and the machine gunners.

We had debarked and fought our way in and the Japanese mortar and fire was knocking the hell out of our companies. We were widely separated, and we knew immediately they had figured our positions. Any elevated point where there was a crevice, a cave, or a dug foxhole, fire was coming and it kept coming closer. My orders were for everyone to take cover.

The 1st Battalion, 29th Marines seized Hill 410 and went on to take Radio Road Ridge. Woody Kyle was ordered to seize Mount Tapotchau the night before we were to land. It wasn't to happen that way. It was so heavily defended, the Japanese counter attacked. We were caught in deadly accurate crossfire, and it was hitting full force. It dawned on us that the lookout was 1500 feet above us on Mt. Tapotchau and they were zeroed in on us. They had concealed positions covering the beach area, manned with automatic weapons and anti-boat guns sited to cover the approaches to the landing beaches.

We reported that we were 75 to 100 yards from the road and meeting heavy machine gun fire, but our landing had been successful. Then mortar became very heavy and I needed to locate a place for my CP (Command Post). I peered over a berm of sand, trying to locate a site, when a mortar shell landed right behind me, killing two lieutenants who were crouched next to me, and wounding fourteen other marines who were in the vicinity. I was knocked out for a few minutes. When I came to, my clothes were in tatters and blood was everywhere. I'm thinking, I must be dead, "Well this is it, this is what it means to be killed in war." My little orderly is scared to death and can't get the morphine needle in my arm, and no wonder. By this time I'm getting a little dramatic, telling him, "Well Zutz, I guess I don't have much longer." Then I began to feel better and said, "Oh God, I'm not going to die after all. Come on Zutz, let's run across the road."

It seemed we had plenty of cover. I got it again; a bullet ricocheted and hit me in the hip. We got to the other side and Zutz saw a corpsman and called him over. I asked him "how bad is it?" He said, "Oh God, Colonel, it looks bad." Again I thought, "Jesus, maybe I've had the course." Zutz went for help across the road. He didn't come back. Worried, I managed to crawl across the road. I saw Zutz's body there. Another mortar shell had landed and caught him. He had been decapitated. This brave little orderly, who had knocked the Japanese off my back at Tarawa, had lost his life helping me at Saipan. There is no way to explain the emotional toll of losing someone who has been serving this close for so long. He was always just two steps behind me, ready with anything I needed. War is Hell.

As I felt better and continued to command, I had a corpsman prop me up against my jeep, he seemed rather new at this and nervous and I'm beginning to wonder if I'm worse off than I thought. I lined up the officers and gave them orders. Then Colonel Riseley arrived and told me I needed to be evacuated because I was losing too much blood. He told me, "I don't know how you are managing to move around." I told him I felt better, I didn't want to leave, and thought I could be taken care of in the field. He tells me again you are to be evacuated. "You've been pelted so badly with shrapnel you are bleeding everywhere, besides your clothes are all blown off. You can't command without any clothes on. I'm calling a corpsman to put you on an amtrac." The first comment by the corpsman was, "Don't move, you have a lot of lead in you, and you are losing a lot of blood." Four corpsmen put me on a plane to the hospital ship.

Half of the Second Divisions' ten original officers were wounded in the first ten hours. Jim Crowe, Lt. Col. Jack Miller, Easley and myself. The worst hit was Jim Crowe; he had been a legend in the Marines for as long as I had been part of it. Now he has been shot through the lungs by a machine gun bullet and was bandaged everywhere, both arms and, I believe, in the legs. We all knew him as one of the worlds' finest rifle shots, a Marine football player and a tough fighter. Predictions were he wasn't going to make it. Then the word went out he died. We knew this couldn't be. Later, when he heard what the correspondent had written " The corps has lost one of its greatest officers on the Saipan Beach." When he heard this he growled, "That is a helluva exaggeration." He lived, went on to serve the Corps with honor for many years, married Mona Quele and together they had seven children. He went on to be an advisor of the film "Battle Cry."

My mind is going back to when I first met this legend. My first recollection, was on a troop train coming from Chingwan to Peking. Next to Korea it was the coldest in memory I have. Later I got to know him and loved him, as every one else did, he was a real role model.   Eddie Albert commented: "We were elated when he received the Navy Cross."

Two hours after I was hit, my executive officer, Major Howard Rice, caught a piece of mortar in his back. Lt. Col. William Keagle commanded until Major LeRoy Huret, Jr. took over. LeRoy lasted until the end of the battle. It was a miracle anyone made it through the day.

I was put on a hospital ship back to Hawaii. After several days, although stiff, I could walk. Walking wasn't the concern of the doctors, and they designated the nurses to keep asking me every five minutes if I could pass gas. A question one doesn't ask. In fact I consider it a rude question in the best of company. I was failing to understand their fascination with this body function, when they told me the shrapnel had taken part of my bowel, and until there was some movement of some kind, my body might close down. They wanted to make sure all the tubing was clear. Then without any warning, I brought a smile to the entire ward. There was no way it could be quieted. I'm embarrassed and the nurses looked at me and smiled as though what I had accomplished was something to be proud of. I'm pronounced mobile again, but the doctors would not allow me to return to Saipan with my unit. Instead I was put on Boeing Clipper and flew back to San Francisco. There, I asked to be sent back to San Diego. I'm bandaged everywhere, draining from my rear end and they tell me to take fifteen days leave and then report to Quantico, Virginia.

Drove my family to Quantico, the pain, unbearable, and on arrival checked into the hospital. The doctor said it would be quite a job ahead of him and I would need to be in the hospital a few days. When he said he could do it now or later, I opted for later as there was a course I needed to attend before I could start teaching Basic school. Somehow, I managed to get through the course, using padding for my leakage, and a lot of aspirin. When I finally checked into the hospital the doctor removed all the shrapnel pressing on nerves, the rest he left in and said it would be a souvenir of my few hours on Saipan.

(I was awarded my first Navy Cross for: Heroism under fire, June 15, 1944 while commanding the 2nd Battalion 6th Marine Division, showing conspicuous gallantry, although seriously injured, Lt. Col. Murray, continued to command his unit.)

The school went well, and through the years I've run into many of the students I taught there. Some I've had with me in battle areas. It was a good time, and time well spent with family.

I was given temporary duty in Washington when President Franklin Roosevelt died. We had a composite group of sailors, soldiers, and Marines plus some of the enlisted from the base Basic school, and made up a temporary battalion. When we arrived in Washington, I was assigned to command the Honor Guard for the President's funeral. It was to be held in the Rose Garden and would follow an itinerary of an honorary sequence.

We presented arms when the body was brought in and again at the funeral. Seemed every friendly nation in the world had a representative, plus the entire cabinet and the Supreme Court. It was very impressive to be standing so near the leaders of all the countries in the world. What an impact this man had had in the world, and he would achieve a very deserving place in our history as one of our outstanding presidents.

Then we were told we would participate in the ceremonies at Hyde Park. We had just one set of uniforms with us so we did what we could to keep them presentable. The troops took off their trousers and for a good part of the train ride, tried to get a crease back in them. This was difficult as we were in our greens.

It was a very memorable and respectful duty and we were honored to be there. In my memory book is a well treasured letter from Eleanor Roosevelt, thanking us for our participation.

I remained at Quantico until we were ordered to become a part of O. P. Smith's special brigade, and moved to Camp Lejuene, North Carolina to organize training for the troops. There was a problem in Haiti and we were worried it might cause trouble. General Smith was replaced by General Minmer, and we were prepared, but the trouble did not present itself. We did continue amphibious exercises in Puerto Rico where eventually we broke up the brigade.

21 August 1946
My son, James, was born.

Shortly after, I was ordered to China but the orders were changed to Hawaii. I'm now the Deputy Chief of Staff to Garrison Forces in the Pacific. General Worton, the incoming general of Garrison Forces, needed a Lieutenant Colonel to go to all the various islands and meet with the commands to help them get organized. He knew me so I was ordered to report.

I'm including the beautiful note I received from Mrs. Roosevelt. This lovely lady found the time to be gracious with all the heavy duties she had to endure during this sad time.

Dear Helen,

I am, at this moment, in an airplane about midway between Guam and Pelelieu. Since I have a few spare minutes I thought I'd take this opportunity to write a short letter.

Our party left Pearl on the 14th for Okinawa. It was my first trip to the island, and I was very impressed. Okinawa is one of the prettiest and most interesting islands I've seen in the Pacific. It is almost out of the subtropical belt, and therefore has no jungles that I know of. We were there for only a day so I was unable to see very much of it, but what I did see was very much like central California, in many respects. There were pine trees and what I took to be fir trees, also, there were many gardens and rice paddies.

Many of the gardens were planted along streams, terraced as is usual in Asia, and utilizing the streams for irrigation. The people are small and look very much like japanese, although I believe they disclaim any relationship. Their villages are also typically Asiatic - that is, the homes are in small groups, built very closely together. The streets are very narrow and winding. I took a few color pictures while I was there, and they turned out well, so I will show them to you when I get home.

From Okinawa, we flew to Tokyo, and then drove down to Yakasuka, the former Japanese Naval Base about sixty miles south of Tokyo. I didn't take pictures there as the day was overcast and drizzly. Tokyo looks grim, great areas are burned out completely, and the temporary structures for the most part are tin shanty town affairs. Everything was so different from when I was there before the war. The people seemed happy, though, and I saw more smiles and laughter than I've ever seen at home.

From Tokyo we return to Guam, and spent yesterday inspecting the barracks. A little trouble seemed to be brewing in Pelelieu, so we decided to take a run over there to see what that was about and inspect the barracks while we there. Will remain in Pelelieu overnight, fly back to Guam tomorrow and then to Saipan, for the inspection, and then back to Pearl.

I'll arrive in Pearl about three days before Eve does and I'm as excited as a school boy. I'm certainly ready for more family life, I'll tell you. I presume you are coming along with your studies. The last report indicated as much anyway.

P.S. I returned last night and found your letter waiting for me this morning. Enclosed is your check for your next quarter. Keep plugging and let me know how you are doing.

Eve and the kids left San Francisco yesterday and will arrive on the 31st.

Love, Ray

April 19, 1945

Dear Mr. Secretary:

I wish to express my deepest
appreciation for the wholehearted cooper-
ation and help rendered to us at Hyde Park,
by Lieutenant Colonel Raymond L. Murray,
of the United States Marine Corps.

He contributed much to the planning
and accomplishment of the arrangements. I am
very grateful for his assistance.

Very sincerely yours,

Eleanor Roosevelt

Chapter Four

Hawaii

1948:

My next orders were to go to China, and then they were changed to Hawaii and attached to the Garrison Forces in the Pacific. My job consisted of many hours of flight time, going from one island to another. The officers were asking for publications and guidance to help solve problems in setting up barrack detachments. I was to find out what they needed, give them assistance in getting it and being an overall advisor. Many of the young officers commanding the islands had attended Basic school in Quantico, had been to war, gotten promoted, but needed to know how to run a barracks. It was my job to help them.

The assignment lasted two years and, it not being a regimental organization, there were no quarters for families. It took seven months to find an apartment that would accommodate a family with two boys one eight years old and one two years old. We got the family settled and Eve tells me we are going to have another one. I thought it would be a good time for my mother to see Hawaii. She had never been very far from home and certainly had never flown, but she had mentioned, to me, Eve should have some help when the baby came. I used her words against her fear because I knew it would take an enormous amount of encouragement, and several assurances that flying was safe, to get her on a plane. She finally consented and arrived in time to be there when the baby was born. We had wanted a girl to go with the two boys we had, but it was necessary to put the name on file when Daniel Walker Murray arrived on June 23, 1948.

Eve was in the hospital and we were all down with the flu, concerned about bringing her home with a new baby. Of course, Eve, being Eve, began looking after all of us. She had been through some tough times before and this was just another one she took in her stride, just happy to get her family together, even for brief periods of time. Now we have a month-old baby, and we are ordered to Quantico for temporary duty on the Marine Corps Board at the Basic School. We knew it was temporary and didn't settle in anywhere. Good we didn't, my next orders were back to Camp Pendleton.

1950 Movie making at Camp Pendleton - The Halls of Montezuma

1949-1950   Camp Pendleton

My orders to Camp Pendleton was as a Lieutenant Colonel to serve as assistant chief of staff, a G-4 and commanding officer of the 3rd Division.

During the time I was a G-4, we were getting what I considered as junk back from China, remnants left by the 3rd and 4th Marines. I was ordered to organize the debarkation of these ships and move troops and equipment back to Camp Pendleton. The ships had to be unloaded on a 24 hour a day basis. I should have known about the 24 hour schedule but I didn't. It was all junk, mostly motor transport pieces; none of it was in good enough condition to roll on its own. Now we needed trucks, qualified drivers who were licensed to drive these big trucks, and people to load and unload them. We had used civilian ships so there was demurrage to consider, so the rush was on, heavy, so thought I should talk with General Erskine. It didn't Help, He just smiled and said, "Keep plugging" We finally got the mess in order and two months later the 3rd Marines were designated the 5th Marines.

We went back to conventional training, with Brute Krulak in command of the 5th. I became his executive and never worked harder in my life. He worked all our butts off. We trained, trained and trained some more. He covered all the areas of training but seemed to focus heavily on amphibious operations; they seemed to be the top priority. I termed this exercise Demon 111. He scripted every move and the rehearsals were tough, he wasn't finished until he thought we could handle anything. We were the best trained outfit in the military, and later we thanked him, every time we were in combat.

It seemed the Marines were playing at war instead of being battle ready. But this was not the case. We were in heavy training as well as providing troops for a film being made at Camp Pendleton. The film "From the Halls of Montezuma" did pull from our more experienced Marines for direction, analysis and review, but it did not weaken our force in any way.

After working this hard and getting the 5th to this readiness, Brute was transferred out. They must have needed his knowledge somewhere else. This was just ten days before the north Koreans crossed the 38th Parallel. This put me, a Lt. Col. as his executive, commanding the regiment.

7, July:

Orders came to prepare to go to Korea, and be prepared to leave on 14, July . We had families to think about and six days to get them situated. Base housing would no longer be available. Most rentals would not allow single parents, and if they would, they would prefer the children not be boys. And we had three boys. We would need to rely on relatives, and as I didn't have the time to help Eve solve this problem, I would be anxious until it was solved. She would be writing me.

From time to time, in different battle areas, a helicopter would appear and Brute would arrive to check on the Marines he'd trained. It was always good to see him, even if we knew he could still be tough on us.

Chapter Five

Pusan Perimeter

In 1948, there had been a probable dissolution of the Marine Corps, supported by President Truman and General Eisenhower. Paul Douglas, a former Regimental Commander Adjutant, was elected to Congress and sponsored a bill allowing a commandant to meet with the Joint Chiefs of Staff when Marine Corps matters were on the agenda. The bill proposed the Marine Corps would stay and have permanent strength of Four Divisions and supporting aviation, giving the Marine Corps equal status with the Air Force, the Army, and the Navy. A campaign began to build up popular support for the idea that the size of the Corps should be fixed by law without reference to numerical strength to the Navy. This was going on in Congress and it was touch and go whether the Marine Corps would win the vote to be a corps of its own standing or be attached to the Navy. We were very heavily into training. General Omar Bradley was questioning the readiness of the military. The Army had just one division, the 82nd Airborne. The Air Force was getting top priority because of the bomb, and at the top of the list of the cutting was the Marine Amphibious Force. The Navy was struggling, being reminded, two oceans protected us from other continents, so therefore was not a top priority. Our military budget, in no way, was matching the Soviets.

My thoughts that existed and conditions we were aware of before the start of the war in Korea, when the North Koreans invaded South Korea in June of 1950, were that United States Armed Forces were not prepared for war. Our marvelous military forces which were in existence at the end of WWII, had disintegrated. What was left, very little. Our Army was on occupational duty. Hardly the type of duty to prepare one for combat. Many, if not most of the men, were young and had not participated in WWII.

The First Marine Division at Camp Pendleton, comprised of but one infantry regiment with corresponding reduced strength in all the supporting forces. Furthermore this infantry regiment, while it had three battalions, had only two companies per battalion and two platoons per company.

The South Koreans, who were thought to have had a well trained well equipped army were overrun very quickly by the North Korean Army, primarily because of the T-34 tanks, which the North Koreans had in fair numbers. We knew these were supplied by the Soviets as they had worked so well against the Germans in the European War. It rapidly became evident, if the South Koreans were to be saved, outside troops would have to be committed. Among the first of these troops, were the Army forces of occupation from Japan, who were rushed in piecemeal, as transport was available. They went in under overwhelming odds, poor intelligence and the fact they were purely on defensive, combined to make the situation difficult to the extreme. Under the circumstances, it was no wonder the first few months of the war, the United States was witness to the awful fact, her Army was driven back by an enemy never considered seriously to amount to anything.

During this early period, the 1st Marine Division was alerted to organize a brigade for deployment to the Far East. The brigade was the first of which, that had been requested by General Douglas MacArthur to make an amphibious landing at Inchon, well behind the North Korean lines. So much was going on it was difficult to keep informed. Startling news did reach us: Forrestal, who had been in charge of the budget, had a nervous breakdown and jumped out of the sixteenth floor of the Bethesda Naval Hospital. Louis Johnson replaced him.

The Americans had pulled their troops out of Korea in the summer of 1949. the Defense Department felt it was best to write of Korea militarily. We didn't want to abandon it altogether, and eased our conscience by trying to train an army in Korea. It takes time to train officers, and a guerrilla type army without proper leadership would not be able to hold its own. An officer can make a split decision and, if he isn't right, has the training to turn things around and save lives. However, it takes strong leadership, the ability, talent and skill to backup this training. The Soviets had equipped and supplied the Chinese Route Army and built an invading force of fifteen Divisions equipped with one thousand tanks. The little Republic of Korea's military force had cleared miles of road and mines. These brave fighters, so outnumbered and lacking equipment, made it impossible to hold ground. It was a defense of sort, but not combat ready. There was support from Japanese/American Army, but neither group was strong enough to defend anything. Stalin knew this and decided it was time to unify Korea. On June 25, 1950, the North Koreans crossed the 38th Parallel.

We were embarrassingly short of everything. We'd thought the war in Europe would end all wars and overlooked what might happen in Asia. Spending for defense was down to 13 billion dollars, and every part of the military had suffered. We were under equipped and weakened. The force itself was down to 1.6 million; manpower had been stripped and under trained, and we also suffered from lack of political intelligence. At first, it

64

was thought that police action by the United States would limit commitment. When it turned out to be an all out war between the Communists and the Non-Communists, this created some very heated political discussions, and some action began to take place. Congress did provide Truman with an 11 billion dollar emergency fund, plus a bill was passed in Congress to extend the Draft. Draft orders were sent to 50,000 civilians in September, and each month thereafter additional orders were sent out. The new recruits were in the front lines within ten days, without training, and some had never picked up a rifle. The Army was the most poorly trained in the history of the United States. There simply was no motivation. We had not been attacked and most of the troops had never even heard of Korea. It appeared to them that it was a civil war and none of our business, but powers were telling them it was to keep Communism from spreading. President Truman signed a Council paper, saying we must defend Democracy at home and abroad, and respond to the invasion of Korea. Kim Il Sung, the dictator, had a record of bloody abuses, killing in cold blood anyone who opposed him. We were backing Syngman Rhee, who was leading a government that was also suspect, but was nearer to a Democracy than the government by the tyrant Kim Il Sung.

Korea was reaching a stage of combat that was no longer a winning situation. MacArthur in Tokyo wasted no time in letting the Chiefs of Staff know that his army needed help or all of Korea would be lost. The Pusan Perimeter was all that was left and it was getting smaller with each attack.

General Erskine received orders to form a Provisional Brigade under command of Brigadier General Edward Craig, and the 5th Regiment was assigned to me. We were a rifle company and short of everything-troops and supplies-but the troops were well trained and battle ready. Preparations for Korea started in June 1950; this was to be an invasion. General Erskine was still in command and General Craig was the Assistant Division Commander. Neither General Erskine nor General O. P. Smith were there in the beginning. O. P. Smith was with the rest of the Division, and it wasn't until the Division had to go to Korea that O. P. came out.

As a Lt. Colonel, I had hoped that I would keep the assignment. General Erskine convinced General Cates that he didn't need a Colonel, that he had someone who could handle it. It was some time before I was able to believe I would keep the command.

Victor (Brute) Krulak and I arrived in San Diego about the same time, I as a Second Lieutenant, fully indoctrinated as a Marine. We both knew this would be our life's work. Brute was an outstanding leader, a man of high character whom I personally admired. We both knew enough about each other to make judgments on how each would act, re-act, analyze and perform, if need be, to a tough situation. We had been working together for a year in a training program at Camp Pendleton. I was lucky enough to be his executive officer. It was my understanding that Brute was to go to Korea, but then his orders came, he was needed elsewhere. Our confidence had to be in the Marines. The 5th Marines were so well trained; we had no turnover for a full year preceding this, and a Regiment that has been together for a full year becomes an extremely well trained outfit. Additional good news came when three Battalion Commanders were assigned. George Newton had the 1st, Hal Roise, the 2nd, and Bob Taplett the 3rd. They were all Lt. Colonels and excellent people. The other Regiment Commanders were Homer Litzenberg and Chesty Puller, both Colonels. I was to meet them both for the first time in Korea.

On Sunday, 25 June 1950, the North Koreans crossed the 38th Parallel. The United Nations asked the aggression be stopped. America, again, sent in Army Troops, (we had pulled most of our support out in 1949) but they were poorly trained and equipped. They could not hold ground against the overpowering numbers and were pushed back to the Pusan Perimeter. This was the news that came back to Camp Pendleton. We were also concerned, when Chaing Kia-shek left China for Taiwan, and within weeks Russia was testing the bomb. China became Communist and Beijing was the first area well under their new form of government. This prompted McCarthyism into the picture, and created a frenzy, McCarthy was looking for communists, in the theatre, the government and in anyone who didn't believe we were about to be overtaken. Russia had been an ally, now a power behind the Chinese. Neither were no longer our friends.

At Barstow, supplies that had been recovered and stored from the previous war were repaired, repainted and made battle ready. Although not new, they were available. We added new M-26 tanks and started retraining the Marines in firing 90 mm guns. The equipment was old and we were constantly being reminded of the Russian T-34 tanks. El Toro supplied the aviators and planes, Quantico the helicopters and pilots. We needed a 3rd Platoon to each rifle company but it was impossible to get, and we knew it would be a serious shortage in combat. We were aware that being short a rifle company and having outdated equipment, we would need to lean heavily on air power. General Craig stressed this strongly when he met with MacArthur.

We spent four days packing and boxing equipment, training the men with some of the new equipment, and making the men aware of some of the training they would need in the M-26 Pershing Tanks and the M20 Rocket Launchers. On July 11, 1950 the 5th Marines, 2643 Riflemen and Combat Specialists boarded the transport ships: The Henrico, the George Clymer and the Pickaway. The dock-landing ships were the Guston Hall and the Fort Marion.

At sea, no one knew exactly where we would be committed to action, but we knew we would be in combat assisting the South Koreans and helping them to ward off the Communists. Army General Walker retreated to what was called the Pusan Perimeter. It hugged the Sea of Japan, the Naktong River and the Naktong Bulge, and there was a border on one side, mountains and rice the rest of the area. It covered a space of about ninety miles one way and sixty miles in another, and was in the form of a rectangle.

The ship I was on, The Henrico, ran into engine trouble. It blew a cylinder off San Clemente Island and had to hobble up to San Francisco for repairs. We did manage to catch up with the rest of the ships and arrived at Pusan, August 2. The 3rd Rifle Company and Platoon were to arrive later. Camp Pendleton was putting this together by stripping all other infantry units. There were three Battalions; each Battalion had two Companies and each Company had two Platoons. This is what we left San Diego with, weak of reinforcing elements with just three tanks in the Antitank Platoon.

MacArthur wanted Marines for an amphibious landing and we would be going as a Brigade. We had expected to stop in Japan, but the plans changed, as the Army was losing ground, sinking fast to the North Koreans. We wondered if they would be able to hold out until we got there. On July 30, General Craig set up a temporary command post and wrote letters to the Brigade to be battle ready when we docked at Pusan. The orders were not received by me until we docked at Pusan. Brig. Gen. Edward Craig was waiting for us as we docked and asked for an immediate meeting with the officers. When he started speaking we knew the situation was urgent. He started with:

"If I asked you gentlemen to be prepared for combat in ten days. I know you would do it. And if I asked you to disembark your troops, unload your gear and be prepare to go into the field tomorrow morning, I know you can and will do it. The perimeter is so close, the noise you are hearing is gunfire, the need is now."

We spent the night unloading the ships. As our orders were to move out at 0600, we were tired as we unloaded 9,400 tons of supplies, including the 3.5 tons in total of rocket launchers and the new M026 Pershing tanks. New equipment had not been made available to General Walker and the Army was being run over. The rocket launchers we brought with us were in two pieces, weighing just twelve pounds, and could be transported wherever needed. They could penetrate armor with accuracy up to 900 yards. These proved invaluable in battle.

On board we had been made aware of the rapid progress the North Koreans were making into South Korea, and we needed to make haste. We split the Marines into three units: the 2nd Battalion 5th Marines from The George Clymer, the 3rd Battalion from the Pickaway, and mine, of course, was from The Henrico. We had 6,534 Marines, three Rifle Battalions with only two rifle companies. Even with this disadvantage, they were well trained

Marines and ready to accept our orders to move to Changwon and stop the North Koreans from moving to Masan.

By the time the Brigade arrived in the Far East, the situation in the perimeter had deteriorated to the extent necessary to commit the Brigade to the defense of the peninsula around the principal city of Pusan,

Pusan, itself, had elements that in the best of times would be considered undesirable. In war times, they had their own black market going in any manner imaginable, and of course offered all this type of service to the Marines. The place smelled not only from the politics but also from the human waste used as fertilizer on the rice paddies, intensified by the hot and humid weather. The landing of the UN and US troops pushed the North Koreans to cross the Naktong on 4, August. We learned later they used sand bags and steel oil drums, and built an underground tunnel that could not be seen from the air. When they crossed on August 4, they brought with them T-34 Russian tanks, 32 tons, and armor plated. These tanks had been successful against the Germans. Each tank had an 85 mm gun. There was no doubt that the Russians were supplying the North Koreans, and we could also see equipment that Russians had revived, as we had done, from the past war when we had been their ally, that was definitely supplied by our lend lease.

When Seoul was captured by the North Koreans, they felt the time was right to find a weak spot along the Naktong Bulge and break through. They did, and as they pushed eastward, the Marines were called on to help. We moved the troops by slow train, and it was a quiet time as they used it to get their equipment and themselves battle ready. Many wrote home, as they might not have had a break to do so later. The maps were all wrong. General Craig used a helicopter to fly over the area.(The first time helicopters were used in a battle area.) He sighted the terrain, corrected maps, located enemy caves, picked up wounded, and kept contact with his commanders. The map correcting was tedious work; the stress was heavy and he needed to rotate his pilots every few hours. He was a hands on general, seemed to be everywhere, and the consensus was he could handle anything.

Within five days of our landing, the Brigade was engaged in its first operation, a breakout from the perimeter to capture the little town of Sachon, which was thirty miles outside the perimeter. It was invaluable as it was our first offensive operation. We had the initiative and there is nothing so effective for creating morale than to be on the offensive. Furthermore we were successful in driving a motorized reconnaissance battalion before us, capturing much of its equipment and eliminating most of its personnel. We had our first fight, it was successful, we were cocky.

We were beating off attacks near Chingchon with our objective just four miles away, and we knew it would be rough trying to reach it by the next day. We moved towards Masan, the anchor of the perimeter near Chindong-ni. Then we moved back and through several towns, just doing what we were ordered. Orders came to hold where we were and return to the perimeter. Artillery Battalion in support of 5th RCT had been cut off, surrounded and wiped out. Here is what occurred:

3, August:

The South Koreans Army and the 8th Army were in serious trouble trying to hold off against the North Korean's move on Pusan. Along with the newly acquired South Koreans troops, we bivouacked at Changwon-ni. There we had a chance to do some additional training with the rifle units and set up a communication system. We were to defend a vital road junction at Chindong-ni, where heavy fighting had been going on with the NK Army; they were headed straight for Pusan. Orders came from General Walker to be prepared for combat by the next evening. Chindong-ni is surrounded by a mountainous range of ragged spurs and the village had been a focus of enemy attack. This was where the Marines were to relieve the Army's 2nd Battalion of the 27th Regiment, attached to Colonel Michael's command.

6, August:

CPQ at Changwon-ni, I called a conference with Lt. Colonel Bob Taplett to proceed to Chindong-ni, and contact Colonel Michaels and arrange to take over. They needed help as General Walker had been taxed to the limit. I also cautioned Taplett that we would be under Army control and it would not be easy as we trained differently and the esprit de corps in the Marines was not easily understood by the Army. Our command post was wherever the fighting was and we, as officers, were there with our men, in direct contact at all times.

Taplett reported that he was unable to contact anyone and had set up a CP on the reverse side of the slope. He learned that the 27th was in the village and had been under heavy attack all night and had driven the NK back to the high ridges. This left our right flank vulnerable and concerned me, as we would be in combat against two Communist Divisions. Taplett's 3/5 moved back into the battle at 0900 with just two LST's with supplies for support, and questioned why we were not provided a hospital LST for the wounded. Ordered to fire on the enemy at 1430, the casualties were piling up as we moved to assist the Army, stalled by heavy artillery and mortar firing. It was an all day battle and we suffered a loss of twenty-five Marines.

7, August:

Lt. Cahill reinforced Army Unit on Hill 342. Lt. Colonel Roise's 2/5 became heavily engaged against the North Korean Peoples Army (NKPA), where we suffered more of the first casualties in the Korean War. The temperature rose to 112 degrees, Men were dropping everywhere from heat prostration and it took its toll. Only 37 of the 52 men reached the crest if Hill 342. The NKPA went around Chindong-ni and cut off the supply road and was putting in some heavy fighting to control the hill. Taplett was driving the enemy off Hill 255 that overlooked and blocked the main supply route. It had taken nine hours of suffering without water in suffocating, sweltering heat, with one third of the Regiment lying on the side of the road, but we finally positioned ourselves on Hill 255. Hot and humid beyond belief, Marines were lying everywhere from heat exhaustion. The hills were impossible, with rough terrain, and slippery rocks. The rice paddies were worse. We were up to our knees in mud and filth, very slow moving. We decided to go down the road, the hill being far enough away that we would have time to react. With heat reaching 110 to 114 degrees, the ridges had been like hot concrete; feet were burning through our shoes, men were dropping from dehydration. More men were lost to the heat than to the enemy. They were dropping everywhere. The rice paddies brought no relief, just required additional effort to move. Those who could had to sweat it out. We called helicopters to lift off the worst cases. Just thirty men and two officers were in good enough shape to get off the hill. The rest just could not make it and crawled under anything they could find for shade. This is why I decided the only way we could move was down the road. We knew that on either side of the road there would be enemy blocks to overcome, and to move a mile took all the strength we had. We did move forward hour by hour through Taedabah Pass, south to Kosong, west to Changchow, and northwest to Sachon.

There was great irritation throughout the Brigade when after three days of success we were recalled into the perimeter because of some successful attacks of the North Koreans behind our backs.

8, August:

Newton's 1/5 moved out of Chindong-ni and ran into a confused Army Battalion, still stalled at a fork in the road where they had taken a wrong turn. The congestion blocked any further advance in that direction, so Newton's orders were changed to a night march to relieve the Army Battalion on Hill 308. To do this he had to veer off the road, becoming totally exposed along a rice paddy and an easy target to be fired upon. The Army Battalion had arrived and were in a hurry to withdraw, without waiting for the Marines relief forces. The Army was totally confused. Newton was quite wordy expressing his opinion of this lousy soldiering. Getting the problem turned around, Newton began advancing the Sachon. Taplett was still in heavy fighting at the rear of the Brigades Command Post.

The war was taking its toll; clothes were being worn for ten days, body odor along with dried blood was awful. We knew that beyond Masan was a boiler, a washing machine, and a portable shower. We could get clean, then leave our clothes and try to find some that would fit. The feeling of being clean again did wonders for the morale.

A letter from home, the first I had received and it was not the best news. The families had been given notice that within two weeks they would have to move from base housing. Most rentals would not take a single parent with children and since ours were boys, it added another negative. The only alternative was to see if we could find a relative to take us in. Eve writes: "You are not to worry. Our problem can be solved in a much easier way than yours. It is just that writing from a different address in the future should not worry you."

9, August:

We broke through after being stalled two days along the Korean south coast. The training is paying off and the teamwork protected by artillery and the Marines air support is making progress. I directed this from a shaded glen with field telephones and radio sets, maps and more maps, and messengers reporting from line commanders. Sometime these commanders came in and brought in progress reports themselves. Our clothes again are beginning to be crusted with sweat and grime.

North Koreans had far more and heavier tanks available than our information provided. They had at least 300 going into the war; our intelligence had estimated 65. The press was reporting our lack of equipment and were ostracized for doing it when it was very evident that we were outnumbered in troops and equipment. The area we were to defend under these conditions, without a third rifle company, needed a positive strategy. The men needed to be positioned in a manner of caution, every man a rifleman, every movement had to count. The North Koreans were determined to take Pusan and wrap up the completion of having all of Korea under Communist control. At this point, the only barrier in their way was the United States Marines.

A farmer dressed in a large white hat and white coat could look very innocent, and might be the one who would throw a grenade at very close range. Some would blacken their faces and walk right up to the field hospitals, firing on the helpless injured. Women with babies were also suspect. We found ourselves relying on Col. Brute Krulak's training, sensing danger by instinct. He had fine-tuned our training to a point where we could see danger in body movements, expressions, smell and hearing, as well as conditioning our bodies for combat. I often wondered if he ever knew how many lives he saved teaching us to sense danger ahead of it happening and how often we relied on it. He had been a tough trainer but the results were positive. Each time we came through a tough situation alive, we thanked him.

10, August:

A tank broke through a bridge and General Craig's orders were to go around it, and leave it there. It would take too much time to clear. Instead, he was to bypass it, move with speed and reach Kosong by nightfall.

11,August:

We reached Kosong. Taplett stayed with the unit and cleared the city ordered an air strike and hit the motorized battalion of enemy tanks, clearing the road from Kosong to Sachon. It was enough of a loss to the enemy that it quieted down the fighting, and three miles east of Kosong, we stopped for the night. At Kosong, General Craig had been informed that two Divisions had broken through the Naktong area. Our 1st Battalion 5th Marines had beaten off the North Korean attacks near Changchon, but our objective was still some rough fighting away. Men were breaking down. They could not understand this war, they were sick of it. In addition, they had just had a shower and clean clothes, but this did not make a difference for very long.

The next orders were to take "Naktong Bulge". It would be a large-scale engagement, the largest yet in the Korean War. My Regiment, the 5th Marines would attack a column of battalions, one in front of the other, with a second battalion in assault followed by the 1st and 3rd. Each would go as hard as it could, then be replaced by the one behind. The enemy would be forced to re-cross the river. They were heavily defended, and Battalion 2 and 3 would be face the worst. Objective One was thought to be lightly defended, easier to seize. On August 12 the 2nd Battalion would seize the Obong-ni Ridge. My orders to Newton the night before were very strong. "We are in a position that we must take that ground tomorrow. You must get on the ridge and take it." Newton answered, "Understood, we will go straight ahead." The men were so tired by this time into battle; I knew we would be lucky to keep them.

12, August:

The enemy attacked again across the main supply line. We needed to formulate a new plan to overcome resistance and went into defensive position for the night. Orders came to begin a tactical with drawl from Sachon east of Paedum-ni We again engaged the enemy north of the road fork and I put Newton's 1/5 in reserve and Roise's 2/5in defensive position at Paedum-ni.

We watched the battle from an adjoining ridge overlooking the battlefield. When the first and third platoons moved towards the ridge, they seemed to be doing all right. When they began to fall from long-range machine gun fire. They were down everywhere, and the casualties were coming from our right flank, the flank that was supposed to be secured by Army Unit 9RTC. They were not protecting it and the enemy was firing into our position. The Marines, who could, made a dash for the wall, some of them carrying wounded along with them. There was safety behind the wall, but exposing themselves, they were targets. The ridge was taken three times, lost three times to automatic weapons fire. We pulled back the second group so we could send in air strikes. They took over. The wounded slipped on loose rocks, rolled down slopes, still firing with whatever weapons they had. This we could see from our hill position; Hill 143 was one of the peaks held by the North Koreans. Obong-ni Ridge was dominated by peaks overlooking the summit. Hill 207 looked down on Obong-ni Ridge from the west. The 1st Battalion 5th Marines, the next unit in line to assault, was moving into position to continue. Fire on Hill 143 was intense coming to Hill 207; phosphorous shells exploded on Hill 143, slowing the fire.

We could count on our hands the men who were able to fight. We saw corpsmen looking for wounded take bullets-one was hit in the chin, one in the arm, and they kept going through fire, crawling on their stomachs from one wounded to another, doing anything to save a life. It seemed the North Koreans got extra points if they killed a corpsman kept them from helping the wounded. There isn't enough that can be said about their devotion to duty, the real heroes in all the wars. By noon, the 2nd was hopelessly stalled. In four hours, we lost 23 dead and 119 wounded. The 1st Battalion was ordered to pass through the 2nd and continue to attack Obong-ni Ridge. The 2nd Battalion moved to a gully between 109-107 that ran down from the summit to a rice paddy below.

The 1st Platoon moved out and seized a portion of the ridge, which helped the 2nd Platoon seize their portion of the ridge. B Company seized Obong-ni Ridge at about 1500. A Company left bank wasn't doing well, suffering from heavy losses when they tied in with H Company. The North Koreans had not been dislodged from the hills. Companies A and H prepared for defense. Night came, the attack ceased, and the rest of the night was rather quiet.

Still: 12, August:

The enemy again attacked across the main supply route. We needed to formulate a new plan to overcome resistance and went into defensive position for the night. Orders came to begin a tactical withdrawal from Sachon east of Paedum-ni. We commenced our withdrawal, destroyed bridges, laid mines and cratered the road. We again engaged the enemy north of the road fork, and I put Newton's 1/5 in reserve and Roise's 2/5 in defensive position at Paedum-ni. Orders came to move the Brigade to Changwon at daylight, and we started moving the heavy equipment at midnight.

14, and 15, August:

Heavy fighting. Heavy losses.

16, August:

Orders were to proceed to Miryang and be prepared to clear the Naktong Bulge. The attack was scheduled for 0800 August 17. Roise's 2.5 Battalion suffered heavy casualties, Newton's 1/5 joined the attack and the objective was secured by nightfall. Although we were to take this objective again we did not disappoint the British military observer. I was given a copy of a cable sent by a British military observer in Korea. This I will share with you:

(Cable sent by British military observer in Korea, August 16, 1950.)

…"THE SITUATION IS CRITICAL AND MIRYANG MAY BE LOST. THE ENEMY HAS DRIVEN A DIVISION-SIZED SALIENT ACROSS THE NAKTONG. MORE WILL CROSS THE RIVER TONIGHT. IF MIRYANG IS LOST…WE WILL BE FACED WITH A WITHDRAWAL FROM KOREA. I AM HEARTENED THAT THE MARINE BRIGADE WILL MOVE AGAINST NAKTONG SALIENT TOMORROW. THEY ARE FACED WITH IMPOSSIBLE ODDS, AND I HAVE NO VALID REASON TO SUBSTANTIATE IT, BUT I HAVE THE FEELING THEY WILL HALT THE ENEMY.
THESE MARINES HAVE THE SWAGGER, CONFIDENCE, AND HARDINESS THAT MUST HAVE BEEN IN STONEWALL JACKSON'S ARMY OF THE SHENANDOAH. THEY REMIND ME OF THE COLD STREAMS AT DUNKIRK. UPON THIS THIN LINE OF REASONING, I CLING TO THE HOPE OF VICTORY."

Naktong

We'd fought before at Chindong-ni, where the Brigade received its baptism of fire, on the long march toward Sachon in the early days of August. While the fighting was vicious and men died, these battles were essentially small scale, with but a Battalion at a time engaged and against odds that favored us rather than the enemy. The U.S. Army had four Divisions along the Naktong River. Question was, could they hold out? We received orders to assist the 8th Army, located about thirteen miles southwest of Chindong-ni. I had put Lt. Colonel Newton in a reserve position at Changwon. At Changyoug-ni I called a conference with Lt. Colonel Bob Taplett, advising him to proceed to Chindong-ni and to contact Army Colonel Mike Michaels; he was to assist the 8th Army and arrange to take over as General Walker was taxed to the limit. I must add here, that Lt. Colonel Bob Taplett was without a doubt, one of the best combat officers I had ever had the opportunity to work with. Many times in the next few months I would thank God for his leadership of his 3/5 Battalion and his ability to take any assignment given him and to excel. He was a man who loved the Corps, but was always aware that he was responsible for his men and did not take the loss of anyone easily.

In his favor was that he had well trained Marines and they were ready to fight. His orders were to slow down the movement of the North Korean Division that was under orders to seize Pusan. The 27th Regiment of the Army had fought hard against the NK 6th, but could not have held had not the Marine Brigade in reserve, at Changyoug-ni, entered the action.

By 1600 the 2nd Battalion left Changwon and the rifle companies moved to Hill 442. Eleven Marines were killed, the hill was held, and the enemy pulled back. The 2nd Battalion launched a night attack and secured Paedum. The enemy left with the 2nd and 3rd Battalions in pursuit. Without much opposition, the motorized column was wiped out.

Earlier there was an ambush at Changdon. Colonel Newton had directed an air strike on the enemy and many of our dead fell and had to be left where they had fallen, something foreign to the Marines, but they could do nothing about it. They had taken the hill and lost it. In war sometimes this happens; an area is taken, lost and taken again. Although something is learned with each battle, it is never easy to leave any of our buddies behind.

Now we were to receive the acid test. For the first time in Korea, the 1st Marine Brigade was to be concentrated in one spot, fighting one battle as a coordinated unit and against odds that any reasonable man would say were outlandish. It is true that the earlier battles had toughened the bodies and the spirits of the entire Brigade, but for the first time we were not only to face the great odds, but we knew that if we did not win this battle, the situation within the perimeter would be desperate, and even a withdrawal from the peninsula could not be ruled out.

The first battle of the Naktong to take shape was when the 4th North Korean Division began pushing troops across the Naktong River in the vicinity of Yongsan between 6 and 10 of August. The entire enemy Division, reinforced by tanks and artillery, had forced the bridgehead some 6000 yards deep on the east bank of the river.

13 August:

The Brigade, which had been attacking in the southern edge of the peninsula towards Sachon, some thirty odd miles outside the perimeter, was directed to break off this action and proceed to Miryang for further offensive action in a new sector. Arriving at Miryang two days later, all hands gloried in a bath in the Miryang, which at that moment had the cleanest, purest water running between its banks that any of us had ever seen.

I must pause here to inject a memory that should be shared, as there are so few things during a war, that when recalled, will bring back a smile. Everyone was ready for a bath, and the river looked like a bit of heaven. Little did we know we would give "Adam" competition. We were a whole regiment of naked men, with not even an olive branch in sight, thoroughly enjoying the cooling bath when Maggie Higgins, a correspondent with the New York

Harold Tribune arrived. This occurrence was to be something that would remain in their tall stories and mine for some time. We underestimated her, though, as she walked through the area as though she did this sort of thing every day. Quite a gal. She couldn't have cared less. Maggie was well respected. She stayed out of the way, had her own sleeping bag and could curl up anywhere; many times the Marines and often times even a General would wake up and not many feet away would be a blond head appearing from under a sleeping bag; she traveled with a comb, a toothbrush, and her typewriter. A dedicated writer, she was after a story and she told it like it was.

After the bath we were given hot food and a change of clean clothes, which made our happiness complete. While this was going on, Brigadier General E. A. Craig, the Brigade Commander, was conferring with Major General Church, the Commanding General of the 24th Army Division, and overall Commander in the area. It was determined at this conference that the entire 24th Division, with the 1st Marine Brigade attached, would attack the bridgehead on the morning of 17 August. The objectives assigned to the Brigade were: first the Obong-ni Ridge, second, Hill 207, which lay directly behind Obong-ni Ridge, and third, Hill 311, which was across a valley from Hill 207 at right angles to the initial axis of advance. Hill 311 dominated the entire bridgehead, and if captured, would require that the enemy retreat behind the river from whence they came.

Obong-ni did not look like a particularly hard nut to crack. It was the lowest of the three objectives assigned and was quite narrow along its spiny serrated ridgeline, precluding any defense in depth. Events were to prove that it was indeed an exceedingly tough nut.

The plan for attack called for a frontal assault by the 5th Marines in columns of battalions against the northeastern edge of the Obong-ni Ridge. The 9th Army RCT, attacking to the right of the 5th Marines, was by prior arrangement between me and the CO 9th RCT, the idea to hold the 5th Marines' attack by fire.

As the 2/5 moved out across the rice paddies separating the line of departure from the objectives, all was relatively quiet. The attack had been preceded by artillery and strafing runs along the Obong-ni's length, which had been lifted.

I must state again, at this point that because of peacetime allowances of personnel, each of the three battalions of the 5th Marines consisted of but two companies each, with each company containing three platoons each, one of which was formed just before the Brigade left California. Not until the Brigade had returned to Pusan after the second battle of the Naktong, some two weeks later, would the battalions receive their third companies. The lack of the third company was to be keenly felt in each of the battalions during the next three days. For each time successes might have been exploited by committing a battalion reserve, there was no reserve to commit.

The advance of 2/5, which had begun at 0800, proceeded up forward slopes of Obong-ni. Suddenly, enemy fire erupted from the front and both flanks. Unfortunately, the expected fire support from RCT 9 did not materialize, for reasons never discovered, of soldiers who'd been available to provide the fire. From Tugock village in a valley in front of RCT9 line of departure, North Korean machine gunners poured a hail of fire into the flank and rear of D 2/5, the right flank company. At the same time, enemy machine gunners from high hills to the left of E 2/5 poured fire into that company's flank. North Korean riflemen began firing and throwing grenades into the front of the advancing battalion.

In the next four and a half hours 2/5 took a terrible beating as platoons and squads decimated by the heavy fighting advanced and fell back. Portions of the ridge were taken, only to be lost again in the face of overwhelming firepower; when it became evident that 2/5 had spent itself against the tremendous volume of fire put up by the enemy, 1/5 was ordered to pass through the exhausted men of 2/5 and continue the attack to take Obong-ni Ridge.

Between 1300 and 1500 the 1st Battalion passed through the lines of the 2nd Battalion and continued toward the crest of the ridge. B Company was on the right portion of the Brigade objective, to which they held tenaciously. On the left, A Company did not fare as well. Receiving heavy and constant machine gun fire from further south of Obong-ni Ridge, the company was unable to advance any further than just below the ridgeline when darkness fell.

At the end of the first day, the balance sheet showed the battalion of the 5th Marines had been badly mauled and another had suffered heavy casualties. About 200 yards of the right portion of the objective was in our hands. The next 200 yards to the left was still in enemy hands, and Marines were within 25 to 50 yards of the ridgeline. It was known that enemy casualties had been heavy, but there was not information as to how many enemy troops remained. Knowing that a night counterattack was virtually inevitable; the men of 1/5 prepared themselves. At about dusk on the 17th, everyone was to receive a tremendous boost to his morale, a welcome change from what had happened during the day.

Four North Korean tanks, accompanied by infantry, were spotted moving down the road from the river to the front of the Marine's lines. An air strike was immediately called for and one of the tanks was destroyed, while at the same time the infantrymen were scattered. The remaining three tanks came on toward the Marine position. Waiting for them were the rocket men of 1/5, a 75 mm Recoilless Gun Platoon, and seven M-26 tanks from A company. As the enemy T-34s came forward they were taken under fire by all the anti-tank weapons, and within a period of a few minutes all three enemy tanks were smoking hulks. Thus ended the myth of the invincibility of the Russian T-34.

18, August:

At 0230 the counterattack came. Since there was not a battalion reserve company, each of the two companies on the line knew they must hold at all cost the ground they had fought so hard to take the day before. Although they were hard hit between 0230 and dawn by hordes of North Koreans, both the left and right flanks of the battalion position held firm. A penetration had been made in the center of the line, but the North Koreans were either unable to take advantage of it or were unaware of the favorable position they had created for themselves.

Shortly after dawn the attack was resumed, and by mid-morning the entire ridgeline belonged to the Brigade. Although no one knew it at the time, the failure of the North Korean counterattack the night before spelled doom for the enemy, and the following morning the Marines of the Brigade observed a sight seldom seen on a battlefield. The remnants of an entire division abandoned all its arms and equipment and raced in headlong flight in front of the Brigade in an effort, largely futile, to escape across the river.

The Army troops, which had been holding a very thin line along the Nakton, had been overrun at a spot near the village of Yongsan, and Hill 311 looked like an anthill with dozens of North Koreans scrambling over the slopes trying desperately to escape the withering fire of every weapon available to the 5th Marines. At the observation post on Obong-ni, I observed tanks firing 90mm shells at individual North Koreans running for their lives. Artillery, mortars, machine guns and everything else that could shoot, was firing at groups and individuals as they frantically ran to the river.

For the first time in the war, I believe, the North Koreans had been attacked by a determined body of troops who would not be denied, and they couldn't take it. Suddenly, in mid morning, all resistance ceased, except for a few riflemen who were covering a commercial Pill Mill. Our mission, was to drive a North Korean Division, which had come across the river, back to where it came from. We did.

All through the afternoon, Marine aircraft bombed and strafed survivors as they tried to cross the river to safety. It was a sight that those of us who observed it will never forget. While the 1st Battalion was mopping up Obong-ni Ridge, 3/5 was ordered to continue to attack to seize Hill 207 (Objective 2), then Hill 311 (Objective 3). By the extremely skilled use of fire and maneuver, and all supporting arms, the 3rd Battalion was able to overcome successive rear guard actions of the enemy with relatively light casualties. By nightfall of 18 August, we had virtually secured Objective 3.

78

By 0645 the next day, the entire objective was secured and the First Battle of Naktong was history.

This battle was important from several standpoints. First, it restored the perimeter, and secondly, it foiled the enemy in his attempt to split UN forces into two parts and drive on to Pusan. If he had succeeded, at this point in the war, the results might have been as disastrous to the UN as the soon to be made Inchon landing was to the North Koreans. Third, it was the first time that a significant portion of the enemy had been driven back, completely demoralized, virtually wiped out in an offensive action by the UN troops. Most importantly, it welded the troops of the 1st Brigade and particularly the 5th Marines into a close fighting unit. The Brigade had been through the deadliest kind of a battle against overwhelming odds and it had not faltered. Never again would there be any doubt in any man's mind, (if there had ever been), whether the Brigade could do its job. For as long as the war lasted, no mission could be assigned that was too tough, nor was there any enemy that could challenge to battle, the men who had been at Naktong, and expect to come out whole.

We had a few hours sleep when the second battle began. The North Korean People's Army had crossed the Naktong again, and now we faced attack in two opposite directions at the same time. The front was fighting Chanchon. During the night, after midnight, there had been a heavy attack on Chindong-ni, where we had our first heavy fighting. The North Koreans did not want to give up this area; it was surrounded by steep hills, an ideal spot for observation, and a local area for communications. It had to be retaken. By daylight, Lt. Colonel Taplett radioed that the ridges were well in the hands of the Marines, and by late afternoon he radioed that the objective was accomplished. The area we were to defend, when we were under equipped and without a third rifle company, became a major concern, and needed to be dealt with. Men were positioned in a manner of caution, every rifleman making every move count. The North Koreans were determined to take the Pusan Perimeter and wrap up the completion of having all of Korea under Communist control. They were, again, well aware at this point, the only barrier in their way was the U.S. Marines.

The enemy was threatening the communications center at Masan. The Naktong Bulge had to go or the entire Pusan Perimeter would be gone. We planned to attack in a column of battalions, 3rd to hold Observation Hill and support the rest of us;. 2nd would seize the first objective, Obong-ni Ridge on the northern slope, the 1st would take back Hill 207, and Hill 307 would be taken by the 3rd Battalion. We moved from Observation Hill under heavy fire. Ten men were able to seize Hill 209, the fighting fierce, casualties heavy: 23 dead, 119 wounded of the 240 fighting force.

The total of the first battle of Naktong cost the Marines: 66 dead,

278 wounded and 1 missing. The enemy was defeated.

19, August:

The enemy found a weak spot in the Army's defense and the Naktong was back under the North Korean control, and all objectives we had secured the day before had to be fought for again. So back to the Naktong went the brigade. The NK penetrated a little further this time into more open country and it wasn't as hard the second time, as the first, to drive them again back across the river. They dropped their weapons and all their equipment and headed for the hills, where our air and ground force was waiting with open fire. They were defeated to the extent the division was no longer an effective fighting force. Our second battle, still on the offensive and still successful, and we were getting a little hard to live with and convinced we were the only ones in Korea doing any fighting. The fact that this wasn't true, was not important. What was important was, we believed it. It was a tough two-day fight, but one by one each objective was again ours. This time when we awaited relief from the Army, we felt we were turning the Naktong over in a more secure position. Now it was the Army's again and they held.

21, August:

The Brigade moved by rail to Changwon, Masan. Waiting there were 800 replacements, replacing the injured and casualties, all eager to get into action. We needed them, as the companies had suffered heavy losses and the enemy had penetrated the line at the Haman Corridor. This brought to the front lines, a visit from General Shepherd. New guidelines were put into effect and with the added force, and for the next three days, we put this energy into completing our objectives.

24, August:

Time was taken out to hold services and proper burials for the Marines killed after the battle at Sachon. President Syngman Rhee was present when 87 Purple Hearts were presented to the Marines, who had returned from the hospital.

30, August:

Rumor began about an amphibious assault, but none of the dispatches reaching me carried any information.

1, September:

Ground was lost by the Army 9th RCT and the fog was so thick we could not contact any air support. Newton's 1/5 going to their aid, got off in the wrong direction, righted itself and advanced against strong resistance. It was tough fighting. The fog was so heavy, the weather unbearably hot, and these conditions hung over the front lines for 48 hours before Newton reported that he had turned the fighting around.

3, September:

I was visited on the front lines about an amphibious landing,

Visitors from Tokyo brought maps, tide tables, weather conditions predicted for 15 September and informed me our Regiment would be responsible for the amphibious landing at Inchon. It didn't make sense landing against a thirty-foot wall, with a limit on the time the tide would be in deep enough to be safe for Amtrac landings. As commanders, we were against it... But to be against it, would be against MacArthur. This wasn't being done.

Walker's command had been split, given over to someone beneath Walker's respect as a person or a military strategist. He couldn't understand MacArthur, as a student of West Point who wasn't remembering our military history and the times in the past when this much risk had been tried. We felt his G-2 and intelligence officer, Brig. Gen. Charles Willoughby, had convinced MacArthur; the Indian ambassador was exaggerating and there was no danger of the Chinese getting into the fight. All information had to be screened through Willoughby and there was no way MacArthur would hear anything Willoughby didn't want him to hear. He wanted Tokyo's plan complete and if news got through to the Chiefs of Staff, a stop would be put on their plans of reaching the Yalu.

4, September:

The enemy retreated, leaving behind cannons, guns, and intelligence data. We were on our way back to where we had fought previous battles, when we were ordered to prepare for embarkation for an amphibious operation. The Army would relieve us. General Walker felt we were still deeply involved in the defense of Naktong Bulge, and strongly opposed the release of his now seasoned Regiment. General Almond assured him he would send the 32nd Infantry to assist him. We were released. But, lo and behold, the NK brought up another division and in the same exact area, again they had overcome the pitifully thin line of soldiers who fought so valiantly, but didn't have the reserves to shore up their long strung out defensive position.

5, September:

We left the front lines at midnight in a pouring rain, back to Pusan to prepare for embarkation.

Now we were to return to Pusan where we were to begin our planning for the Inchon Operation. The Division was headquartered in Japan and the 1st and 7th Marines were en route to join up with us for the landing. The third rifle company has joined us, plus our anti-tanks, which we had not had up to this time. We had a tank company but no tanks.

We are embarking on 12 September. Just six days away and all the planning to do for the operation. I don't know exactly how it got done, but it did, and we were in high spirits when we set sail from Pusan.

Inchon Landing

During this time the Marines were asking to be given a voice on the Chiefs of Staff. The President let it be known that the Marine Corps would continue to be the Navy's Police Force. Again, we were aware, we had been fighting with the peacetime force, two rifle companies to a battalion instead of three, four guns to the artillery instead of six, and we did not get our third company for the three battalions until just before embarkation for Inchon.

MacArthur's favoritism in men was profiled in his selection of aides and executive officers. And the Marines were busy tagging descriptive names of these favorites. At his headquarters in Dai Ichi, Tokyo, his staff consisted of an intelligence officer, Willoughby, who was nicknamed "Sir Charles." Adolph Charles Weindenbach came to this country from Germany when he was eighteen years old and joined the U.S. Army as a private, changed his name to a more American version of Willoughby, left the Army after his tour, went back to school, and reentered the Army as a second lieutenant. From there he gained favor with MacArthur and came up the ranks to Brig. General. With MacArthur as his mentor became one of the commanders at Corregidor and was now in third position on MacArthur's team..

.   General Almond, a very ambitious Chief of Staff, the Marines referred to as the "Anointed One," MacArthur put a great deal of responsibility on Almond, and trusted his opinion enough that the rest of the staff suffered from his outlandish ego and arrogance, and could take him or leave him. Every time he spoke he let it be known it was as though MacArthur was giving the order. He served MacArthur with complete loyalty. Whatever he seemed to be, this presence seemed to appeal to MacArthur. His record in Europe had gone well, but he had not achieved the three-star status he was striving for. There he had proved himself a valuable commander, bragged about being an SOB and knew how to be tough on subordinate officers.

We had to be good listeners and overly cautious not to comment, as neither Willoughby nor Almond had any respect for each other. Each telling us how inadequate he thought the other one was. They were struggling for first place with MacArthur and in time it was Almond who won out.

Almond would often comment on Willoughby's monocle being silly and doubted his connection to the gentry, and he really resented Willoughby's telling everyone America was responsible for China becoming Communist. My conclusion was not to cultivate either as friends.

The Army put together was one of the worst the United States had ever put into combat, under trained, ill equipped and not combat ready, and he was throwing them in against what he called the barefoot laundrymen. Those barefoot laundrymen turned out to be one of the best trained and, with the Soviet backing, one of the best-equipped armies at that time. At one of the briefings Colonel Puller, known as a well-qualified combat leader who had suffered many baptisms of fire, got to his feet and growled, "You people are lucky. We used to wait ten or fifteen years for a war, now you want one every five years. You have been living by the sword; by God, you had better be prepared to die by the sword." After this, he walked out of the meeting.

Tension between Almond and General O.P. Smith, was often visible. Because of Almond's superior behavior, (Smith, the seasoned warrior, had more logic and savvy, and it seemed to annoy Almond.) Almond, because of his close association with MacArthur, was given the command for the Inchon Landing, added to his duties of chief of staff. It seemed to be the command wanted to keep all decisions in a close circle.

It is difficult not to question the command of the ways things are done, but to schedule a landing without a plan should be questioned. A landing plan must be in place, setting up waves, the best way to climb a ladder in high tides, anticipating possible hazards. I wondered if anyone in their right mind would try to land against a good-sized city, and over a sea wall of thirty-foot tides. There should have been some rehearsal. We had a short time for planning as the brigade had landed 2 August 1950, and the next three weeks had engaged in two hard-felt battles in widely separated areas of the Pusan Perimeter. My staff and I hardly had time to look at some aerial photographs of Inchon when we were ordered back to the Naktong Bulge. On 1 September, we left on a new combat assignment, back to fighting in the Pusan Perimeter, with a landing scheduled for 15 September, without any time to make plans. We as commanders were against the landing , but, again, to be against it would be against MacArthur. This simply wasn't done.

About 3 September, on the front lines I was visited by a small group of officers from the Brigade and a liaison officer form Division Headquarters in Japan. I was briefed on the operation, including what intelligence in the division scheme had on the enemy and the hydrographic conditions in the area. I was also given the division's scheme of the maneuver for landing at Wolmi-do at the morning tide and then make simultaneous landings of the 1st Marines and the rest of the 5th on the evening tide twelve hours later. The 5th Marines landing was to be made on a fairly narrow beach alongside the causeway, which led from Wolmi-do Island to the mainland. The 1st Marines would land several thousand yards to the southwest of our landing and then the two regiments would join in attacking Kimpo Airfield and Seoul.

I was asked what I wanted as my scheme of maneuver for the landing and after studying the map for a bit, decided I wanted to land battalions abreast, in columns of companies. Since we were landing at dusk in both directions, after landing I felt that Battalion Commanders would have better control if I landed the battalions abreast, with one battalion attacking to the left and the other to the right. I was asked to nominate a battalion for the Wolmi-do landing and I nominated my 3rd Battalion. It was understood by the Division planners and myself, that practically all the planning for the operation except the actual landing of the 5th on the first wave, would have to be done by the division, without normal input from our Regiment. In all my years in the Marine Corps, I was never given an order without any advance preparation of orders. We were told time simply did not permit the concurrent planning that normally takes place. After this conference, I returned my attention to the battle that was going on. Finally, on 5 September, we received word that we would be returning to Pusan. Commencing at dark, the Army units would relieve the regiment in place at midnight and we would withdraw to assembly areas and to embarking trucks for the return to Pusan. This movement was completed in pouring rain and by the next morning, we pulled into our assembly area at Pusan.

I didn't learn until much later that a tug of war was going on between the 8th Army and the Division over the brigade. General Walker wanted the brigade in the Pusan Perimeter and it wasn't until 3 or 4 September that the decision was finally made to release the brigade on the 5th so it would return to Pusan to complete its planning for the landing. This is how close we came to reading about the landing instead of participating in it.

At this time, I was informed that a Battalion of Korean Marines was to be attached to the 5th Marines, for the use initially in mopping up Inchon, after we passed through the city. This was no big problem, but unfortunately, some were just taken off the streets, some were just kids who had never fired a rifle, and few of the men of the ROK Marine Regiment attached to the division had ever fired a rifle. One whole battalion had not been issued rifles until just a few days previously. There was also, a language problem. The brigade hastily organized a training group and gave the shortest course in marksmanship history, with each Korean Marine being allowed to fire eight rounds. I was quite skeptical of the value of these Korean troops and would have just as soon someone else be bothered with them, but need not have worried. I like to think being around the Marines rubbed off on them, and they became great fighters.

Between 6 and 12 of September, when we went aboard ship, I occupied myself primarily with visiting various units, going over problems we might run into, and greeting replacements and the newly arrived 3rd rifle companies. I knew that the new personnel had read about our battles in the papers and had heard about them on the radio, prior to arriving in Korea. This I used as a motivator for them, telling them how fortunate they were to be joining a unit that had battled continuously for the past six weeks and had won every battle. I don't know whether that inspired them or not, but certainly when the landing was performed they performed magnificently.

Meanwhile the regiment and the battalion staffs were working feverishly to complete embarkation plans and the boat assignment tables for the landing, with the 3rd Battalion making its plans independently of the division, dealing directly with the brigade. As I recall, this was the only planning done on the Regimental and Battalion level. All the rest of the planning was done by the Division staff, including the landing plan that featured the landing with the assault waves of eight LST's loaded with heavy equipment and supplied needed for the first day of battle. These LST's would remain until the next high tide, when they would be retracted. During this period, prior to embarking, we held a rather public hearing for all hands on the landing at Kusan, a city several miles south of Inchon, in hopes that it would confuse the enemy as to our intention to land at Inchon.

Finally, after six days of very heavy hectic activity, on 12 September, we embarked and set out to meet the unknown. By the unknown, I'm referring to how little time we had for planning. We'd just been handed a few maps and some tide tables, and were told we could use these to study. There were just three days to prepare for a landing, a landing predicted by experts to have just one chance in a thousand of making it. What I thought was to give us added confidence and wish us luck on the landing, when I was told Almond was on the phone, turned out to be the opposite. General Almond, on 12 September, came in with his orders in a manner I considered un-necessary and overbearing. (He should not have even spoken to me. He was always preempting General Smith and we wondered at times just how far he would go.) I picked up the phone, and after he inquired how things were going, he began his tirade. "You are the amphibious Marines. Just remember the success or failure of this landing is on your shoulders. I want no rebuttals. We want a clean landing. I will talk to you later." He hung up. I was happy I didn't need to answer him; he was famous for his tantrums and I didn't want to waste any time listening to anything more. We had a landing to plan, and he was telling us we would be in deep trouble if it didn't go right, and he knew who to blame if it didn't. (I'll jump ahead and relay the 5th Marines made this thousand to one chance landing, made the assaults and for the first ten and a half hours, was the only regiment on shore. (Almond's Army didn't land until three days later.)

Our three-day trip from Pusan to Inchon was uneventful, except for one thing. There were fifteen or twenty correspondents embarked in the ship I was on and I decided to give them a briefing on the operation before we landed, in hopes they would write more accurate stories if they knew what was planned. They seemed to appreciate it very much and I like to think that better stories came out of the landing as a result.

A young doctor, Chester Lessenden, asked if he could have a few minutes to be briefed in what is expected in field medicine. I did the best I could and tried to explain the primitive conditions he would be working under. I feel the hour spent with the good doctor, was the most productive hour spent, during the Korean War. This man was a real doctor, dedicated to his oath with an inner knowledge of the worth of every individual, and the combination of this love and his skill performed more miracles than any one other person in the war. Many times with injuries and his feet frozen worse than the patient he was treating, he was still working without more than a few hours sleep. He caught on to field medicine under pressure, would use anything available, stretcher, sleeping bag, torn underwear. When coming across a new-born Korean baby, would use a sleeping bag cut into swaddling clothes. (Years later I heard the doctor's comments on his service. "There are few things in life I can feel as proud of as my service in Korea. The Navy needed doctors and I happened to be one of them. I was doubly proud I was there and assigned to the 5th Marines.")

During the three days on ship I did issue instructions, practicing some of the problems we might face. The sea wasn't all that smooth moving from Pusan to Inchon; we practiced climbing ladders against imaginary sea walls, each Marine giving assistance in imaginary situations. With the short time we had in planning, it became one of the most remarkable operations in history. I wanted to land with two battalions abreast; each battalion in a column of companies, and that meant each wave was comprised with troops from two different ships. News was coming in all the time the landing was not something the Chiefs of Staff were happy with. They knew the odds.

Ridgeway had been sent to Tokyo to reason against the Inchon Landing, but MacArthur was steadfast, and would not consider giving up his plan. President Truman, against his better judgment, decided not to interfere. From a political standpoint, MacArthur was riding high and was making a lot of noise about running for president on the Republican ticket. He was using his star quality to get his name in the ring ahead of any of the nominations and Truman, politically, was a little shy at that time of reeling him in.   (28 August, MacArthur received the consent of the Joint Chiefs of Staff with a written sanction from the President for the landing at Inchon.)

As I have said before. The invasion force was given to General Almond, who was also holding the title of Chief of Staff, closing all possibilities of anyone getting into his inner circle. This did not go well with the Pentagon, as it became a lockout of information to Washington and the Chiefs of Staff. Come hell or high water, MacArthur was going through with the landing.

When it was brought to the attention of the Navy experts, they reaffirmed their evaluations that it was one chance in a thousand that it would work. There was a typhoon to deal with as well as the mud flats. The channel approaching Inchon Harbor was narrow, so we would need to anchor at least seven miles out. Each operation was timed by the tides, with just four hours to complete the landing, as the beach must be hit at high tide. During low tide, it was a mud flat. We had to worry about two hundred and sixty transport ships, sixty war ships and six aircraft carriers. Six destroyers would go within range of the shore to draw fire and trick the enemy, and the naval guns would do their job ahead of the assault. Any miscalculation and we would lose the entire fleet plus all our Marine Corps, ending up as a shooting gallery for the Communists. All these negatives were not easy to deal with when we were fighting battles in the Pusan Perimeter, and had not been given time to study weather reports or maps to plan a landing. We were to sail on 12 September, and land on the 15th. Every calculation had to be correct and we had just four hours to complete the landing. MacArthur admitted to General Smith that it was a helter-skelter plan but he felt the Marines had the training to go ahead. His reasoning was if we waited until we were militarily ready, we would not have had a chance to re-unite Korea and we would have lost. He kept admitting it was risky but he felt a successful landing would demoralize the enemy and win the war.

With all that was going on in Congress, the Marine Corps was fighting for its existence and felt this was an opportunity to prove themselves. A second typhoon was following close behind Jane and we would need to sail early as the route to Inchon placed us squarely in the path of the oncoming oriental hurricane. Gen. Smith was concerned that the operation was being squeezed into an impossible short time frame. There should have been months of planning, and this glory ride was not to his liking. Rehearsals were considered essential and his men were being put in a situation where the entire Marine Corps had a chance of being in peril, as well as an entire fleet of warships. What was the hurry? Nevertheless, there was no time to practice landing of the LST's and they were gambling the typhoon Kezia would veer to the south. Our ships did struggle against 125 mph winds of the typhoon, with MacArthur in command on the Mount McKinley, and giving orders to all ships to maintain radio silence. On the 5th day of the air and naval bombardment and just before dawn on 15 September, we hit Wolmi-do. We knew the Russians had supplied mines, and this was a major concern, as there was no time to send in minesweepers. The only thing that could be done was to have the destroyers open fire with 40 mm guns and explode the mines. They did what they could and reported Wolmi-do safe to land. MacArthur was having a few uneasy moments as he realized his reputation could be in jeopardy if his calculations had been wrong. He was up all night standing by the rail of the Mt. McKinley, smoking his corncob pipe.

My note to Eve:

Dear Eve,

I can tell you we are going over a rough sea wall of boulders. Our landing craft is light, and the stones are a threat. What is in our favor is the wall is twelve feet above the water line. The Marines will scale the wall with ladders attached to steel hooks. You can give thanks your husband has long legs. That is all I can tell you now, and won't mail this until sometime in the future. All my love, Ray

.

We programmed three landings. At dawn, the first would storm Wolmi-do on an Island causeway. The evening schedule was Red Beach, a sea wall south of the city. We were to seize these areas and push to the city outskirts. The shore bombardment started at 0545 and by 0600, the 3rd Battalion, under Lt. Colonel Robert Taplett, was ready to go ashore. The Marine Corsairs swept the beach. The island seemed to explode. Then the landing began. I had put the best I had out there, and if it could be taken, Taplett and his battalion would do it. At 0800, the high ground was secured and Taplett radioed the Mt. McKinley that Wolmi-do was secured. We were informed of a sad tragedy, and the gallantry of Baldomero Lopez, when reaching the top of the ladder, was wounded, and couldn't throw a grenade, shielded it with his body to save his fellow Marines..

Taplett called me and said, "I knew it would be a tough landing, but the callousness of Almond's orders stunned me. He ordered me to continue until 82.3% of my force were casualties. What kind of an idiot would write an order like that?"

I was told later an ensign, George Gilman, was heard to comment, "Here we had his highness aboard, and none of our officers had any experience operating under tidal conditions, and no one ever had been involved in an amphibious landing. As we approached September 15th, we realized we had all the ingredients for a disaster on our hands. Four Generals were watching from the bridge and were fascinated how it seemed to fall into place. As the landing progressed, we could see the 5th Marines knew what they were doing and their landing was timed, programmed to the last detail. They were landing in a manner that was beautiful to watch."

All went relatively smoothly and the initial boat waves started for the beach on time. As it turned out, there was a mix up with some of the later waves and a few of the troops were landed on the wrong part of the beach. Nevertheless, this was soon overcome and the attack to seize objectives began. They spent the rest of the day on the island covered by naval fire and aircraft, waiting for us to land. Now was the long wait for the evening tide and not much to see as the island was covered with smoke. That evening as the boat waves formed it looked like an inferno ashore; several buildings

Inchon, showing the narrow strip we needed
to maneuver to get into the harbor, and
the devastation war brings to a city.

Instructing the Battalion Commanders on our attack.

Over the wall at Inchon.

Col. Lewis "Chesty" Puller, commanding officer of the 1st Marines, appears to be buttoning his coat up against the bitter Korean winter.

Photo by Gen. Edward A. Craig/ Courtesy Maj. Jack Buck

were on fire and some oil tanks located between the landing beach and the city were burning. Preceding our landing the naval gunfire and air strikes had done their job. I went along with my headquarters with the eleventh wave and actually came ashore on the causeway between Wolmi-do and Inchon.

At 1730, the rest of my regiment would land at Red Beach and seize the O-A line 3,000 yards from Cemetery Hill. Roise was to continue to the British consulate with the inner portion of the tidal basin. We had just two hours to get this done, and darkness was already starting to settle in.   The 1st and   2nd battalion, Newton's 1st and Roise's 2nd would land abreast across Red Beach and the South   Koreans would follow. They would be coming in off the Henrico and the Cavalier by landing crafts and over the sea wall. Landed, they were assigned to Cemetery Hill and the northern part of Observatory Hill. Roise was to continue on to the British Consulate and the inner portion of the tidal basin. A lot to accomplish with just two hours of daylight. I moved my CP into trenches built by the North Korean defenders, and good location along the beach. Soon I was receiving word of capture of more and more of our initial objectives, with the exception on the extreme right flank where the bulk of the enemy opposition seemed to be centered. By 2200, the Battalion Commander called me and said that his patrol in front of his lines was meeting with very little resistance and he was moving out to secure his assigned objective.

MacArthur radioed the flagship, Rochester: "The Navy and Marines have never shone more brightly." On the ninth wave, Brig. General Craig, now an assistant commander, came ashore and moved his command post into Inchon alongside an airstrip   being bulldozed. He selected this because he felt it would be a good place to receive information and keep an eye on supplies. Litzenberg's 7th Marines went ashore on Green Beach on Wolmi-do and raised the flag on Radio Hill. The 5th Marines led the advance on the north side of Inchon and the 1st Marines took the southern side. The Marines had established themselves before the first hour of darkness.

The 7th Marines, from everywhere, who had not landed with us, finally arrived. Six tanks entered the cul-de-sac and with this additional strength, Hal Roise kept going and had gone through the city before daylight. The next day we moved out towards Ascom City on our way to Kimpo Airfield. Between Ascom and Kimpo the Corsairs brought down three Russian tanks, we thought we had them all.. Rumor had it that many, many Chinese were going to attack us. There was a natural setting, a long corridor much like a cul-de-sac with hills on each side, where the 2nd Battalion was set up. Hal Roise had set up at the other end with six tanks for support. Then the North Koreans came in from Seoul at daylight, with six tanks, and entered the cul-de-sac. There were over 200 NK troops behind them. The trap was sprung; they were no more.   MacArthur arrived at this moment and turned to his aide and said, "Get this man's name; I'm going to give him a

Give a Silver Medal to "That Man"

Pointing out crevices and caves where the North Koreans were hiding.

Silver Star." Almond snorted, "You damned Marines, you always seem to be in the right place at the right time." General Shepherd grinned and said, "Well, Ned, we are just doing our job." I heard this, and it was good to hear because I had been catching hell from his command post for several days that the landing had better be a masterpiece. But then to make a statement that he didn't know my name, and did not bother to find out, when he knew I was the commander assigned to the landing, well, my ego kicked in and I wondered the value of the Silver Star. And I was a bit puzzled for receiving a Silver Star for just doing my job. Through the years, as I reflected back, I've wondered if he felt obligated in some manner to recognize the 5th Marines for the smooth landing at Inchon and this way he sidestepped any reference to the 5th Marines part in the landing, other than the early statement that the Marines had never shone more brightly.

MacArthur started to leave, than his jeep squealed to a stop and he announced he had to take a leak. He started for the bushes, was almost shot, and would have been if a Marine had not intervened and shot the North Korean. Seven more NK's were hiding under a bridge not twenty feet away, ready to finish the job had they not been detected. After this scuffle, he calmly asked, "Now, can I take a leak?" You could not help but admire the coolness this man shows under pressure. He seemed to give the impression that he was indestructible, an admirable quality, but a heavy load for his subordinates to carry. The leak taken care of, his entourage of Army jeeps with the Marine escort, turned around and headed back to Inchon. (Dr. Lessenden's.comment " He called our Colonel, That Man, and didn't ask the doctors how they were taking care of the wounded, or how many casualties we had, Just walked right past us.")

We were still nineteen miles from Kimpo. The Korean Marines had gone ahead and were fighting hard on the other side of Ascom City. Taplett moved in the 3rd Battalion and the resistance subsided. Roise ran into some resistance, but a further problem was that the road map was wrong. Eventually, he did find a road that would lead to Kimpo Airfield, and by 1800 was on the southern end of the runway. The Battalion settled down for the night, and then, at 0300, the NK's attacked Roise. Then a second attack came in from the west and east, a third came in from the south. Newton's 1st Battalion moved up to the right and turned the enemy around. Taplett was still two miles away, but coming in as a strong backup. The enemy fled to the Han River. We knew it would be some hard fighting and they weren't going to give up their airport very easily. Roise had the airfield secured by 1000. In 24 hours he had 1 4 Marines killed, 19 wounded, taken 10 prisoners and left 100 enemy dead.

My orders were to bring the 5th up on line abreast with Colonel Puller's 1st Marines. We were a distance apart, so far, I had not met Colonel Puller, and I looked forward to working with this legend.

Liberating Seoul.

Almond was getting anxious to cross the Han and arranged a meeting with General Smith. Their strategies were not the same. Almond wanted Chesty Puller to cross the Han first; Smith wanted the 5th Marines to cross first. General Almond visited me and asked me how I would plan the crossing. (Why was he asking me?) I told him if I were planning it, we would be crossing in a column of battalions, using amphibious tractors, amphibious trucks, and pontoon floats, and it needed to be at the ferry crossing northeast of Kimpo. Being a narrow area, it should be in the morning when they least expected it. Most assaults are done at night; this had to be a surprise attack. We then would have a clear view of where the Kalchon River meets the Han.

So much for telling him my plan. Orders came that we were to seize the hills and Chesty was to cross the Han. Almond had a way of pressing for information, called it his inspection. He was always trying to find out what esprit meant and how the Marines came to be such a close brotherhood. I'm sure he never found out.

17 September:

We had much of Kimpo Airfield and were coming into Yongdung-po on the south side of the Han. We were fighting on the ridges when we got orders to go to the north and cross the Han north of the city. The 1st Marines had been fighting on a ridge in front of us and had a bloody battle taking Yongdung-po. Then orders came for Chesty and me to coordinate our attacks. At this point in my service I had not met Colonel Lewis Puller; he was a legend in the Corps, a tough fighter, leader, well respected, in tune with his men and usually with them on the front lines. His real first name was Lewis, but his stature, rounded chest, and his manner, contributed to his nickname to the point that no one ever heard his given name.

When I flew in by helicopter I had no idea what to expect. The first question he asked me was, "How many casualties do you have?" I answered, "Quite a few." He must have taken this as we, too, had been in the heat of the battle and were qualified to help take Seoul. He seemed to judge the severity of the fighting by the casualties. He was easy to talk with, every inch of that rounded chest, a Marine. I was looking forward to working with this legend and it was easy to figure why his men were so loyal to him. We came to a battle plan not to use more artillery than was needed. Things did change later when pressure was applied to liberate Seoul by 25 September. If MacArthur could do this in this time period he would be presidential material, the best qualified for the office. He had already dabbled in politics and had been very successful at it, redoing the Japanese Constitution, getting them back into the world where they were again respected. He could handle the job. He was the best candidate out there, and he told us so. Harold Stassen, Robert Taft, and Tom Dewey, were all being considered and Eisenhower's name had also been mentioned. He considered them all dull candidates, especially Eisenhower. The nation would be at a loss with him at the helm. (Seems you could catch a touch of envy when he was speaking of Eisenhower, maybe this was his way of leveling the rank.) In a way he was already running for office.

Each and every time there was a photo-op, MacArthur appeared. When supplies were delivered to Kimpo Airfield and any time the Marines made any progress, there was an oratory and the news people would gain a vast amount of material to work with. Now his next big job was to get the Marines to liberate Seoul.

19, September:

There were so many reporters in my command post it was impossible to give briefings. MacArthur was big news but it was interfering with progress. I had to ask the press to leave. We had orders to take Hill 125 and the intelligence was scanty. I've read somewhere that I told an intelligence officer that the only way to find out what was on the other side of the river was to swim over and find out. The scouts did and ran into some heavy fighting but were able to bring back enough information to put us on the banks of the Han. This was 20 September, going into day 6.

I set up CP Quarters and shared it with Lt. Colonel Hays. We were trying to get some rest. He was on a cot across the tent and sat up when all hell broke loose; a mortar and fragments hit the tent and so severely injured Lt. Colonel Hays that he had to be evacuated. I came out luckier with only a deep cut on my cheek and a small tip of my nose left my face, other than losing blood, I wasn't hurt. A corpsman, David Howard, took care of it and advised me it was a clean cut and dressed it, with a warning to keep my head down and find a safer place for my CP. This I did and moved the CP into a hillside cave.

MacArthur was getting more active and difficult to keep up with. Wherever he was there was an entourage of jeeps, manned by soldiers, four in each jeep, and armed for protection. Traveling behind the Army jeeps was a jeep with two Marines, each with a machine gun, a BAR, and grenades. He was no longer taking his afternoon nap, being back in action, and there was a certain swagger about him and an energy that made it difficult for younger men to keep up with him. They were wearing out protecting him from himself and the chances he was taking. We began to notice a palsied hand that he tried to keep in his pocket, and heavier dark glasses, but his stance was erect and his posture always upright. His speeches didn't get any shorter; he seemed to love giving speeches and he would let us enjoy them from time to time. His presence would dare any filmmaker or actor to move in on his lines; and when on camera he was at his best. The press was always there for his speeches, and his eloquent words were in their typewriters and on their way to the newsrooms in minutes.

Almond was getting upset, a little edgy, because for the first three days the Marines were getting all the press, plus MacArthur was referring to the Marines as "his boys." On 18 September, three days after the landing, Almond pressured Admiral Doyle to land "his boys" the 32nd Regiment and the 7th Division. They were now part of the war party, though poorly trained, and new in combat, and, in time, this would be a concern.

We, the 5th, were forced to fight through the hills west of Seoul, never easing up and never giving the enemy a chance to regroup in the center of the advancing line. In the end, it was the line of supplies in slow moving amtracs that compelled the 5th to hand over the crossing of the Han to Puller's 1st Marines. Almond must have thought I had given him good advice because he used my plan for the leathernecks to attack at the ferry, eight miles below Seoul, at 10 a.m. Most assaults are done at night, so this took them by surprise. Only 400 Communists were there, and they broke and headed for the hills. Never thinking that the Marines would try landing where the landing area was so narrow, and only possible to land two amtracs at a time, it left a weak spot. Two tanks crossed the river, and within two hours captured Haegju, then swung eastward toward Seoul, six miles away.

MacArthur wanted to be there to see the crossing. He arrived and I could not believe what I was seeing. A jeep, driven by Almond, bounced out of a rice paddy, then back on the road in a cloud of dust, with MacArthur hanging on for dear life. Almond's driving must have provided him with as much excitement and highs as the war. They almost missed seeing Chesty, who was waiting to give his report. Behind them, in another cloud of dust, was a truck laden with furniture and equipment in the event he wanted to set up an office and living quarters in Seoul. The truck drove right up to the industrial area of Seoul.

25, September:

We were all catching hell from Almond this morning because we were supposed to occupy Seoul by now and we had fallen behind. Almond seemed to be constantly pushing the 5th Regiment, starting with that order he threatened me with on the Inchon Landing. (I believe he was sorry it went so well.) We had been fighting, without letup since Pusan, and he was pushing again that we had to take Seoul in 24 hours. Never mind how many bodies we left behind, it had to be taken by 25 September. MacArthur had sent out news releases that it would be secured by then, and Washington had the same report…any delay and the news media would have a different story. So, if we didn't make good progress in the next twenty-four hours he would relieve us with his 7th Army Division. Heaven forbid. Where had they been up to this point? O.P. said the man was completely ignorant on what goes on at the front and, never to his knowledge, had an Army Regiment taken over a front line from a Marine Regiment, especially one so poorly trained. This was the second time he threatened me, so may I be forgiven for thinking he should hop-skip over the dead bodies on Hill 56, through the rats, the dogs, and the stench, get himself back to his deluxe trailer, shower, bring out his best linen and order dinner with his large staff attending, and let us do our job.

Litzenberg's 7th arrived and O.P. Smith now had a full division: 20,000 strong, 3 veteran infantry regiments with just 24 hours to secure Seoul or be replaced by Almond's 7th Division. My 5th and Chesty's 1st had been holding and making progress, but now we were in full strength. Chesty was to take the center of the city, followed by the Korean Marines, who would mop up, and take care of the stragglers. Litzenberg's 7th would police the left bank and seize the ground northwest of the city. I was still on Hill 56 with an intelligence report when General Smith called a meeting. He was waiting for me at the command post. He started with, "Ray, we have to come up with something, find a weak spot to break through, a break, any break to put Almond back where he is out of our hair, so we can get on with this war." Again, we had been warned about the premature news that Seoul had already been secured and repeated that the news people might come in with the exact opposite of the news that was being released from Tokyo. Chesty, under orders, was being pushed by Almond, began to use a lot of artillery, and you could see the boundary line between the two of us, the smoke coming up from his sector and very little from mine. I'm not saying that I was right and he was wrong, by any means, but what I'm saying is that we had two different philosophies. The military opinion seemed to be in Chesty's favor but I felt the Communists wanted us to appear worse than we were by burning out and destroying shacks that were the homes of these people. I later heard that Chesty commented. " These people will hate us for burning their homes these shacks are all they have."

MacArthur wanted Seoul taken quickly. Anything in the way became a devastated area, to be included in the fighting. But the Communists had been there before and the carnage was unbelievable. They had come into Seoul from the north, south, and west, and headless bodies, women and children, were piled in heaps and trenches. The stench was beyond belief. This was happening after MacArthur sent out the news report that all was secured. We had captured the high ground on the western flank of Seoul, but it was costly; we had been in Korea for forty nine days and six of my commanders had been evacuated; I was now left with just one rifle company. The toll had been heavy on the platoon leaders; we had started with eighteen in South Korea, four had been killed and thirteen wounded, now on the forty ninth day, of the officers involved when we landed, in Pusan with twenty four officers, twenty two were casualties.

Now, as we were going through the city, we saw the lower windows of homes had been sandbagged. Behind them it was almost a certainty there would be a North Korean with an automatic weapon. Some of the houses we broke into were vacant, others had families all huddled together and hoping they weren't going to be included in the fighting. Some buildings had several floors where doors had to be kicked open, always wondering if this one would be the one with the machine gun ready to open fire. Tension was building high from the suspense of the unknown, always in the backs of our minds hoping to keep innocent people from being casualties. Every home was a fortress. Marines went through every home, street, alley, and outbuilding. Some of the Marines came out, others we would not see again.

The street was a real war zone. Puller had his hands full and wasn't taking any nonsense. The scouts were reporting it would be worse when we reached the business area. What kept us going was that we were capturing the most important city in Korea.

27, September:

We, the 5th, reached the capital building. American tanks moved up and advanced, and the 1st Marines raised the American flag over the U.S. Embassy and the French and Soviet Consulate. The 1st Marines set up a CP

Our ship into Inchon.

100

on the grounds of Duksoo Palace thinking the war was over, when the North Koreans launched a counter attack using grenades and killed 4 Marines and injured 28 more. The Army finally arrived and reached the southern flank of the X Corps and the Communists seemed in full retreat.

We had not destroyed the Blue House, which is their White House, and they were grateful for that. Most of the city was a disaster, but the Blue House gave them a place for their ceremony. MacArthur announced the liberation of Seoul and had a dramatic speech prepared, with many prayers and large tears streaming down his face and onto his uniform as the government was returned to Syngman Rhee. News reached us. The Joint Chiefs of Staff were not pleased with this display of drama. Then they were told that a special pontoon bridge had been built, ordered by Almond, to make it possible for MacArthur to drive directly from Kimpo into Seoul. This was an extravagance that did not go over well in Washington.

Almond, with orders that came directly from MacArthur, was to keep Marines away from the news media and away from the cameras. This did not go over well with Chesty and he was getting testier all the time. When he arrived in his field uniform, after a tough battle, after the loss of so many men and knowing this battle was far from over, he wasn't about to take any sass from an Army Sentry, all spit and camera polished, who told him he wasn't in a staff car and he wasn't properly dressed. Only four Marines were invited to the ceremony: Smith, Craig, Puller, and myself. Craig voiced his opinion, "It looks like they would have the decency to give some honor to the men who captured this damn place."

Fortunately, my aide had found a clean uniform for me and I went through the inspection and waited for Chesty to come through. I knew there would be some reaction to his field uniform. Chesty told him in no uncertain terms that the "Marines had taken this real estate," and then added a few new words to the Sentry's vocabulary. Then he told his driver to go on through. By this time the Sentry screamed at him that he would deal with him later. Chesty got really huffy and told his driver to go through and, to make sure to get his uniform dirty. The Sentry jumped aside and Chesty attended the ceremony.

The reporters caught all this and made a point of how the Army was taking all the credit for the liberation of Seoul and was not being respectful for the Marines part in the battle. Of course, there were a lot of retractions and denials later, but a point was made.

.   What a day! I took a minute to write home, knowing Eve would be happy to learn we, the Marines, had something to do with the success of taking Seoul, at least this far.

My Darling , Eve.

Our orders were to let MacArthur take his bows. This was as much a part of his character as oratory, acting, and breathing. You couldn't help but feel sorry for him, a great general in his day, trying hard to live up to or surpass his father, but like a prize fighter who has stayed in the ring too long, judgment seemed to be lacking where it was needed most. The Army took all of the credit for the liberation of Seoul, gave speeches ignoring the participation by the Marines, even gave orders that Marines were to stay out of camera range. In a way it was sad that this great general needed this adoration so much.

The Marine generals and their commanders knew that no other Infantry existed that could have made the landing at Inchon, against the highest, most vicious thirty-foot tides in the world. The 5th not only did this but were the only Regiment holding the ground for ten and a half hours until the rest of the Division joined them. There is certain warmth in knowing the truth and not making a show of it. Honey, you can be proud of us and we still have a lot of work ahead of us before this area is secure.

Love you and my little family, Ray

As Chesty predicted, this was not the end of taking Seoul. The Marines were to lose hundreds more in door to door fighting, holding ground and taking more, always with the feeling that if this weren't finished, it would need to be done over. Some of the reporters, Keyes Beech among them, said, he was going to write an article, a scathing one, on how the Marines were treated, and I'm sure he did. The rest of the reporters stayed with the Marines and told it like it was, and then were reprimanded for contradicting the news that had been sent from Tokyo. Each day MacArthur would inquire if any Chinese had been sighted, and since none had, thought the worldwide Communist offensive was unfounded. He told me that the Communists would melt into the hills and the war was going pretty much as he had planned. He was still glowing from the reflected glory of the genius of the Inchon Landing. Our next orders were to move to Wonsan by sea, so we were to turn around and get back to Inchon to follow this command. There was unsettling in the command and felt at all levels. The divided command did not go well with General Walker. He thought there should be a unified ground authority. General Almond, MacArthur's appointed Chief of Staff, was always overbearing and a pain in his side and he wasn't too quiet in expressing his opinion that Almond was obsessed with glory. Because of this, he thought Almond would not be using good judgment.

The 8th Army's news from the south, under General Walker, was hoping the Inchon Landing would send the enemy north to defend Seoul and would weaken their lines in the south. But it did not happen, and the fighting was still intense along the Naktong River. Almond's newly formed X Corps, up north, wasn't making the showing Almond wanted. Then there was a turn around, and the 14th Army Infantry Division and the British Brigade drove the North Koreans back across the Naktong.

I assumed at Seoul we were going to stop. We had given the South Koreans the territory that had been taken away from them, plus given the North Koreans enough of a lesson not to try it again. Nobody had any idea we would be going on to North Korea, and certainly not any idea we would be fighting the Chinese. Most military men, especially the artillery men, would say, "Don't get in a foot war on the Asian mainland, there are too many of them. Also, facing a winter in the coldest part of Korea wasn't too bright an idea." I never thought we would go beyond the 38th Parallel, as we were under-equipped and not prepared for a winter in that climate. The 38th Parallel was still the division line and Washington was questioning the military advantage of a victory in North Korea.

I had mentioned in my last letter to Eve that there was a possibility we would leave Korea after securing Seoul. I wrote her about this foolhardy notion to cross the 38th.

Dearest Eve,
Before we left Inchon, I had a rather heated discussion with Joe Alsops against crossing the 38th Parallel. We have been told it would be the South Koreans who would cross and infiltrate to see if the Chinese had entered the war. They would act as a patrol. We have also been warned if the UN crossed, the Chinese would enter the war. I was against it and Joe was for it. We argued and disagreed violently. I couldn't see what the hell we would accomplish by going there. If MacArthur is really after the presidency, and if he plans it right he should stop here. He is riding high on the success of the Inchon landing and the liberation of Seoul. Talk about walking on water. If he stops here, my bet the presidency would be in his lap. He has been riding high for such a long time no one dares tell him he could be wrong.

It is a rough sea so I won't be writing much until we reach Wonsan. Take care of the children and yourself. As you know, my family is always foremost in my mind every minute of the day.
Love you, Ray

Seoul, Korea

Raising our Flag at Seoul.

Lt. Col. Murray, of S.D., Among Heroes at Seoul

Forces Used In Softening Hill Defenses

SEOUL, OCT. 1 (Sunday)

When the final story of the bloody fight for Seoul is told, two of the greatest heroes will be a Marine Colonel who fought his way into the city and one who did not.

It was a grizzly bearded 50 year old regimental commander, Lewis "Chesty" Puller who tricked the way into Seoul after 8 days in which other leathernecks led by Lt. Col. Raymond Murray, of San Diego, had battered the wall of Communist Artillery and mortar fire.

Puller's First Marine Regiment jumped across the river last Sunday at a point where the north bank is a series of steep Palisades and the beach is too narrow for a couple of Amtracks to land at one time.

SPOT NOT DEFENDED

The Communist, never thinking the Americans would try a landing here, left the spot virtually undefended. The Marines landed at dawn and began a seizure of the South Korean capital. Murray and his Fifth Marines were forced to fight their way through the ring of hills west of Seoul and soften the North Koreans. Despite a dreadful line of supply stretching back to the

Navy vessels at Inchon harbor, Murray's Marines, followed their corps dictum to the Letter, never easing up on the enemy, never giving him a chance to Regroup in the center of the advancing line.

RESISTANCE TOUGH

The American command had expected the resistance at the center to be the lightest. Instead it turned out to be murderous and on the second day the South Koreans were forced to withdraw 1800 yards.

Murray, a tall, raw boned officer, so young there was not sufficient time to promote him to a full colonel's rank, had only praise for the South Korean troops.

In the end, it was a tenuous line of supply over washed out dirt roads, mined bridges, and across the Han in slow moving amtracks which compelled Murray to hand over the job of taking Seoul to Puller

MACARTHUR VISITS HAN FRONT AND PRAISES MARINES

"Perfect Job,"
He Tells Them

BY PERCY WOOD
(Chicago Tribune Press Service)

INCHON, Korea , Sept 20

Gen. MacArthur today assured himself by personal visits forward that his troops were approaching Seoul after a successful crossing of the Han River. The supreme commander watched elements of the 1st Marine Division take landing crafts across the stream and join the already sizeable force which proceeded them at daybreak.

The Americans suffered only light casualties in this vital operation, while killing, wounding, and capturing hundreds of the enemy.

Told by the regimental commander, Lt. Col. Ray Murray of San Diego, that a North Korean battalion was believed still in the hills between the Marines and Seoul, MacArthur replied, "They'll all evaporate shortly. You've done a perfect job."

SEES SEOUL FROM FRONT

This compliment was repeated in essence an hour later when MacArthur stood on the narrow road only a few hundred yards behind the front lines of another Marine regiment and looked at Seoul across the chimneys of Yongdung, a suburb of the capital, on the western bank of the Han.

Snipers were still operating in the area and the big guns were laying shells in rapidly. A large oil tank had been hit and sent a column of smoke upward.

At this point, MacArthur was only two miles from Yongdung and four from Seoul. His proximity to the enemy brought looks of concern to the faces of the officers who accompanied him.

Col. Lewis Puller told MacArthur that "one of my boys got two tanks, then was killed trying to get the third." MacArthur shook his head. "That's too bad," he said.

Almond was at the wheel of the MacArthur jeep today, Almond who has a distinguished record as a soldier, drives as if he were being pursued by the devil, despite heavy war time traffic.

Chapter Six

Keyes Beech

Chicago Daily News
Yonpo Airstrip Korea.
December 9, 1950:

(Authors note: An insight into the next chapters)
MARINES DIDN'T BREAK ....THEY FOUGHT AND SAVED
THEIR WOUNDED.

Remember, drawled Colonel "Chesty Puller" whatever you write this was no retreat, All that happened was we found more Chinese behind us than in front of us. So we about faced and attacked. I said "so long" to Puller. After three snow bound days with the 1st Marine Division, 4,000 feet above sea level in sub-zero weather of Chosin Reservoir, I climbed aboard a waiting C-47 at Koto Airstrip and looked around. Sixteen shivering Marine casualties, noses and eyes dripping from cold, huddled in their bucket seats. They were the last of more than 2,500 Marine casualties to be evacuated by the U.S. Air Force, under conditions considered flatly impossible.

Whatever this campaign was, retreat, withdrawal or defeat, one thing can be said with certainty, Not in the Marines Corps long and bloody history has there been anything like it. And, you will pardon a personal recollection, not at Tarawa or Iwo Jima, where casualties were much greater, did I see men suffer as much. The wonder isn't that they fought their way out against overwhelming odds but that they were able to survive the cold and fight at all. So far as the Marines themselves are concerned, they ask that two things be recorded:

(1) They didn't break. They came out of the Reservoir as an organized unit with most of their equipment.

(2) They brought out all their wounded. They brought out many of their dead.

And the ones they didn't bring out they buried.

It was not always easy to separate dead from the wounded among the frozen figures that lay strapped to radiators of jeeps and trucks. I know because I watched them come in from Yudam to Hagaru, fourteen miles of icy hell, five days ago. The same day I stood in a darkened corner of a wind-whipped tent and listened to a Marine officer brief his men for the march to Koto the following day. I had known him for a long time, but in the semi-darkness with my face hidden by my parka, Ray didn't recognize me. When he did the meeting broke up.

When we were alone I could see tears in his eyes. After that he was all right. I hope he wont mind my reporting he cried, because he is a very large Marine and a very tough guy. He cried because he had to have some sort of emotional release because all his men were heroes and wonderful people; because the next day he was going to have to submit them to another phase in the trial by blood and ice. Besides he wasn't the only one who cried. In the Marines twelve day seventy mile trek from Yudam at the "bottom of the hill" strange and terrible things happened. Thousands of Chinese troops, the Marines identified at least six divisions; totaling 60,000 troops boiled from every canyon and rained fire from every ridge.

Sometimes they came close enough to throw grenades into trucks and jeeps and ambulances. A whistle sounded and the Chinese ran up to throw grenades into Marine foxholes. Another whistle and the Chinese ran back. Then mortar shells began to fall. The 3rd battalion of the 5th Marines was reduced to less than two companies but still ordered to "attack regardless of cost" " We had to do it" said Lt. Col. Joe Stewart, of Montgomery, Alabama. " It was the only way out"

Fox Company 7th Regiment was isolated for three or four days. Nobody seems to remember days or dates. But they held at a terrible cost. One Company killed so many Chinese the Marines used their frozen bodies as a parapet. But for every Chinese killed there were five, ten, or twenty to take their place. "What'n hell the use of killing them" said one Marine, " They breed faster's we can knock them off"

The Chinese had blown bridges and culverts behind the Americans. The Marines rebuilt them or established bypasses under fire. No part of the division escaped, including headquarters sections composed of file clerks, cooks and bakers. Bullets plowed through a Korean house in Hagaru occupied by General O.P. Smith

Always the infantry had to take high ground on each side of the road to protect the train of vehicles that sometimes stretched ten miles. When the Chinese attacked a train, the artillery men unhooked their guns from their vehicles and fired muzzle bursts from between trucks at the onrushing foe. This was effective, but rather rough on Marine's gunners, who had set up their guns on the railroad tracks 5 or 20 yards in front of the artillery.

If there was an occasional respite from the enemy, there was none from the cold. It numbed fingers, froze feet stiff, through layers of clothing froze and crept into the marrow of your bones. Feet sweated by day and froze in their socks by night. Men peeled off their socks and the soles of their feet with them.

About the men of the 5th Marines. Lt. Commander Chester M. Lessenden, Jr. from Lawrence, Kansas, A Navy Doctor, became a hero in everyone's mind. "Lessenden is the most saintly, Godlike man, I've ever known" said Stewart. " He never seems to sleep, always on his feet and never says it can't be done, and yet he is suffering from frostbite worse than most of the men he is treating" (Lessenden is a graduate of the University of Kansas, where his wife teaches. They have two daughters.)

In their struggle to keep from freezing the Marines wrapped their feet in gunnysacks or pieces of old cloth, scrounged from the countryside. When they could, they built fires, but this wasn't often, because fires would give away their positions. When they camped in Koto before the final break-through to the sea, they made tents of varicolored parachutes, used by the Air Force to drop supplies. The red, white and green tents, looked like Indian wigwams. Some covered themselves with Japanese quilts dropped from the air, but they were warmest when they were fighting. Combat was almost welcome because they forgot the cold. The cold did strange things to the equipment. Because of sub-zero temperatures, artillery rounds landed as much as 2,000 yards short. Machine guns froze up. Men tugged frantically at their frozen bolts. The M1 rifle generally held up, but the Marines cursed the lighter carbine. Communications gear broke down because, like men, can only stand so much. Canteens burst as water froze inside them. Despite all these things, the men who walked down from the reservoir still could laugh. " It was impossible for us to get out because we were surrounded, encircled and cut off" said one Lieutenant. "But we never got the word, so we came out. That's us, we never got the word"

INCHON TO WONSAN TO CHOSIN

(Author's note: I've printed Keyes Beech's report ahead of the chapter, as a bit of a warning of what is to come when we cover the war in North Korea.)

When we secured Seoul and it was turned over to the Army, orders were to go to Wonsan by sea. The most feasible route, better and faster, would have been overland, cross-country. Instead it was back to sea in antiquated LSTs from World War II. Most had been stripped, were not even air-tight, and it was a miracle we arrived without sinking the craft. We yo-yo'd up and down the coast while the Navy swept the mines. The Navy lost two mine sweepers making it safe for us to land. We were recovering from our defense of the Pusan Perimeter and the Inchon Landing, tired and hoping to get some rest, and it seemed we were about to be in combat again. We unloaded cargo and the next morning moved to establish a command post.

There was a feel of autumn in the air and we knew winter this far north was to be feared. It soon became evident that the plans were to cross the 38th Parallel, which was against my better judgment. If we did cross, I felt the Chinese would feel threatened and come into the fight. We were not prepared for this kind of war. We were undermanned, under equipped, and going into freezing weather without adequate clothing. It would be two divisions against what could be a million Chinese, and as soon as we left they would take over again. I was convinced we should stay south of the 38th and keep it secure, at least until spring. I did not feel that area was entirely secure, and, if, we didn't secure it, we would need to come back and do the same thing again. I hoped MacArthur would talk with some of his commanders and reconsider.

The Indian ambassador to the United States had warned Congress that crossing the 38th Parallel would prompt the intervention of the Chinese. President Truman related this to MacArthur when they met at Wake Island, but he assured the President that the Chinese would not attack. They had no air force and they were trying to get to Pyongang; they had just finished an internal battle and were not able to take on another commitment. On the front lines Major General Almond was constantly telling us we could handle what little trouble the Chinese would give us.

Maps, maps and more maps were studied, trying to analyze the terrain and lines of communication. North Korea is seventy percent mountainous, with spiny paths called roads winding to nowhere, and there was some talk of Lieutenant Colonel Roise finding an overland route through this to the Chosin Reservoir. It was also suggested he find a way to block the Sinhung Corridor. There was some talk of Lieutenant Colonel Newton doing an amphibious landing at Chongjin, further up the coast. Then Almond cancelled this plan and Newton rejoined the Regiment. Roise reported back that there was no overland route to the Chosin and returned to his Regiment. There was a joke about the orders changing every few minutes; if you left the room for a few minutes you would need to be briefed before the next order came in. Finally a decision was made and we were ordered to move north to Hamhung.

Hamhung and Hungnam sound alike when spoken but they are in fact very different. Hungnam is a port on the north side of Songchon River, an estuary, and has an airfield. Hamhung is a rail and highway nexus, and the entry to a dirt and gravel road that stretches seventy-eight miles from Hamhung to Yudam-ni. This two-lane, sometimes not more than a path, would be known to the Marines like no other. No other route was found so this one would have to do. I ordered Newton and Roise to concentrate forces along the road that was to be our MSL (Military Supply Line) before starting the uphill climb to the reservoir.

Colonel Litzenberg, Colonel Puller and I were in the vicinity of Wonsan for a short time fighting some of the North Koreans who were struggling to go north. Then I was assigned a zone behind Litzenberg's 7th and Chesty Puller was assigned 1st Regimental Commander. Leaving Wonsan we kept wondering why our orders were to keep climbing when the promises were to be home for Christmas. The higher we climbed, the more we could feel the presence of the Chinese. Occasionally they would be observed in small groups and when they spotted us they disappeared.

The 8th Army had crossed overland ahead of us, and by 9, October had crossed the 38th Parallel. There had been heavy fighting for a week, then the fighting ceased. By this time the command had been divided, the tactical and the 8th were still with General Walker. The X Corps had been given to General Almond at Inchon and we were to stay with his command. The first report received from General MacArthur was very firm and issued from his headquarters: "All orders were to come from Tokyo." He issued press releases: "The war is almost over and the boys will be home for Christmas."

15, October:

Truman had met with MacArthur at Wake Island and gave MacArthur his fifth distinguished cross, and was assured by MacArthur there was no danger of the Chinese entering the war. They had just come from a civil war and had no interest to get involved in another one. Just five days later, on 20 October, the 8th Army had secured Pyongyang and reported atrocities beyond belief. Bodies were stuffed in walls, body parts were everywhere. Taking care of the carnage, considered stable, the Army was given orders to press on and cut off the fleeing North Korean stragglers. The first airborne paratroops began bringing in cargo, thousands of parachutes dotted the sky. Some paratroops met with resistance and were able to escape, some were taken prisoner. Some we never saw again.

With previous warnings from China if the Americans crossed the 38th Parallel, China would enter the war. So it was our understanding, only the South Koreans, who were in the 8th, would be the only ones advancing anywhere near the Mongolian border.

24, October:

MacArthur lifted the order and urged the commanders to secure all of North Korea. Doing this, he was changing U.S. policy, and ignoring orders from the Chiefs of Staff. But, they did nothing to prevent the order. China began getting ready for action.

25, October:

The UN troops are pushed north and seemed to be scattered in every direction. A prisoner was taken on 25 October and reported, " Chinese were in the nearby hills and another ten thousand were in the backup, and many, many more were coming." His story was dismissed in Tokyo. Hadn't the UN troops reached the Yalu and peed in the river? No one seemed to be aware of the trouble they could be in. The war was about to take a menacing turn.

The troops had a visit from Almond, accompanied by Maj. Gen. David Barr, commander of the 7th Division. This visit was for a news relief and picture taking. MacArthur congratulated Ned Almond and asked him to tell Barr, " his division had hit the jackpot."

While they were basking in their glory, Prime Minister Chou En Lai, made good his promise to bring in the Chinese, by night, and brought in a 150,000 man force in one of history's smoothest troop movements. While, Prime Minister Chou En Lai was warning Washington not to cross the 38th Parallel; Truman was being assured, China would not commit, they were crossing the Yalu. Always under the cover of darkness, carrying everything needed on their backs. Nothing moving could be seen from the air. Any Chinese soldier moving in the daylight and seen from the air would be shot. They hid in caves and nooks, and on their backs were 80 rounds of ammunition and a week's ration of food.

General Nich Yen Jung, China's acting chief of staff, had warned Ambassador Pannikar: "China will not sit back and let Americans come across their border, and they can never defeat us on land. We outnumber them two hundred to one" Not heeding these warnings, MacArthur lifted all restrictions on going to the Yalu. Omar Bradley had warned MacArthur on extending the war into China. "This would involve us in the wrong war, in the wrong place, at the wrong time, with the wrong enemy." MacArthur kept insisting that China lacked the industrial might to wage a modern war. He would follow through.

The UN was hit and cut off; 875 men escaped, 2700 were killed or captured, in three days the ROK 6th Division was wiped out as a unit and the 11th Corps collapsed. This exposed the entire right flank of the 8th Army. Headquarters felt this was a flash in the fighting and Major General Willoughby is telling his commander and Washington, "the Marines are over-exaggerating the numbers they are fighting."

Divided by a mountainous range, we were miles out of contact with the 8th Army. General Smith felt he had too small a force to do what Almond was demanding. Almond was pushing too fast and we needed to send patrols to see what was ahead. Smith knew the Chinese were there, but how many? He was stalling, protecting his men until he could pull up the 1st and 7th Marines. He needed this additional support to meet the demands.

The last of October, the night temperatures were dropping to zero and warm clothing was needed. On 28 October some arrived, not adequate, but better than we had. Dramatic as ever, Almond used the map to demonstrate how we would wrap things up, then leave the South Koreans to take over, and pull our Divisions out of Korea. We wondered if this were true, then why were we continuing north?

The reporters were coming up with more information and warnings to be cautious, as the news was available to them (and we wondered why the Chiefs of Staff ignored it.) The NKPA (North Korean Peoples Army) was a force of fourteen divisions, well trained and mechanized. Since 1945 they had trained ten thousand troops in Russian schools, based in Siberia, and, year after year, added a stronger base in several phases until it reached one hundred and twenty thousand strong. By 1950 they had built the force stronger by adding well trained junior officers, ready for combat.

South Korea had stabilized its economy, rapidly becoming anti-communist. North Korea was seeing the rapid growth and felt, if they were going to do something about merging the north and south before South Korea became better prepared militarily, now was the time to strike. They were doing this while our Defense Department, headed by Secretary Louis Johnson, was trimming every aspect of our military. Then, by MacArthur's analysis, "On 25 June, they struck like a cobra and crossed the 38th Parallel."

MacArthur gambled on the North Koreans being afraid of our air power and our sophisticated weapons, and discounted the support from Russia in equipment and China for manpower. We were soon to learn, and such a bitter lesson, how wrong these assumptions could be. Also a factor was not heeding the advice of the Indian ambassador that China was prepared to intervene. MacArthur had been riding high after the successful Inchon Landing. In a position heeding public opinion, it made it difficult for the president and the chiefs of staff to reel him in.

When we landed at Wonsan, and I had studied the maps, I personally thought there was no need to go further north. We could secure Wonsan, Hungnam, Hamhung and Pyongyang, which were the only areas of military value. We had the war won. By holding them, we could cut off troops coming in from the south we missed and also supplies coming into the port.

Our supplies and our force were inadequate but strong enough if we held a seaport, where we could be re-supplied, and waited for better weather. We could kick the hell out of anything they sent us. It seemed to me if we went further north we would be in a vulnerable fighting position and freezing our butts off, possibly getting into a situation that would be disastrous. I discussed this with my three commanders and they saw the reasoning. Being a Lieutenant Colonel under orders of the army, there was only one other person who might be interested in my theory. I wasn't the first to have these doubts. General O. P Smith said it worried him and wondered why it wasn't being considered. But we were under army orders and they were calling the shots. It seemed Almond's main objective was not to be upstaged by the Marines, and the old general was still making speeches, this being his finest hour, and at times so spellbinding, so forceful, it would have rivaled Sir Winston Churchill. There was no way this strategy would be changed.

I knew the forces would be so thinly scattered that even a few Chinese, if they came in, would be a threat. It seemed the Army would need reinforcements if they were to cover all the real estate assigned to them. We already had news the guerrillas were attacking the Army's rear bases. Why would an entire division be piecemealed in enemy territory we knew could be hostile? What was the reasoning in weakening forces in this manner? Also, O.P. was apprehensive and none of the commanders could understand how a war could be won when all decisions were coming from Tokyo, never going to a battle front, and commanding with strategies from maps alone. Tokyo had split the Tenth Corps away from the 8th Army, weakening Gen. Walker's command. Then they gave orders to split the Marine regiments. A real disaster in the making. Even the maps, if read in Tokyo, could tell you the Chosin reservoir was a trap. A battle survival was impossible; it was like putting troops in cages and closing the door. As we pushed further into the trap, O.P. cautioned us, "Take every precaution, be prepared every minute, day and night." He felt the worst was about to happen.

It would not be long until we found what happened to weakened forces. There didn't seem to be a workable plan, just bulldoze in and take real estate. We should have turned around and gone back to Wonsan or Hamhung, fortified it, stabilized, and come up with a more workable plan. It would slow us down but what we needed was to send out patrols from each flank and move out when it was clear.

We had not observed many Chinese, but then, on November 2, they appeared with heavy tanks, from everywhere. Heavy fighting began on the west when the 7th Marines were attacked by the Chinese near Kanu-ri. Litzenberg had run into heavy combat at Sudong when a regimental force of Chinese cut them off. It was the toughest fighting thus far, and in fact was so heavy that, with the help of the 11th Marines and the air strikes, it took two days to secure Sudong. While we were climbing where the 7th was fighting the Chinese, we ran into Olin Beall, with the Motor Transport Battalion. Right on the spot we decided what we needed, and Olin did all he could to keep us supplied.

Koto-ri was to be set up as a base operations for Colonel Chesty Puller and his 1st Marines. It was a collection of shacks loosely put together from whatever material the Koreans had on hand, and it seemed to be a lot of scrapped shavings, bits of lumber, rocks or pieces of cement put together as somewhat of a shelter and a way of getting out of the freezing weather. It was a godforsaken country, enormous high mountains, deep rocky valleys, impossible to negotiate, pathways for roads. I honestly couldn't imagine anyone would have any desire to live or own such a place. It was freezing and useless, beautiful scenery but nothing else. Beyond Koto-ri the Chinese seemed everywhere and the numbers kept growing. No matter how often we reported this to Tokyo, there was never any acknowledgment in any way that they were worried.

The pull was strong to touch base with Eve and tell her about Colonel Williams. It was so hard to find time for even a note and I feel I must do better.

Koto-ri:

Dearest Eve,

Have I told you about O.P. Smith's Executive Officer? He is Colonel Williams, takes no guff from anyone and especially none from Almond. He is short, erect and someone you would want on your side in a fight. No one crosses him. He knows there are Chinese out there and doesn't mince his words when he has a chance to confront Almond. Being a Marine he knows his promotions don't depend on Almond's evaluations, and speaks freely. He told Almond that anyone can smell the presence of the Chinese and it is time we paid attention. I've only run into him five or six times and he stressed that Almond wasn't interested in the facts. Almond flies over in the daylight when the Chinese are in their caves. They fight at night, this he won't believe. Never visits the front during a battle. I'm beginning to feel MacArthur's cohorts are afraid to tell him the truth. Eve, what I write in letters to you are not to be publicized. It is just nice to have someone who is not critical to lean on in stressful times.

The weather has turned cold and we have been issued some warmer clothing so don't worry, I'll keep moving fast enough to keep warm. Miss you so much and thank you every day for being so understanding of the times I'm away. Know it is difficult coping with three active boys and thank God every day that I have you to take care of them.

All my love,

Ray

1, November:

By now the Americans were freezing in their summer uniforms, inadequate blankets and sleeping bags. It was risky to get a few minutes sleep. The Chinese used horns, bugles, and loud banging noises to find our position, then moved, by moonlight, to bayonet the troops in their sleeping bags. We went to work trying to figure out their code. The loud banging and bugle noises were their way of communicating as they had no radio communication. This had to be their fighting orders, gongs meant one thing, bugles and insults others. We never figured which one was the bayonet order or the one to disappear back into the caves We hoped we would be on our way home before we did. When this didn't work, they really became nasty, saying insulting things about Babe Ruth and Shirley Temple. The perils of war.

4, November:

We knew this war would be a tough one; it grew larger every day, and headquarters told us, we were exaggerating.

5, November:

Although he had been warned about China entering the war, now on 5, November, MacArthur is outraged because he knows the Chinese have crossed the Yalu. He is now indignant and wants to bomb the bridges at both ends of the Yalu. Washington, said NO, there will be no escalation of the war. Washington was feeling uneasy. MacArthur had miscalculated, in the worst way. They knew something was wrong and by doing nothing had missed the best chance to halt the devastation. No one, it seemed, wanted to take on MacArthur and the chance was lost. MacArthur still honestly believed the Chinese were beaten because they were withdrawing. He made a mistake, not bothering to supply the 8th Army. General Walker was short on ammunition and rations and his army was also freezing in lightweight clothes. MacArthur did not re-supply him and he could not hold with what he had.

Mike Michaeles, an honest leader, who had learned directness and truthfulness from his leader "Ike," was always direct with his men when he felt there was a mistake being made, and commented, "This war is a mockery, men massacred in hopeless fighting. Platoons of twenty men down to three, because of nothing to fight with, in a war no one can understand, under trained, improperly equipped, soldiers reluctant to fight as they are being tossed into battle unprepared."

10, November:

We entered Koto-ri on the Marine Corps birthday. Colonel Puller cut the cake with his sword and there was a short celebration. Then, I received orders to concentrate on the MSR leading to the Chosin Reservoir, twenty four miles further north. Newton's 1st Battalion, coming out of Chigyong on 10, November, was to move to Majon-dong. Newton's battalion was ambushed before it could get to the village and had to be rescued. On the 13th they ran into a company of Chinese that killed seven Marines and wounded three more. We were on our way to Chinghung-ni; it was as desolate as Koto-ri, and it didn't get any better from there up to Hagaru-ri, to Yudam-ni, and to the Yalu River. This is the area that is referred to as the Chosin, an area we would learn was infected by hordes of Chinese. It was evident we would be fighting on torturous mountains roads, with hairpin turns so narrow any breakdown would be traumatic.

I had never seen the sun perform with so little energy, no warmth

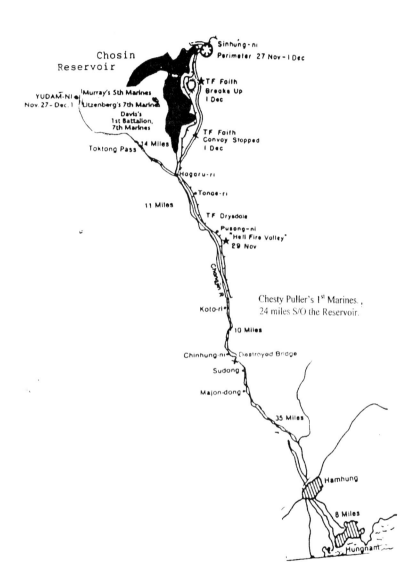

Chosin
Reservoir

Sinhung-ni
Perimeter 27 Nov-1 Dec

TF Faith
Breaks Up
1 Dec

YUDAM-NI
Nov. 27-Dec. 1

Murray's 5th Marines

Litzenberg's 7th Marines

Davis's
1st Battalion,
7th Marines

TF Faith
Convoy Stopped
1 Dec

14 Miles

Toktong Pass

Hagaru-ri

Tonae-ri

11 Miles

TF Drysdale

Pusong-ni
"Hell Fire Valley"
29 Nov

Chesty Puller's 1st Marines.
24 miles S/O the Reservoir.

Koto-ri

10 Miles

Chinhung-ni Destroyed Bridge

Sudong

Majon-dong

35 Miles

Hamhung

8 Miles

Hungnam

at all, and the temperature had dropped to 20 below zero. Korea consisted of forbidding mountains, rising in height to 9,000 ft. The valleys were never straight, but twisted and tangled through and around mountains. Roads were disguised as single paths, and, when iced over, the hazards were intensified. These paths, a.k.a. roads, were carved slits almost under the mountains. The overhang kept the sun from melting the black ice and any misstep or swerve could cause you to drop hundreds of feet, into icy crevices below.

Roise's 2nd battalion came out of Sinhung Valley and Lt. Col. Robert Taplett was at Chinhung-ni with his 3rd battalion. We felt it was much too quiet and the worst was yet to come.

Maj. Gen. O. P. Smith also had doubts, wrote the commandant his worries: " I believe a winter campaign in the mountains of North Korea is too much to ask, and I doubt the feasibility of supplying troops in this area during the winter or providing for the evacuation of sick or wounded."

15, November:

The 7th Marines had occupied Hagaru-ri, fourteen miles south of the Chosin Reservoir. This is where General Smith gave orders for the Marines' engineers to begin building an airstrip. He stressed the main supply route from Wonsan would be exposed to guerrilla attack and, there were fifty-four miles without patrol, except for South Korean counter intelligence, and stringing so few Marines on a single mountain road over two hundred miles in zero temperatures could be leading to a disastrous trap. He was enough of a warrior to know that a winter campaign at below zero temperatures had made history in many war stories and had never won a war. He kept preparing for the worst.

General Almond kept stressing that the Marines could handle the few Chinese that had been spotted and the orders were to keep advancing. O.P was apprehensive to a point that he started hoarding food and ammunition, and stressed the need for more suitable clothing for his men, doing everything possible to save his men.

Sometimes, arrogance and not giving your enemy the respect for intelligence due them, can lead to your own downfall. They had been studying us seriously, more than we were studying them, and they hit us as far north as we were because they knew we would be without supplies. It was unbelievable, the more you thought about it the more unreal it became. What we had to do was the most ill-advised unmilitary operation I had ever been ordered to do in all my years in the military. We felt, Almond sensed it was a trap, but wouldn't face facts and kept the truth from MacArthur. He seemed to be caught in a frenzy, knowing we would be facing annihilation, yet, still convincing MacArthur of the Chinese lack of military ability. His information had come from Willoughby, making it suspect.

It had been leading up to this for some time, do to Willoughby's enormous power with the command and manipulation of his intelligent reports. We all knew there were 300,000 Chinese surrounding us and he threatened to close down any source of information other than his reports to MacArthur. If you crossed him, he let it be known your career was finished.

We became aware we would not be home for Christmas when the 5th and 7th had joined, and the two regiments bringing the force to almost ten thousand, had orders to continue north and join the 8th Army. We still had to conquer rocky Toktong Peak, the highest point on the road to Yudam-ni. In a short space we were climbing 4,000 feet in elevation on a snowy, icy road with heavy packs, heavy equipment, slipping and sliding, spending half our time getting up and battling the climb again. The road all the way was narrow and covered with ice. By this time, I did not have happy Marines. They were half frozen, Chinese all around them, and readied to take on almost anyone who was responsible for putting them there. I spent most of my time calming outbursts from their frustrations, hearing anger in every form. The questions they were asking were:

"What kind of stupid bastards are there in Tokyo running this damn war? Our feet are freezing and they are in Tokyo going over maps and congratulating themselves on being military geniuses, why aren't they out here? Who's fighting this war?" They didn't calm down as more Chinese appeared and Tokyo kept saying there weren't any. Plus we couldn't get air support because of the low visibility, and most of our fighting equipment was still at Hagaru-ri. We all felt we were sitting ducks.

Our orders, for the 5th, were to push to the east of the Chosin Reservoir, on a narrow, one way path of road. It was another rough climb and we were to continue on to about five miles past the reservoir, without replacement of supplies. Any seasoned warrior has an inner warning instinct, especially one who has been on the front lines; it is an inner system that says something is very wrong. It is entirely too quiet, and we knew the Chinese were there, you could feel it, smell it. The weather was changing and there was no way to get out of a trap ready to spring. Concerned most was O. P. Smith, a veteran of so many battles, but still orders were to advance. Taplett's 3/5 led the way to Sinhung-ni, four miles north of Pungnyuri-gang inlet. This was where we were served our Thanksgiving dinner.

The day after Thanksgiving, General MacArthur flew in and issued press releases that the war was progressing as he had planned and the troops would be home for Christmas.

24, November:

I received the following communique:

HEADQUARTERS X CORPS

APO 909   US ARMY   OUTGOING MESSAGE   UNCLASSIFIED

24 November 50 241120 1 INFO: CINCUC   ARMY EIGHT

Cite X 2952. The following Communique from General of the Army, Douglas MacArthur will be relayed to all troops of X Corps. "ZX 26755

Communique Number 12.: The United Nations Massive compression envelopment in North Korea against the new Red Armies operating there is now approaching its decisive effort. The isolating component of the pincer, our air forces of all types, have for the past three weeks, in a sustained attack of model coordination and effectiveness, successfully interdicted enemy lines of support from the North so that further reinforcement from there has been sharply curtailed and essential supplies markedly limited. The Eastern Sector of the pincer, with noteworthy and effective tactical movement and has now reached a commanding enveloping position, cutting in two the Northern reaches of the enemy's geographical potential. This morning the Western Sector of the pincer moves forward in general assault in an effort to complete the compression and close the vice. If successful, this should for all practical purposes end the war, restore peace and unity to Korea, and enable the proper withdrawal of United Nations Military Forces, and permit the complete assumption by the Korean people and nation of full sovereignty and international equality. It is that for which we fight. Signed: Douglas MacArthur, General of the Army, United States Army, Commander in Chief. The Corps Commander takes this opportunity to again express his appreciation to the officers and men of the X Corps who have contributed so well to the tactical success referred to by the Commander in Chief.

Confirmation Copy Distribution "E" Plus ROKA"

I asked my Exec. to file this communique. There was no way I would tell my men we had the war where it would be over in two weeks. This is the only document I've saved from Korea. It is framed in my office. I didn't send it out because of the reports we were receiving, that 800,000 Chinese were on the border with 200,000 backup. True or not, these reports were interesting enough to take notice. And if so, I knew I wouldn't be facing a court-martial for holding it back until we had confirmation of the amount of Chinese in the war. Locally we were doubting anything coming from Tokyo because Bill Barber's F2/5 outfit with Ray Davis had been left on the hill to guard the pass dropping down into Yudam-ni. They were into fighting with everything they had. We finally got to them, and they cut across the mountain into Yudam-ni.

25, November:
The Chinese offensive slashed the 8th Army, hurled them back and stripped protection of the Marines' western flank. Their objective was to divide and conquer; at this time there should have been someone from Tokyo reassessing the weakened forces instead of ordering them further into a trap. We had two regiments, they had two divisions, and our supplies were cut off. The 5th and 7th were at Yudam-ni and were ordered to link up with

Railway and narrow passage called a road,
leading into the trap at the Chosin Reservoir.

Photo by Gen. Edward A. Craig

the 8th Army. We were miles out of contact with the 8th Army and the mountainous range divided the forces. At times the 5th and 7th Marines were fifty to sixty miles apart, and the forces were too small to cover this much mileage.

We could never understand why MacArthur had described the Chinese as "determined to annihilate the UN Forces" and it was becoming a different kind of war, when he saw us going into a trapped situation, and would not give credit to the Chinese intelligence to see the advantage of the trap. Disregarding his own evaluation, two weeks later, he ordered troops into the very trap he felt was about to happen. Our forces were too thinly spread from Wonsan, on the coast, to the frozen area of Chosin Reservoir. Twelve thousand troops over a two-hundred-mile radius left openings for the Chinese to pick any spot they saw to break through, and the guerrillas were attacking the rear bases all the time. The Chinese kept broadcasting that the only troops they had in Korea were volunteers. Headquarters fell for it. Our orders were to pursue the North Korean stragglers, when we were being surrounded by hundreds of thousands of Chinese, thirty divisions, we were later told.

The newspapers were beginning to pick this up and commenting on the incompetence of the generalship. They speculated: was MacArthur getting the wrong information from his intelligence sources?

The next news we received was that eighteen divisions of Chinese had counter- attacked General Walker. How many Chinese do we need to report before they will recognize that the Chinese are in the war? And they were here and well equipped to fight.

Two days after Thanksgiving, at Koto-ri, Col. Chesty Puller had engineers hacking away at the ice-covered earth, building an air strip. The 1st Medical Battalion, under Commander Howard Johnson, set up a clearing for the helicopters to bring in the wounded. They also set up a field hospital that was the first Mobile Army Surgical Hospital that we now know as M*A*S*H*. Orders were for: The ROK (Republic Of Korea) troops to advance to the Chinese border. The 3rd Infantry Division was scattered all over North Korea, under General Soule. Some weird orders had come through for him. He was to be on the right flank of the 8th Army, support the 1st Marine Division, protect the harbor, the air field at Wonsan, and the flank of the X Corps. No way that much territory could be covered by an infantry division. The field commanders didn't think much of these orders.

Lt. Col. Ray Davis with his 1st Battalion 7th Marines, defending Toktong Pass, ran into several hundred Chinese and used air and artillery to defend the pass. By late on the 25th, Litzenberg and Davis reached Yudam-ni. My 5th was ordered to join Litzenberg. We are now aware of Mao Tse Tung's boast to annihilate the 5th and 7th Marines and we planned to arrive in semi-darkness; making every effort to conceal our positions, also to secure our perimeter, and set up defense positions for the night. We started up the road to the reservoir and met with Lt. Col. Faith and explained that all three of my battalions were now on the east side of the reservoir. Taplett was in the lead and radioed that he had met with a small party of Chinese.

Lt. Col. Faith set up a Command Post Battalion in a small hut on the lower slope and waited for the arrival of his commanding officer, Colonel MacLean. When he asked me what might be his next orders, I cautioned him. " Do not move further north without direct orders from the Division, wait for Colonel MacLean to arrive."

Faith was a handsome young man and had some heavy duty fighting behind him. He had been an aide to General Mathew Ridgeway, commanded the 1st Battalion 32nd Infantry for more than a year and had been recommended for the Distinguished Service Cross for Inchon and Seoul. His officers were well trained and we considered them of the highest quality. His only problem, as with the rest of us, was the language barrier between the officers and the untrained South Koreans.

The next news we received was eighteen divisions of Chinese counterattacked General Walker. Frustrations grew. How many Chinese do we need to report before they will recognize that the Chinese were in the war and ready to fight? General Smith was getting more apprehensive, " Murray, I'm warning you again to be cautious." The 5th was to launch an attack at the northern end of the reservoir on Monday, 27 November. The 7th would continue its advance to the Yalu. The problem, occurring to General Smith, was that with these orders it would separate us by one hundred miles. We were a weakened force as it was, and this could be a disaster.

I replaced Newton. He damned near killed himself staying awake and doing a top notch job. I was afraid he was going to collapse. He never rode, always walked, because he wanted to stay awake. There comes a time when a commander can see someone who has pushed himself to the limit, to a point of burning out. I replaced him with Lieutenant Colonel Stevens. Lt. Col. Joe Stewart was my executive officer and rightfully the command should have gone to him. The problem was, he was too good an administrator and I couldn't replace him.

During this transition there was a breather and the troops began telling stories about winter wars and Napoleon's fate, and some added the story of Genghis Khan. Another claimed a foot war with the Asians in the land of the Mongols in dead winter would need to be commanded by someone who didn't know military history. The stories ended there.

Then, all hell broke loose. The Chinese were coming across the lake and headed for the Regimental Headquarters, which was only a makeshift tent. We became aware and came out firing. Bodies were falling everywhere and the snow was turning red with blood. There was fighting in every direction Then suddenly they broke and ran, not bothering about their wounded or dead. We had been subjected to night attacks throughout our operations in Korea, so at first I thought it was just another local action. Then, another attack. The command post came on fire, and we knew we were in for some serious fighting. So my exec and I got the hell out of there.   I dove behind a small mound and had enough phone line to keep in touch with my commanders. I tried to get Taplett on the line and he told me to call back as he was under attack. Two of his platoons counterattacked. I pulled Roise's 2/5 and tied him in with Harris's 3/7 on the left of Taplett's 3/5, that was on the right, hoping this would save lives.

The Chinese wanted Hill 1286 and kept charging. They were so close we could hear the crunch of every move, and the Marines on the hill were so isolated it seemed this was going to be their last battle. The fighting slowed a bit at 0200, and they pulled back. Bodies were everywhere, some still alive and groaning. The next assault began an hour later and many times during the night we did not feel we would get out of this one alive.

We held until daylight and threw everything we had at them. Then, as each time before, they disappeared. They were night fighters and would creep up on us from nowhere, always doing the same thing, generating the loudest racket possible by banging and yelling profane language to get our location.

It became evident that thousands came into North Korea by crossing the Yalu at night, then hid in caves during the day. We learned from one prisoner that if they moved during the day and were sighted, they could be shot. He said they moved at night in white robes, carrying whatever food and ammunition they would need to fight the next night.

When they ran out of supplies or were killed, a few thousand more would be sent in under the same plan to take their place.

The Chinese would dig foxholes, leave them, and disappear, very convenient for the Americans on patrol or someone looking for a place to dive for shelter. They would sneak back at night and bayonet anyone who happened to take advantage of this, and I came very near to getting the full treatment myself one night. I was missing men and afraid they might be wounded, so went out on patrol after dark. Fortunately my hearing was good, and I heard some Chinese before they saw me, and dove into a foxhole, turned over and waited. They walked past and didn't seem to notice, maybe because I don't think I was breathing. I didn't dare move because I knew if I did, I was dead. I finally heard them leave and I was so stiff and sore from not moving, I could hardly get to my feet. My back was killing me as something had been poking me in the ribs the entire time I was hiding. I discovered my mattress had been a dead Chinese and the pain was caused from an elbow on one side and a weapon someone had left in him from the other. I didn't investigate any further and I was happy to part company with that foxhole.

Where we had rifle companies in the hills, fighting was bad. On Hill 1240 the Dog Company, 2nd Battalion began the night with two hundred men and six officers; by morning one officer and sixteen men were still alive. I sent another platoon to join them and they took back Hill 1240. It wasn't theirs long, as the Chinese came in in full force. The Dog Company was no longer a fighting force. A few troops, ten or twelve, still able to walk, bloody and wounded, stumbled in. The rest of the company on the hill were dead. An entire rifle company had been lost in one night. No Chinese?

The day after MacArthur issued his communique; he issued a statement to the press. He was so comfortable with his plan he sent out a news release world wide, divulging the plan: " He would put the 5th Marines on the west side of the reservoir. And Barr's 7th in a position to attack from the east. This would have the enemy between the pincers and the war would be won." With this information, the Chinese came up with a battle plan of their own. They had given us just enough harassment to allow us to get further into the trap. NOW THEY WERE READY.

The nights of 27-28 November, unable to dig through the frozen earth, the Marines had no way of digging any type of foxhole for protection and fought all night without any shield from the freezing cold. They stood there in their inadequate clothes and fought with rifles and bayonets. Our supplies were cut off, we were isolated, and the 8th Army was retreating, stripping us from protection of our west flank. The mission of the Chinese, surrounding the Marines, had one thing in mind, to annihilate us to the last man. We were seventy miles from the sea and we had made it to the Chosin Reservoir. But at what a cost, for what? We knew there was a bill in congress to abolish the Corps, but this was a hell of a way to do it. Seventy miles of Marine blood was spilled along the way. We wondered if Almond or MacArthur had ever suffered a wind chill and a minus 75 degree chill factor. They were safely in Tokyo, swearing there were no Chinese in Korea. This did not make our fighting any easier. We had facts, there were hundreds of thousands of them. If they thought it was so safe out here, why did they pull the Army back?

The wounded could not be treated, because removing their clothes for a few minutes would freeze them to death. The best way to treat them was to let the blood freeze and close the wound in that manner. To keep from freezing we used everything, parachutes, any clothing we could salvage, even stacking up dead Chinese bodies and using them as a windbreak against the chill. The wounded could not escape, the enemy was throwing phosphorus hand grenades on the trucks carrying them. Again heroism beyond my ability to express, wounded helping wounded, many times risking their lives to save a buddy.

The enemy then blocked the road and hit us with full force. By midnight the first attack was over, then they hit us again at 0300.   Lt . Col. Roise lost Hill 1403 and he was outflanked. The main Marine force at Yudam-ni was also under attack. Each had to hold their own, help was not coming from anywhere. There wasn't any.

Hill 1403 overlooking the MSR had been lost to the enemy. Roise was still in position of his portion of the line and I ordered him to continue the attack at daybreak. If Taplett held, he was to come up on the right side flank in assault. At dawn it was clear that the strategy had to be changed from offensive to defensive. We had come very close to annihilation. Had we gone into the hills to join the 8th Army, I would have lost my regiment and my life.

Thinking back, there had been early warnings. The enemy would strike the supply lines, re-supply their equipment and then disappear. It was evident there was at least one division. This amount MacArthur was comfortable with   But it was grossly underestimated. No airpower is enough when the battle is fought on the ground, and the ground force is outnumbered by the thousands   Not only did we underestimate the number of divisions, we were unprepared, thinking our air power and the bomb were the answer. They were backed up by millions, and they had enough strength in numbers to attack, attack and attack again. Their pattern never changed; they avoided any frontal attack, and by traveling with whatever weapons they needed on their backs, they could move easily and disappear fast. With three under-strength battalions, we were vulnerable against six divisions, and at times, estimated to be as high as thirteen to fifteen divisions. That is a lot of Chinese. They were prepared for a strong war and Almond's evaluation of the supposed untrained laundryman was wrong. We were up against well trained Chinese, who could drive a truck, fire a machine gun, and lob a mortar with the efficiency of any well trained Marine.

When I met with Lt. Col. Don Faith, who was commanding the 1st Battalion, 32 Infantry, I informed him he needed to go another eight miles to catch up with his Regimental Headquarters.   Taplett had sent a patrol to observe a hydroelectric plant; a major source of electricity for China and heavily guarded by Chinese and North Korean forces. Taplett was now four miles on his way back when I had some advance news that Taplett would be moved and Don would be moved into Taplett's vacated position. But it didn't seem logical that Faith would be able to cover all the spaces left vacant by Taplett.

26, November:

Mid-morning on the 26th MacLean arrived at Faith's position and set up a command post south of where Faith had his. MacLean was a West Point graduate, just forty three years old, and a veteran of the European Theatre. He was a well trained officer and up to the command. MacLean was also undermanned and stretched out over ten miles, with all his lines weakened. He was ordered by Almond to lead the attack to the Yalu. Almond wanted the Army to reach the river before the Marines. MacLean ordered Faith to attack Kalchon-ni. Faith reported while planning the attack, to take place at dawn, the enemy came in from every direction and they were fighting for their lives. The temperature had dropped to twenty below zero and we all had orders to keep advancing. The Marines were spread thinly over thirty miles through small inlets and mountainous passes. A wind chill of seventy degrees below zero was forever present. Day temperatures seldom reached above zero. Weapons were freezing, grenades failed to explode, mortar tubes cracked, blood plasma froze solid, and fuel oil froze.

The Marines, the 5th and 7th now had a force of eight thousand on the west side of the Chosin, the Army had three thousand on the east side. We were surrounded by one hundred and twenty thousand Chinese. They hit like the Siberian wind coming in from everywhere. We were in a trap with no exit, fought for fifteen hours and gained only fifteen hundred yards. The road to the rear was cut off. We were completely surrounded on all sides. I got a short note off to Eve, just in case.

Dearest Eve,

Too many decisions have been made by maps alone. Many of these orders from Tokyo are tactical failures. When MacArthur went on the air revealing his strategies for winning the war, making us face the enemy, who has advanced knowledge of our offensive plan, he has put us in a position of losing this battle before it begins. If he can tell the world, I can write something to you. Thank God, we have an excellent General in O.P. Smith. A person who listens. We need to get our heads together. Don't worry too much, your husband has been in tough spots before, but a prayer would be helpful. I think of my wonderful family almost constantly, and pray it won't be long until we are together again.
Love you with all my heart, Ray.

We lived through many of General Willoughby's patrols and his negative responses to the Chinese in the area. As MacArthur's intelligence officer, he would fly through the area in the daytime when the Chinese were in their caves and report back to Tokyo that " the presence of the Chinese is a Goddamn Marine Lie." He made no bones of his dislike for the Marines.

Then if I didn't have enough to worry about, my Exec. Joe Stewart, calls me into the CP. "Ray, we have just cleaned out the carnage of dead and wounded from the worst night of fighting we've had. In daylight, of course, all the Chinese disappear. Willoughby shows up. Wants a little chat with "the boys" and you can't believe what the troops say he is telling them. The idiot goes into a drivel about who should have won World War II. According to him, America had no business getting into the war. Britain rightfully should have gone to Germany and if we hadn't stuck our noses in the war, it would have gone to Germany. The reason we are here now is because America allied with Russia. This makes you responsible for China going communist, and if you don't agree with me you are communist sympathizers!" The carnage we cleared were the Communist we fought all night.

"Ray, we are surrounded by hundreds of thousands of Chinese, we are not likely to live through another night and the men were still reeling from the loss of their buddies. I'm afraid if we do live another day, and he comes back, the Marines will likely tell him to shut up or they would stick his ridiculous monocle up his ass and turn him over to the Chinese who aren't there. I think he wanted them to talk back, so he could have us all court-martialed, and he is mean enough to do it." I assured Joe, "The next time, Sir Charles appears. Call me. I'll handle it. I really don't believe we will see him soon , it is getting to be heavy enough fighting to keep him away. Joe, from my judgment of people, this falls into the category of: Someone never forgives someone they've done wrong, they continue to find fault to prove themselves right, but for his own safety, don't let him anywhere near the troops."

President Truman wasn't being fooled. He did not want a war with China and kept asking about the Chinese intervention. Willoughby's response was always for him, "not to be concerned." Then the president began questioning, asking for unit names and the names of the Chinese officers. He started getting the correct information, and told the Chiefs of Staff, " That bastard, Willoughby, is lying; he isn't reporting the facts here or to Tokyo, also Almond, the other part of the Troika, has no patience with the black troops or the Marines and is making it known, they are all he has to work with. He also reported O.P. Smith was driving him crazy, saying he was too cautious, had to think out every move, and this was what was slowing down progress." O.P., concerned about his men, didn't like the way they were being used, sent north without a secure left flank. He also stated, Almond's orders to MacLean did not make much sense and there was a possibility he would lose MacLean's regiment. Battles should be thought out. He often said " speed is an enemy and a companion of errors."

The fighting was always at night in the freezing cold. This was when the enemy would attack. We soon learned not to move at night, just maintain our position until daybreak. We were ordered to keep advancing, while the army was in full retreat. This put the Marines in a position of fighting for their lives. My orders were to pass the 5th through the 7th and lead the advance. To where? We were surrounded and the minus twenty degree temperature was having an effect on the men, the machines and the weapons.

I cancelled all orders. I will never forget, many bleeding from bullet wounds themselves, would crawl back and rescue a Marine they considered more wounded than themselves. The corpsman would take over, but many times before we could lift them to safety, they froze to death. On the morning of 28, November, the situation was desperate. Almond says, "we are exaggerating the number of Chinese." He flew to the east side of the reservoir and confronted MacLean and Faith. They had fought all night and had been hard hit and lost the high ground of the perimeter. Almond's orders were always the same, "keep attacking and don't let a bunch of Chinese laundrymen scare you." They were then given orders to retake the high ground and to continue to attack north. He handed out three silver stars one to Faith, one to a wounded Lieutenant, and one to a Mess Sergeant. Faith ripped off his medal and threw it in the snow. He felt this would show his men what he thought of Almond's orders. Back at headquarters, Almond eventually learned of the 8th Army retreating and he was not happy.

Our survival seemed bleak. Almond left orders to defend the objectives. The north and south were not defended and, being on one of two unprotected prime routes, would lead to problems. All units on the valley floor were also unprotected and it was this condition surrounded by Hills 1420, 1286, and 1384 that almost led to the destruction of the 1st Marines. We set up tents, hoping to get some rest. This was wishful thinking; as night fell the Chinese came in with all they had. Mortar fire, red and green rockets, flares and bugles. They hit all the Marines' positions west and north of the village, attacking in massive numbers and pushing us off the ridges Each time we counterattacked and sent the Chinese back. It was back and forth all night. By morning we had the high ground but paid dearly for it, with hundreds dead and hundreds wounded. It was deadly fighting, our casualties were heavy, and we were constantly hearing from Tokyo to press further north. First, though, we must get out of this mess. They attacked again that night. There was no way of knowing how many Chinese were out there. They were attacking from all sides, north and west and from every cave and hill. Our rifle companies of both 5th and 7th were down to half strength.

General Pang Dubai of the PLA had made us aware of his intentions early in the morning, by revving up and flexing their muscles for battle with another enormous amount of noisy insults, bugle calls, tremendous banging, insulting profanities, through a PA system and if we could have understood, would have made us aware we were not going to live long if he had anything to do with it. They were determined to seal our fate to the last man. We were surrounded on all sides and the only way out, if one could call it that, was more of a trail than a road, capable of one-way traffic, a treacherous, and dangerous road. Sharp hairpin turns, critically narrow bridges, when covered with snow and hidden black ice, could plummet you into the beyond.

129

MacArthur was still playing down the presence of the Chinese. The President was still pressuring for correct information, and his inquiries were getting more and more often. Then on 28, November, the President received a hysterical call from MacArthur: " We are faced with impossible odds and conditions have become disastrous."

In fact, the country was divided for some time about the crossing of the 38th Parallel and questioned the reasoning for it. MacArthur knew this and at 1730 on 28 November, called a conference at his headquarters in Tokyo. He wanted Almond and Walker to be there. Almond was still optimistic and wanted the Marine and Infantry to continue to the Yalu. MacArthur finally disagreed with him. He had also been pressured by the President. He orders a withdrawal.

Earlier in the day, General Smith had flown by helicopter to open his command post at Hagaru-ri. A half hour later, General Almond , accompanied by his aide, Captain Alexander Haig flew in on his "Blue Goose." At that moment we were still trapped at Yudam-ni, in the beginning of five days and nights of fighting out of nightmare alley. It was to become the worst battle of survival in Marine history. The rest was minor to that. Night after night at Yudam-ni I never thought we would see daylight again. Our guns and vehicles were frozen, carbines jammed and no easy way of getting replacements. Some were flown in and a few made it to our area, but much was dropped outside the perimeter and fell into the hands of the Chinese. They didn't need to be supplied, we were furnishing what they needed. It was their aim to cut us off. The Chinese 59th came in from the southwest and cut off the supply line to Yudam-ni. The road had been active until this time and some of the empty trucks were on their way back to Hagaru-ri. Hill 1403, overlooking the MSR (Main Supply Route) had been lost to the enemy. Roise was still in position and I ordered him to continue the attack at daybreak. If Taplett held, he was to come up the right side flank in assault. But at dawn, it was clear the strategy had to be changed from offensive to defensive if any of us were going to come out of this alive. To keep from freezing, the corpsmen carried two bottles of brandy, one for cleaning their hands if reaching into a wound, the other for a healthy slug for instant warmth. This kept them going and help revive many Marines. Woolen caps under helmets, kept our ears from freezing, also parka hoods over the helmets kept the warmth in. If fingers were exposed outside the mittens, they would freeze to anything they touched. Shoe pacs had felt linings, not a good idea; when they became sweat soaked they would freeze, bringing on frostbite. Body elimination was a problem; any part exposed for more than a few seconds would freeze.

Once the Chinese chose to enter the war, as we have said, their numbers were overwhelming. There was no other avenue but to consider how we could save as many men as possible and still break through this solid wall of entrapment. Our X Corps Commander, Ned Almond, was unwilling to admit the forces were not strong enough to hold the position, and was constantly blaming General Smith for everything going wrong. We were trapped and the division had not sent anyone to evaluate the condition. Buzz Winecoff was finally sent and he came back a shaken man. The only report the division had was: Winecoff's and he had not seen the whole picture. Somehow the news got back to a fuming President, who was still smarting from the wrong information MacArthur had given him at Wake Island, and there was a feeling the President had been pushed to the limit and something was going to give.

Daily, I wondered what we were doing there in the first place, getting our tails whipped and not understanding why. To this day it is difficult to understand MacArthur's reasoning, unless it was simply hoping for positive publicity, since we had earlier learned from his speeches his desire for the Presidency.

The only food we had, not frozen solid, were cans of fruit cocktail and Tootsie Rolls, being dropped by the fly boys, We put the candy next to our bodies to keep them soft enough to eat. The sugar in both of them gave us the energy to keep going. During this time the Chinese had very little supplies of their own, even with some of ours falling in their area. They continued to move silently and quickly, carrying everything allotted to them on their person. When the supplies were gone or they were killed, a few thousand more would be sent in under the same battle plan. The fanaticism of their officers toward communism and the extent they would drive their men to indoctrinate their troops to care so little for their lives, was beyond the realm of reasoning.

29, November:

During a sleepless night and silent prayers, it came to me. The Chinese made the mistake against all military training. They had not kept their strength where it was needed and, by surrounding us on all sides, they had weakened their lines. They thought they had us trapped, my only hope was they would continue to make the same mistake. I knew there was a possibility of breaking through. It was time for Colonel Homer Litzenberg and me to get our heads together with a workable plan, if we were to get our men and ourselves out of this trap alive.

When officers looks at reality, the awful truth must be faced. We were undermanned, under equipped and completely surrounded by at least one hundred thousand Chinese. Should we push on and lose our regiments? Or, should we look to the first duty of a commanding officer and save as many men as we could.? The attack to the west could not continue, and we had to get this through to General Smith. On our own, we consolidated and traded forces where they would do the most good and if one of us didn't make it the other would take over the command of both regiments. There was some talk of withdrawing separately, but, had we done this, it would have been suicide. We were now on our own without division guidance. We put riflemen on the ridges and being in for heavy fighting we lost whole platoons; our supplies, by that time, were completely cut off; what was dropped was supplying the enemy. We were facing the same problems, steep sided valleys, icy roads, Chinese on all ridges, guns and vehicles frozen, ice on mortars, jammed carbines, and vehicles without fuel.

There is a time when you know with whatever certainty there is, death could be imminent, and with this realization, a calmness takes over and you start thinking clearly. These regiments were in our care and they were going to be saved. We can break out. We stopped thinking of the faulty generalship responsible for this mess. We knew the Chinese made a mistake. We needed to use every bit of training we had to out maneuver their battle plan. We had a new challenge.

Sung Shi-lum decided he would finish off the Marines and the Army on both sides of the reservoir and sent his 81st Division in to add strength to the 80th, isolating Colonel MacLean. We were in a rough spot, but so were MacLean and Faith. At 1:00 PM, 29, November, they were in for some heavy fighting attacks on all their companies. MacLean ordered the battalions to withdraw and fight their way back to the inlet. Faith put the wounded on trucks and started moving out at 4:40 AM. MacLean was up front in a jeep, when they came to what appeared to be a road block. MacLean got out of his jeep and walked around a bend to a concrete bridge. Captain Bigger reported, " I saw MacLean fall several times on the ice, then the Chinese came out from behind some bushes and pulled him back." No trace of MacLean has ever been found. Task Force MacLean, became Task Force Faith.

Litzenberg and I issued a combined order for a breakout. Our units 5th and 7th were intermixed, but no one was specifically in command. Colonel Litzenberg was my senior and put his 7th in the center of Yudam-ni. The spot left was the northwest corner of the village. We drew up plans. If I had troops on one hill, he put his on the other, so it made a good perimeter defense. We became aware there were more Chinese coming into the fight and we were now surrounded by two more divisions, the 79th and 81st. We were also aware the 59th Chinese division was on the south side cutting off our supply lines to Toktong Pass. Many people have asked, since Litzenberg was a full colonel, why didn't he assume full command? I can't answer that. There was a division headquarters over the hill, so we had a common head. We decided to operate closely, and we did, but soon we were out of touch with other divisions and operating without their guidance.

We put 2/5 into the perimeter west and south of the village, 1/5 to the east and 3/5 to hold Hill 1286. The Chinese continued their fighting on 1286. Taplett blocked the fork of the road and turned them back. We were so short of supplies we scrounged for anything and everything we could find in ammo and grenades. We held on. Each hour looked bleaker, supplies getting lower, utilizing half frozen Marines just capable of thirty percent of their potential, but we knew what was in our favor was the thirty per cent was all heart. These men would take a command and do whatever we needed done. Every Marine was a rifleman, and without supplies, it became a hand to hand, bayonet to bayonet, life or death battle.

How many people are completely oblivious to war and its devastation? Where is the limit to human endurance? Where does the struggle for survival give up, or do we fight to save our bodies from freezing? Low temperatures caused the loss of ears, fingers, toes and feet, as body warmth went internally to protect heart, lungs and brain. Men were staring and not seeing, trying to speak, and couldn't speak, trying to walk and couldn't move. To stop for even a few minutes would have been disastrous. They would have frozen where they stood. Stragglers had to be pushed, pulled, kicked, anything to keep them moving. If they stopped they wouldn't move again.

At nightfall, General Smith officially sanctioned the actions Colonel Litzenberg and I put together. We were ordered to attack to the south and reopen the MSR to Hagaru-ri, and we were to plan a joint defense from Yudam-ni and breakout to the south. We regrouped our regiments, organized a provisional battalion of Companies D and E of the 7th and Companies A and G of the 5th. Dog Easy was freed from Colonel Ray Davis and became part of our battalion. Roise's 2/5, covered by air and artillery, held a line from Hill 1426-1282. Then, under heavy resistance, fell back to 1426. And 1294. Harris's 3/7 moved to the MSR south of Yudam-ni.

This was everybody's war. A priest, Father Griffin, with the 7th, was always where he was needed. Very adept, he would fill in helping the corpsmen, bringing comfort to the wounded, and, when his rank remained the highest in the battle area, he wouldn't pick up a weapon or a rifle, but he would take over and direct the command. He always carried small bottles of brandy and often said, with a little blessing, it worked as holy water bringing warmth and life back to the freezing troops, and easing pain from the wounds. It wasn't the way he would have chosen to serve the Lord; always praying the Lord would understand and His will alone would be done.

Almond arrived. He had heard of the ambush and disappearance of Colonel MacLean. He appeared to be a changed person when he realized Task Force MacLean had been under his orders to advance when he was not properly manned or supplied. He became concerned about Task Force Faith.

133

1 December:

Faith's dispatch:

Lt. Col. Don Faith loaded his wounded on trucks, set fire to any equipment he was leaving behind and started his withdrawal. When they were leaving a plane mistakenly strafed the area and showered them with napalm, a flaming gob of jellied gasoline, ignited, burns so quickly, by the time the troops could roll in the snow, they were already casualties. The ones who didn't survive were buried in a nearby ditch Now his men are getting out of control, instead of holding their posts, racing every direction to safety. Faith radioed for help and was told the only help available was air cover, as every command was involved in intense fighting. He tried to rally his troops, and was forced to threaten them to being shot if they didn't stay and fight. He started out on his own, hoping his men would follow. He was badly wounded. They loaded him in the cab of the truck, picked up other wounded and strapped them on in every available space, two and three deep, on hoods, bumpers and roofs. Faith kept commanding, but was getting weaker from loss of blood. He kept urging his force to make it to Hagaru-ri.

He almost reached freedom. They found the truck and Faith in the cab, where he had bled to death from his wounds.

Taplett had pulled George Company from Hill 1282, where they had been fighting hand to hand and grenade to grenade, and assigned two of his companies to take another hill. He was not happy when we radioed his orders had been changed. He was to pull two companies from the hill' and lead the attack to Hagaru-ri, and seize the ground on both sides of the road. By this time he was fuming and I asked his good friend, Father Bernie Hickey, if he could calm him down. He listened, and I'm certain he considered his orders to be lousy, having changes made when he had his objectives where he wanted them. Father gave him advice, and he often referred to it as saving his life. " When the going gets tough, make the sign of the cross and say, "not my will, but Thy Will Be Done, and you will be successful."

Litzenberg's 7th, moved overland and the 5th Marines moved along the MSR. We put the strongest force we had out there, Taplett's 3/5, by now down to half size. He was to take the road led by a solitary Pershing tank, which had reached Yudam-ni on a trial run. At dawn, Davis's Battalion was attacked again. A few Chinese were in back of his column, but strong enough to give him serious resistance. The wounded were being brought out on litters and we lost our regimental surgeon, Navy Lt. Peter Arioli. He was killed by a sniper's bullet. Lt. Col. Roise was having problems in the rear guard; night fighters had hit him hard and the fighting had continued all night through to mid morning. Roise gave up his position and continued south. Lt Col. Jack Stevens was fighting east of the road with the Chinese who had crossed the reservoir behind us.

134

With bridges out and engineers targeted, the losses were heavy. The Chinese were aware the engineers and the corpsmen played a vital part in keeping the battalions moving, putting extra effort into killing them, if they could get them in their sights. We had started with forty-eight engineers and were now down to seventeen. Six inches of snow fell through the night, and Taplett could tell the draining effect this had on his men, and knew he must get some strength back into the forces; he collected the remnants of Dog-Easy and George Companies, then returned the command to Lt. Charles Mize. Item Company bore the brunt, not only the freezing frostbiting weather, but the loss of most of their company. They still had not reached Hill 1520. But George Company had made progress, clearing the MSR and was starting up Hill 1520. Hill 1520 had to be secured, as this is where the Chinese put their strength and the only way out of the reservoir. Fighting was heavy, getting there one thing, holding the Hill another. The fighting went on all night, corpsmen doing what they could. Taplett put Item Company in the lead, followed by G and H, but when they had not gone far they ran into the 7th Marines. Taplett had been informed the 7th was supposed to be ahead of him attacking Hill 1520, and asked them " what the hell are you doing here, you are supposed to be ahead of us." Their reply was " We were slow getting started." Taplett took over, switched, put his How Company in the lead followed by Item Company and George, with orders to clear Hill 1520, so the rest of the 5th and 7th Marines could get through to Toktong Pass. There was heavy fighting and the resistance was strong. A dark night, frozen snow, icy and treacherous, made every step fear for one's life. Davis's 1/7 had joined them and was put out front. The map finally indicated they were on Hill 1520. Davis stopped there, gave his men a rest, and radioed his position. Capt. Harold Schrier, with the Item Company, was running into stiff resistance on the reverse side of Hill 1520. He fell back in a better position to protect the MSR and was hit by a mortar fire. His wound was through his neck and he was only able to say " everybody has been killed." He had been wounded earlier in the day, which he had played down so he could continue to command his men. This was too much; bleeding and in serious condition, he had to be evacuated. He was replaced by 2nd Lt. Willard Peterson. Taplett moved in George Company into the defense position behind Item Company. All night the fighting became more deadly and at daybreak the enemy reached 342. We had also taken a heavy losses. Peterson was down to twenty men still able to fight. There were just two platoons left in George Company. Taplett did some switching around and by noon Capt. Chester Hermandson had taken Hill 1520.

The attack had to be renewed; all companies were down to half strength. I sent a tank and enough force from remnants of other companies to form a composite company. Taplett was leading the way with the composite company he named the "Damnation" and fighting for every inch of the road. One of the companies was stalled near a demolished bridge. George Company managed going around it and secured its objective on the left side of the hill. Taplett radioed he had to keep his men moving. They must keep moving; they had not eaten, they were freezing and if he didn't keep them moving they wouldn't be able to move. Worse still, he felt the fight had gone out of them. They were so beat they didn't give a damn anymore.

We knew our main objectives had to be Toktong Pass and Hill 1520. Every inch would be launched by the enemy. They had completely infested the hills. Six more inches of snow had fallen, and the enemy had blocked the pass. Taplett had commanded to this point and felt the Pass should have been his to clear. And it should have been. Each time he had come on a problem, he had helped the officers figure a better method, and had brought them through some rough fighting. Colonel Litzenberg gave the command to Colonel Ray Davis, and his 7th Marines cleared the Pass and positioned the 7th in the lead.

Bringing up the rear, and still back at the reservoir, one hundred and twenty thousand more Chinese moved in to surround us and hit the 5th and 7th on the west side. We were in desperate need of anything that would help us to continue to fight. Smith ordered Colonel Puller to form a task force at Koto-ri, open a supply line and fight north to Hagaru-ri. A 922 man force was put together, The command was given to Colonel Douglas Drysdale, of the British Commandoes. He brought with him fourteen officers and two hundred twenty one enlisted men. The rest were Marines. At 1:55 PM, Task Force Drysdale, headed by a tank unit in the lead and a dozen tanks in the rear, began their climb to Hagaru-ri. They ran into heavy fighting almost immediately, covering only four miles, when they radioed Colonel Puller for help. With additional tanks, they made some progress but were attacked again and the casualties were heavy. The heavy fighting was in a small valley, where many of the trucks were on fire. Drysdale aptly named the valley "Hell Fire Valley." The hills they had taken earlier were retaken by the Chinese. It was deadly, bloody, and the losses were enormous. About fifty British and American troops were taken prisoner.

Jack Buck, a historian, with the San Diego Marines, who had been an aide to General Craig, was a Marine assigned to Drysdale. He had flown over the area with the General many times and remembered the territory, the terrain and its many pitfalls. He also remembered narrow paths and ledges with overhanging areas where, if they could escape and keep out of sight, they would have a chance of getting back to Koto-ri. Vehicles were catching fire and some of the troops used this to break to the right, but they were taken prisoner. " I gathered up as many of the forces as I could, some from the Army, the Marines and a few Royals, and broke to the left. It was a small

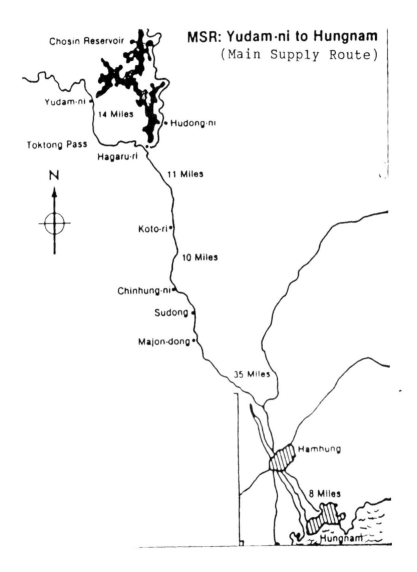

MSR: Yudam-ni to Hungnam
(Main Supply Route)

Chosin Reservoir

Yudam-ni

14 Miles

Hudong-ni

Toktong Pass

Hagaru-ri

11 Miles

N

Koto-ri

10 Miles

Chinhung-ni

Sudong

Majon-dong

35 Miles

Hamhung

8 Miles

Hungnam

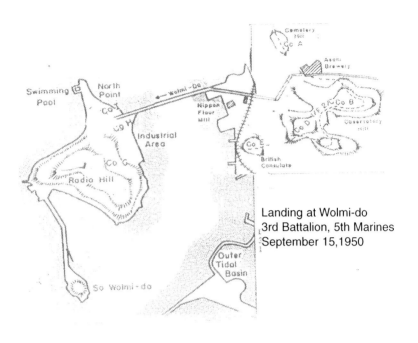

Landing at Wolmi-do
3rd Battalion, 5th Marines
September 15, 1950

The observatory tower in Inchon,
after the capture

Leading the rear battalion away from Yudam-ni.

Leaving Yudam-ni in freezing 40 degree below zero temperature.

group, but we would try to save as many as we could. I kept in mind the embankment; if it could be reached, we would have a chance of getting away. Before we moved very far, we were spotted. I noticed a figure coming across the road, it looked as though it might be a Marine, so I told the troops to hold their fire. It was a Marine, who had been taken prisoner, and the news to us was to surrender. He called out:! "Surrender, you don't have a snowballs chance in hell." I told him 'we can't surrender.' Then, he related he was a sergeant with the supply platoon, and repeated again for us to surrender. Then, Lt. Col. Pop Seetly, of the Motor Transport, came across and said they had shot a forty-five right out of his hand. I brought to his attention he had a higher rank and it was now his call. He said he would go and talk with them. In fifteen minutes he returned and said, "you have just ten minutes to surrender or be blown to bits" I remembered the ledge, and thought if we had a chance to reach it we could stay out of sight long enough to get away. We would not be taken prisoner if there was a chance of preventing it. We certainly had the motivation to move a lot of distance in ten minutes, and we did. The river we needed to cross was frozen, and at this point we welcomed the freezing ice, as we were praying it would hold our weight. I tested it, it held. We crossed and climbed to a high area where we could not be seen and hid in some trees. Ten minutes passed and we heard the firing, the firing that was to blow us to smithereens. We followed the ledge until we were out of sight. We were in enemy territory, constantly alert, trying to hold up, and in some instances carrying the wounded. Ten o'clock the next morning we were back in Koto-ri and had our wounded where they could get some help. Chesty called me into his tent and ask for any information that would be helpful to him. We chatted for a few minutes, and he gave me a stiff drink in a canteen cup; asked if I needed anything else. I asked for a toothbrush, and he reached under his cot and pulled out one.

Task Force Drysdale had left Koto-ri with 922 troops, reached Hagaru-ri with 400; 162 were killed and an estimated 300 got back to Koto-ri, 159 were wounded and 44 were taken prisoner. Colonel Drysdale was wounded by a grenade fragment and his force was down to 100. He recorded: 61 British Marines as lost, 321 casualties of the combined forces and 71 vehicles destroyed. Forty-one of the commandoes became a garrison reserve and were assigned to me.

The grand offensive was shattered. Almond did not make the Marines aware of this. The troops had a different names for him now, he was no longer the " anointed one."

Yudam-ni is surrounded by hills on three sides with a shoreline of the Chosin Reservoir on the east, this is where we are now surrounded. We had been falsely promised to be home for Christmas, and knew MacArthur had miscalculated. For two days there had been no response from Tokyo.

Stories were, MacArthur was sending cables to the White House, asking if he could use the bomb. There was some talk about it, but the chiefs of staff and Truman did not want to be the reason to start the Third World War. It was never used. It was a foot soldiers war and a bomb was not the way to win it. It was time to withdraw and regroup.

MacArthur's next press release, in his own voice, reflected the news of the 1st Marine Division being trapped and he made a statement to the press. He had no help to send them and his Army had retreated. The Marines at the Chosin Reservoir were lost and presumed dead.

The Chinese gloried in this press release. Peking radio got into the act and announced, " the annihilation of the 5th and 7th Marines trapped in the icy waters of the Chosin Reservoir." Other radio news we heard: " The Marines annihilation is just a matter of time." Well, we weren't dead, and it would take more than these news releases to make it so. By then MacArthur should have known the Marines, as he had made this same statement before in Guadalcanal. We will make it. We are Marines.

First I wrote to Eve. It may not get to her, but it released some of this frustration.

Dearest darling Eve,

We are in a tough spot, possibly the worst the Marines have ever found themselves. MacArthur's judgment should be questioned. He has been surrounded by people, from what we are learning, who having been playing to his ego, believing he can't be wrong. There is a chance he has met his match with the Chinese and they will knock him down to their size. Our concern has been, why did he use the Marines in this abusive manner? You know how much I love my family, the guilt I carry for being away when our precious Michael died. You have always carried the heavy load, and taken care of everything. We've had so many beautiful memories and some sad ones. And I know some of the problems have been heavy. Please watch the children in the same loving manner you always have. This war can't last forever. Looking forward to coming home.
Love you, Ray.

Almond ordered General Smith to withdraw and destroy all equipment. Smith couldn't believe what he was hearing. How could a general give such an irresponsible command.? If our equipment was destroyed, how could we have gotten out of there alive.? We needed it to bring out our wounded, and the equipment to fight with, if we were going to get out of this trap. This is where Smith, took charge, and told Almond, he would make the decisions, on what equipment to keep, and how he would order his commanders to break out. The dead were frozen stiff, laid out in rows stacked four feet deep. The earth was frozen, so we bulldozed a burial ground and had a field burial for eighty-five Marines. Both Catholic and Protestant Chaplains officiated blessing the bodies and the burial area. We would not leave them for the Chinese to disrespect them by stealing their clothes or bayoneting their remains. There weren't any flowers, but their buddies' prayers were heard and the hollowness and emptiness felt from their loss could be seen in every comrade there.

General Smith was in command now. He was making the decisions, and ordered a pull back. It had to be handled well as he did not want it to be a disaster. He made up his mind he would not lose an entire division and his orders were: "One unit anchors and secures its objectives, before the next moves south; then it can be leapfrogged by another when the unit reaches its objectives. I don't want two units moving at the same time. If we have a problem, we don't go on until it is taken care of." He gave these orders to his commanders, knowing they understood and would take care of details. The Chinese had two rifle companies surrounded and trapped. If they could keep them there the X Corps would have no defense. They were without supplies, fighting with whatever they had, securing small areas with anything available. If vehicles broke down with the road so narrow, one small turn would send equipment down hundreds of feet.

Almond had not been happy when General Smith set him straight, less so when he heard about what Litzenberg and I had worked out. Smith stressed his regimental commanders knew the fighting had to be turned around from offensive to defensive and he agreed with them. Almond still believed we should press north, but he didn't press the point. An aide said, "Smith had had it and it looked as though Almond grasped, sensed it, and wasn't disagreeing." We thank God Smith took command, as this was the only way we would get out of this debauchery alive. This saved the Marines MacArthur said couldn't be saved.

We fought for five days and five nights without rest. Our prayers were constant. I could hear the Catholics saying their Hail Mary's, the Protestant's reciting the Twenty-third Psalm, and my prayers took a turn with all of them. At daybreak, I looked at these tired, beaten, worn out men, half frozen, some already with frostbite, others with wounds so painful I wondered how they were walking. In my mind, I went over again my thoughts when we landed at Wonsan, and I had studied the maps. I had personally thought there was no need to go further north. We should have stayed in the Wonsan or Hungnam area, secured the area and come up with a better battle plan. I thought, again, these cities were the only areas of any military value. We could have kept supplied and kicked the hell out of anything they sent us. Instead we had been ordered north into an area where we had no business being, freezing our butts off, and fighting our way out of this trap.

MacArthur had gambled on the Chinese being afraid of our air support and our sophisticated weapons. This would not suffice when forces were so thinly scattered, that even a few Chinese would have been a threat. Now they were coming in by the thousand; different quotes have estimated from ten to thirteen divisions, pitted against our three regiments. The 8th was spread so thinly, the Chinese would have broken through anywhere, and the guerrillas were attacking the rear bases. On a pitch black night the planes strafed and rocketed the enemy within one hundred yards of our position, and in daylight, a lot closer. We did the Marine rear duty under fire, with the equipment needed for the breakout. We heard later, it was called the most valiant action of the Korean war.

The Chinese, all in white, seem to wave and blend with the scenery. Their white coats were padded, looking bulky, but seemed to keep them warm enough. Their shoes were tennis shoes. Frozen feet would break the shoes open, and their feet would be black and frozen, minus parts of flesh, coming through the open spaces. Even with these handicaps the Chinese could move over mountainous peaks, rocks, and impossible crevices with the agility of mountain sheep. In our favor they had moved most of their fighting equipment to the Yalu, thinking that was where they would finish us off, and were fighting only with what was on their backs. Much of the news reaching them had been from our own sources indicating we would be crossing the Yalu.

Taplett radioed his orders to Captain Williamson to fight the Chinese overland. The fighting would be tough getting through these impossible peaks, the snow was waist deep, and the men were exhausted, but there would be no stopping. Taplett fought through the night and was within one hundred yards of Toktong Pass. Davis climbed all night through the snow and Drysdale, weakened by the loss of half of his men, caught up with them. The enemy had lost Toktong Pass. It had been taken by Fox Company, and held for three days. There were still seventy-five Marines on the hill, all injured, propping themselves up to be able to hold a rifle. They held. Then three Chinese divisions following us, joined the remnants of the Chinese left on the hill, and took back Toktong Pass. Davis, with the added strength of Taplett and Drysdale, moved in, took back the hill and cleared the MSR. With the taking of Toktong Pass, we broke out of the trap .The place was a frozen hell, and took its toll on the enemy, as well. We would see Chinese, frozen standing, with rifles still in their grip; frozen stiff with their eyes wide open; feet, black from the cold, breaking through their tennis shoes.

We had fought through five days and nights of unspeakable horror, fighting for every inch we gained, through masses of yellow humanity and dozens of roadblocks. Those five days and nights through nightmare alley were the worst thing that ever happened to the United States Marines. We brought our wounded out any way we could get them out, piled high, so each body could bring whatever warmth it had in it to help any other it touched. We tried everything, but many froze before we could get them to a hospital unit. Most of the troops had been depressingly assailable and isolated, leading to unnecessary bloodletting. Taplett's battalion was down from 2000 to 326. He'd led the way out and paid dearly. There were impossible passes and torn out bridges ahead of us, but also new hope as the three battalions banded together for additional strength.

The survivors of Task Force Faith caught up with us. The men remarked they had one can of C rations every three days. Some fell through the ice on the reservoir, some were machine-gunned and burned, many just froze. Some were minus most of their clothes. The Chinese had taken anything usable. Easily understood why so many of them froze to death. Our own clothes were not the best for these temperatures and the reason we lost so many to frostbite or freezing..

We could see Hagaru-ri in the distance. Going north, it did not have the appeal it had now. We saw the peasants' huts, with smoke curling from the chimneys, giving the illusion of warmth. It appeared as a beautiful postcard. Warming tents had been set up, where we knew we could bring feeling back to our bodies. We must have been a sight, our clothes hadn't been changed since our climb up the hill, some just hanging in shreds, hadn't shaved for days, faces raw and bleeding from the cold, famished and suffering from frostbite, our bodies wracked by diarrhea , dehydration, oozing sores from lice bites, what was left of our clothes, permeating from diarrhea and urination; some were supporting their buddies, holding them up so they could stand and walk in with dignity. We are told, a nice doctor, with tears streaming down his face, commented, "Look at those bastards, those magnificent bastards." The best compliment the Marines ever received.

A MASH unit was there where we could get some help for the wounded and an airlift to evacuate them. We were hoping for enough additional support to get some rest. Everything I've written here happened in seventy-nine hours, without sleep and very little food. Our bodies had taken unthinkable abuse. We knew there were miles ahead of us and there would be some tough fighting but the worst was behind us. We had gone through the greatest odds the Marines had ever faced, brought in fifteen hundred wounded and frostbitten troops, carried our dead for burial, and the wounded to the hospital..

We were still the rear guard with more Chinese behind us than in front of us, but the combined forces of Taplett's Darkhorses, Davis's Roadrunners, Drysdale's Commandoes and the rest of the 5th, gave us the moral support and the military strength we needed to put us back into serious fighting. We counted our combined losses, in the seventy nine hours of fighting of the Marine and Army, at over five thousand, from frostbite, amputations of arms, legs, toes and fingers; dead and missing. Inhuman exhaustion, certainly not for rewards or promotions, honor or glory, but for the simple obedience to duty. The losses stood at more than Tarawa or Iwo Jima. We were rewarded now with some hot food and coffee something we hadn't had since Thanksgiving.

Four thousand five hundred of our wounded were flown out of Hagaru-ri , and these were only the seriously wounded. Anyone who could walk, anyone who could even stand and hold a rifle was needed to fight through the solid wall of Chinese defense. When I observed them I wondered how many would be able to walk the final walk. They had to. This was the only way they could be battle ready. It would take too long to get from a vehicle and be prepared to fight. Walking, their reactions would be in a split second and this would save their lives. I could feel the negative thoughts going through the troops, just wondering themselves if they would be able to make it. The officers as well, after being through what they had just gone through, seemed down, but we had to go on. They were hollow-eyed from fatigue, knew what it was to be without food and water. My feelings were, with reinforcements, we could make it and I must make them believe they could. I felt my eyes tearing, and I wasn't ashamed of it. The heroism of these men will be in my memory for as long as I live. They should be allowed to be home, raise families and be the citizens our country can be proud of. I tried to collect my thoughts, why were we here? We came to Korea unprepared. Syngman Rhee's warning words were "Your Government must learn as we have, there is no compromise with the Communists. It will be a trick for them to negotiate peace to get extra time to prepare for war. " MacArthur thought two divisions would hold Korea, again underestimating the enemy and the strength of the supplies brought in by the Soviet Union. Any negative news received by MacArthur was made light of. Rumor had from the start, the Chinese and North Koreans were bringing in 13 to 15 divisions, well armed and ready to fight. He tried to convince President Truman we could hold them with ground troops. This is why we were here.

It would be a miracle and whatever we could do as well trained Marines to come through against almost impossible odds, freezing conditions, bombed out bridges and whatever I could do to get these men, who had no fear of death, just not to let down their brother Marines. I needed to get them back on their feet and keep them going. I started with: "We advance to the rear. Those are division orders. We are going to come out as Marines, not as stragglers, We are going to bring out our wounded and equipment. We are coming out, I tell you as Marines or not at all. Any officer here who does not think so, will kindly go lame and be evacuated. I don't expect any takers"

It took everything it had in me, to appear to them that we could get out of this mess, and, with God's help, be a strong leader they could depend on.

I noticed Keyes Beech, a familiar face. He was a press photographer and a war correspondent, and had been with us through most of Korea. I walked back to talk to him and mentioned he should have been with us at Yudam-ni, he really would have had a story. His comment was, "I'm damned well glad I wasn't" He also added: "Almond had to know he was sending the Marines into a trap, I've said it before and I will say it again. Almond is the meanest son of a bitch, in the military or outside of the military, I've ever had anything to do with. But, he loves to give medals."

4, December:

General Almond flew in and decorated General Smith, Colonel Litzenberg and myself with Distinguished Service Crosses. Then flew to Koto-ri and decorated Colonel Chesty Puller and Colonel Ready, with their Distinguished Service Crosses. Nine others would receive Silver Stars. My Regiment would take over the defense of Hagaru-ri and Colonel Litzenberg would march south.

At Hagaru-ri there was a power plant built in the side of the hill, and over it was the road, right on the roof. To stop us from coming and going, the Chinese had blown it twice, just another obstacle to overcome in battle. We got around it in good time. Litzenberg, with some flank security, led the way out from Hagaru-ri. The 5th became the rear guard again, and stayed behind another day. The divisional CP (Command Post) was at Hagaru-ri, mine at the end of a ledge, on a bridge, leading out. A very vulnerable position. When the 7th moved out we had hordes of Chinese attacking, and it went on all night. We had tanks firing at them and machine guns firing down the road. The next morning we walked down the road, and as far as we could see there were dead Chinese. It was a horrible sight; almost a full regiment had lost their lives. My exec's comment was: "It could have been us." We began to move more easily, but the real devastation was moving out of Hagaru-ri. The 7th had been hit again, but was able to drive them off.

Our problem was, we had no flank security, so we were vulnerable on all sides.

But there was no better fighting force than the 5th and this reflected on the outstanding reserves. You couldn't tell the difference from the regulars. They fit right in. Since World War II, reserve training had been improved, and they were kept current, and as a result, they were superior to any training received before. They were battle ready when they arrived, and could think fast in combat, knew their job and did it. I will always think this was the best combat regiment I ever commanded. The officers were outstanding, and the regiment, the best trained outfit in the military. They certainly proved

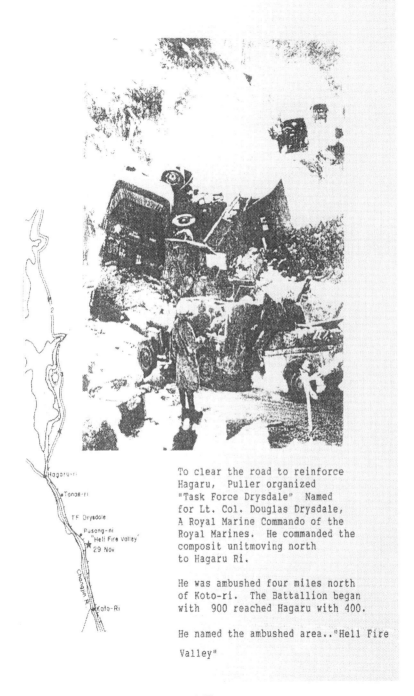

Hagaru-ri
Tonae-ri
T.F. Drysdale
Pusong-ni
"Hell Fire Valley"
29 Nov
Changjin R.
Koto-Ri

To clear the road to reinforce
Hagaru, Puller organized
"Task Force Drysdale" Named
for Lt. Col. Douglas Drysdale,
A Royal Marine Commando of the
Royal Marines. He commanded the
composit unitmoving north
to Hagaru Ri.

He was ambushed four miles north
of Koto-ri. The Battallion began
with 900 reached Hagaru with 400.

He named the ambushed area.."Hell Fire

Valley"

147

themselves during the breakout from the reservoir, and back down to the sea. My hopes are: Our entire military will always be this ready.

Colonel Puller would continue to stay in his position and hold Chinghung-ni. Everyone else would march south with two days rations and their rifles. All excess supplies and equipment were put in a bonfire. Casualties were being flown out but a new group was being brought in every day. The 7th Marines moved along the MSR, alert that seven Chinese Divisions were still being rumored in the area and were moving to defend Funchilin Pass, also aiming to move against Colonel Puller at Chinhung-ni.

From Hagaru-ri to Koto-ri we passed Hell Fire Valley and dozens of burned-out vehicles. The devastation was everywhere, showing the extent of the fighting Colonel Drysdale had faced with the Chinese in great numbers, with superior supplies, supplied by the Soviets, and played such havoc on Colonel Drysdale's forces.

7, December:

Our division is in Puller's perimeter. Twenty four miles below the reservoir. The first fourteen had taken us seventy nine hours, and it has taken us thirty hours from Hagaru-ri. Fighting all the way. We lost 103 dead, 506 wounded and 7 missing. When we arrived at Koto-ri we were relieved on the hills by the 1st Marines. We knew the march to the sea would not be a cake walk and we would need our tanks and brought them with us. Puller took me aside and said, "Ray, when will the truth ever be told?"

Maggie Higgins, the New York Herald reporter, was there for her story. She was a dedicated reporter and seemed to bounce back, every time she was ordered to leave the front lines. She always wanted to be where the action was, wanted a story and worked hard to get it. Puller and Smith were not happy with this additional worry, so they sent her out on a C-47, with the wounded. Two days later, she was back with General Shepherd. They both wanted to walk down the hill with the Marines. Again this did not go well and they were discouraged in a hurry and flown out. The plane they were in was fired upon and had engine trouble. They had some exciting stories to tell when we caught up with them again. I must have been a fright, Maggie looked at me and said" Ray you are just a ghost of the commander who made the triumphant landing at Inchon" I commented, "we have covered a lot of real estate since then" The commanders had additional concerns, bridges blown out, roads blocked, wounded to worry about, bodies needed to be buried, and the march down the hill would take three days.

8, December:

We left Koto-ri, tired and down in strength but determined this trek back to the sea would be accomplished. The night temperatures dropped again to twenty below zero. The road was still covered with black ice. It seemed if it could be made more difficult, it was. News came: A major bridge

THE SAND DIEGO UNION
SAN DIEGO 12, CALIFORNIA
★ Thurs., Dec 7, 1950

Contempt for Cold
Battle-Weary Marines Sing About Plight

NORTHEAST FRONT, Korea, Dec.7 (Thursday) (UP)

U.S. Marines, marching toward possibly the bitterest fight of the corps long history, showed their contempt for the weather and the enemy today by writing a song about it.

Undaunted by days of fighting around the clock while trapped at Hagaru in Northeast Korea, and by the killing cold, the days without food and terrible casualties from both enemy fire and weather, some were singing this to the tune of "Bless Them All."

....But we're saying good-bye to them all,

As home through the mountains, we crawl.

The snow is tail deep to a man in a jeep.

But who's got a jeep? Bless them all.

The unbeatable attitude of the leathernecks was expressed by a young intelligence captain. "There is almost enough Chinese in the hills to make it a helluva fight."

From Hagaru the leathernecks and the 7th Division Infantrymen with them made an uphill fight through a narrow valley to a mountain pass which spills into a canyon five miles south of Koto. Then they must pass through a steep gorge if they are to reach the comparative safety of rolling hills about 20 miles north of Hamhung.

The historic march is commanded by Lt. Col. Raymond Murray, San Diego, commander of the 5th Marine Regiment. Murray has been senior officer since Maj. Gen. O.P. Smith, 1st Division Commander, flew to Koto to direct the fight from there.

149

Bombed out Bridge.......Two thousand foot drop

Repaired and on our way

had been blown, a very crucial one. There would be no way of going around it. It spanned a canyon dropping over two thousand feet to the valley floor and we would be trapped again, if an immediate solution couldn't be worked out. Fortunately there was a concrete building on one side of the canyon that could work as an anchor. Our engineers were excellent and they came up with a solution: Treadway Spans. They could be flown in by helicopter and dropped into place. Two were lost and ended up in the canyon, but six made it to the bridge. The engineers went to work and within hours had the spans in place. It was a tight fix. By flashlight and sometimes with just an inch to spare on both sides, the vehicles and equipment crossed. Thousands of troops followed and crossed the narrow span, then the engineers had to destroy their beautiful work to keep the Chinese from following. They blew the bridge back down the canyon.

We were leading with rifle companies, followed by a strange combination of: tanks; refugees with babies, cows, sheep; and Marines. Still, the Chinese came in close enough to put grenades under tanks and we lost three. One of the tanks skidded on an icy curve and we lost another one. On the way to Sudong we ran into more Chinese; the Army had not protected the MSR and we were ambushed. They destroyed trucks and blocked the road. We drove off the attack but eight more Marines were injured. Finally, the last of our equipment reached Hungnam. When our tank column arrived, we were all together again. Waiting for orders.

Chesty Puller set up trailers, with showers and assorted uniforms. We had not had a change of clothes since our climb to the reservoir, and we were ready to shed those clothes. Major Jack Buck remembered, and related the story: "I was sharing the trailer with Lt. Col. Murray, and we both were looking for anything clean we could find, fit or misfit. It wasn't difficult for me, as I'm of average size, but the Colonel was six-foot-three and there wasn't much to choose from. He finally came up with a corporal's uniform and was able to get it on. It was clean and he offered no complaint about the stripes, just grinned and commented, he had had a promotion. He was some kind of an officer. When we walked out of the trailer I heard a Marine comment: "Those stripes carry the respect and dignity of a Five Star General." This met with the applause from every Marine in earshot. We saw tears in his eyes as he turned and walked away.

The prose , 'to rout', is not to be applied to the Marines. When we turned our fighting from offensive to defensive we fought our way out, and it was the first time in history the toll taken was more on the enemy, six divisions of them, than it was on the Marines. When MacArthur decided to withdraw all forces from Hungnam, this did not go well as we felt we were on the winning side. We had destroyed the six divisions and could see by the conditions of the POWS we had captured, it was all over for them. They were in a sad state, frostbitten and hungry; all the fight had gone out of them, and they were completely demoralized.

It was not easy for us either. The toll from our force of 15,000;

561 Killed
2894 Wounded
182 Missing
3657 Injured from frostbite.

Timing had been wrong, Had we waited for better weather, taken the three cities of military value, reinforced our troops and supplies, we would not have paid such a price in lives lost. Time magazine brought the horror of the Chosin battle to the attention of its readers, saying: " The running fight of the Marines from Hagaru-ri to Hamhung was a battle unparalleled in United States History." I, DISAGREE completely, for I was there.

The worst battle was fighting out of the trap from the Chosin Reservoir at Yudam-ni to Hagaru-ri, but there were no reporters there. Many times during this defensive fighting, when the Army had retreated, we gave thanks to God, not only for another day but for every hour or minute we remained alive. When we reached Hagaru-ri, and had additional support for the breakout, we knew we had the worst behind us and there was a chance we would reach the sea. (Maybe this will be recorded as there were no news people there, and the bravery of the troops, both Army and Marines cannot be forgotten)

Refugees followed us, and there must have been another thousand of them. We had destroyed their homes, but they seemed to have more faith and confidence in us than in the communists. Some, who had been forced into the war, would pop out from holes and hand over their rifles; anything to get away. They were sick of the war. We loaded as many on the ship as we could. The ship by now was cramped quarters, overloaded many times the capacity. We were crammed in like sardines, but we were warm and allowed good food.

(I often reflect on the wisdom of General O.P.Smith, and the courage he showed, determined not to lose the entire 5th and 7th Regiments. He knew there was trouble before we had advanced very far; used every bit of savvy he had, finally taking over, he put his career on the line to save them.)

BACK TO THE BEAN PATCH:

The voyage was uneventful. We docked at Pusan on 15 December and moved on to Masan, back to the Bean Patch, another tent city. We were able to get medical attention, supplies, and a space to work, getting our troops "Back to Battery." Warehouses were filled with equipment, fresh food of the quality we hadn't had since we arrived in Korea. We had fought all this time from Pusan, Inchon, Seoul, Wonsan, the Chosin, in steaming weather and freezing weather, almost the length of Korea, now we were right back where we started. It was depressing, as nothing had changed except the loss of so many lives

15, December:
General Walker was killed in a road accident and General Mathew Ridgeway took command of the 8th Army. This also included command of the X Corps. MacArthur had reassigned all units under Almond's command to General Walker. They were now with General Ridgeway. At first I was not impressed. I had listened to so many long-winded speeches, without any substance I was weary of them. Every speech sounded the same. It wasn't long , though, until I changed my mind. Here was a real General. He had the sluggish 8th turned around in fighting order in no time and had them believing they could do anything. He also wasn't taking any guff from Almond. He was a General in charge, and these were his troops to command. Always there, he knew what was going on. Each day I found myself having greater respect for this man. I don't believe, I have ever met another man like him.

Christmas 1950:
General Smith had a gathering for officers, offering cocktails and his best wishes for a Merry Christmas. We were allowed time for a call home and letter writing, and the cooks prepared a Christmas feast, complete with all the trimmings and enough turkey to stay on the menu for several days. This was all prepared in a make-shift tent without any amenities, but they did themselves proud and we had a wonderful meal down to dessert and coffee. The Navy had supplied Christmas trees with handmade decorations and for a few hours the war was forgotten.

Note: Although I was in Korea from 2 August, 1950, I did not start this journal until New Years 1951: Masan, Korea.

We had been back at the "Bean Patch" seventeen days, working to reconstitute our equipment and doing some further training with the South Korean Marines. Colonel Lee, of the South Korean Army Liason, invited me to a party he was giving at a Korean hotel. The hotel was typically Korean and cold. The food was standard, with the most exotic dish being boiled octopus. The party paled after a couple of hours and I returned home at 2200.

2nd and 3rd January 1951:
Masan, Korea. "We continued the rehabilitations and the reequipping of the units. The weather, as we remember was steaming. After

the frozen area we just left, any degree above zero seems hot. There was no projection of any move, and the news we are getting was: The Chinese have broken through the UN defense line near Seoul. The information was sketchy.

8, January, 1951:

Masan, Korea. Captain John Ford, USNR, a.k.a. a movie director, spent the afternoon with us taking movies of the Navy and Marine Corps. Spent some of this afternoon asking questions about the Chosin then changed his visit to entertaining us with some very witty stories of his own experience. Nice afternoon.

I met with General Ridgeway, the commander of the 8th Army. He looked very fit, and seemed to be aggressive, and gave me the impression he was not as much of a politician as the others. He gave the standard pep talk. The effect was largely lost on the group of Marines present. These were the ones who knew what a real fight was.

10, January, 1951:

Masan, Korea.   The 1st and 2nd Battalions are finally moving out by LST to Pohang. I was happy we were leaving, but feel we would be going back to some cold weather, yet it would be a new area and a chance to see more of Korea.

15 January, 1951:

Pohang-dong, Korea.   Arrived yesterday morning at 0700. This is a beautiful spot, the most beautiful I've seen in Korea. Yongil-man is a deep bay, bordered on the north and south by hills, and on the west by a broad flat valley. The bordering hills rise to some rather high and, at this time of the year, snow covered mountains. We landed at a fishing village, about fifteen miles from our campsite. The road between the two, winds around through low, pine-covered hills. A welcome relief from the dismal appearance of the Masan area.

17, January, 1951:

I've commenced a system of extensive reconnaissance patrolling throughout the 5th Marines patrol sector. The patrol consist of six to ten men who remained out two to three days scouting throughout the back country. We needed to know what was out there and gain considerable training value as well as warning of enemy approach.

24, January, 1951:

Pohang-dong, Korea..   No change. We continued to patrol extensively throughout our zone but with no contacts. The patrols got some valuable training.

15, February, 1951:

Yongchan, Korea.   Prepared to move north, probably to counterattack the Chinese who were in the midst of a major counteroffensive.

I've come to a conclusion recently; the average Marine officer cannot solve a tactical problem. We simply call on all the supporting arms fire we can get a hold of, and then, our men, with superlative guts, just start moving toward the enemy. I've written Joe McHaney asking him to push for more instructions relating to use of supporting arms in the schools. Ridgeway has launched a new offensive, he termed, "Operation Ripper," a whole new strategy he presented to MacArthur, and was using it to drive deep into central Korea, pushing the Chinese into withdrawal from Seoul. The strategy was working, and Ridgeway was soon hearing MacArthur's announcement to the press that "Operation Ripper" was all MacArthur's own idea.

1, March, 1951:

Yongchan, Korea. I had a long talk with Major General Frank Lowe, a couple of days earlier. He was Truman's Personal Representative in Korea. He was very interesting to talk to. He described Truman as a very well informed constitutional liberal, whose politics are practical, and a man of character. General Lowe believed the salvation of the country lies in having Truman or someone like him in the White House. An honest man.

Our last move was made much like the rest, everybody scrambled on the roads. The cure: The highest echelons had to get involved in an effective coordination. General Shepherd, Brute Krulak, Joe Burger and General Puller visited the CP. Trivial "Visiting Talk" conference with commanders, stressed salvage, and proper employment of weapons. They thought the junior officers were not utilizing the capabilities of the weapons properly. They thought the Marines were relying more on guts than the intelligent use of fire and movement to attain objectives.

6, March, 1951:

Hoengsang, Korea. I awakened to find four inches of snow on the ground and it continued to snow all morning, not clearing until around two o'clock. Been informed Dick Hayward would relieve me. I was eager for him to do it. I wondered, of course, if he is as eager to be here as I am to go.

8, March, 1951:

Hoengsang, Korea. It snowed again last night, but not as much as on the 6th. The day was mild, snow melting, and we were in a sea of mud. The 1st and 7th are moved forward. There didn't seem to be any organized resistance.

11, March, 1951:

Still in Hoengsang, Korea. Dick Hayward arrived today. We talked all night. I wanted to brief him as rapidly as possible, so I could get out of there.

12, March, 1951:

General Smith said, " You can leave tomorrow" First, a phone call to Eve. Then I wrote my family.

Dear Don,

I made it. My relief finally arrived on March 11. It looks as though I fly into Japan for one night, on to Honolulu for one night and arrive in San Francisco the morning of the 11th. Eve will meet me at El Toro, a Marine Air Station, near Santa Ana. I'm looking forward to visiting the folks and the rest of the family. Will be writing Jack to see if he will arrange a dinner party for later in the week. Eve said she will make a tamale pie, maybe sister Helen will do her famous banana pie and Jack and Wilda the salad and coffee. We can all gather at Jack and Wilda's and have a nice visit. Things seem to be shaping up here. The patrols discovered the enemy has moved away from Seoul, and the capital of South Korea has returned to South Korea. Hanchon also fell to Smith's Marines, so we are okay, making progress in our objectives.

Seems everything is happening today. I have my orders to go home. A Catholic Priest, Lt. Commander Sporrer, had sent a story to a California magazine about the luxury a senior Army officer is enjoying while the Marines are without even the basics. All hell has hit the fan. Army pressure was put on the Marine commanders to deny the story. The Priest stood firm and wouldn't deny it, the Marines wouldn't deny it. Everyone stood by the story. The newspapers came in and took pictures, ran their story about Almond's headquarters, and the worn tent that serves for every purpose of the Marines needs. This told the story. All this excitement and I'm going to leave. Guess it is time to go home.

Say Hi, to everyone.

Ray.

13, March, 1951:

Departed Hoengsang today at 1030, by jeep to Wonju. The roads were rough. Then traveled by air from Wonju to Pohang, where I visited with and ate lunch with Dick Bird. Pohang to Chinhae by air and Chinhae to Masan by two-and-a half-ton truck. I am staying with Wally Walseth tonight

14, March 1951:

Itami, Japan. Left Pusan at 1330, had lunch with General Harris and General Cushman at K-1. The air wing had a nice camp, but they were worried about the rains coming in. General Harris was recovering from the loss of his son. We all felt his sadness. Met Don Taylor when I arrived and we had a nice visit. He is one of the nicest people and one of the finest Marines, I've ever known.

15, March ,1951:

Left Itami at 0600 and flew to Tokyo, stopped a few hours waiting for a plane to Bakers Point. Left Tokyo around 1500 and arrived Midway around 0400 the same day. Crossed the 180 meridian. Left Midway around

0530 and arrived at Bakers Point around 1200. Brute Krulak and Toots Henderson met me at the airport and we returned to Brute's home. Saw General Shepherd and Joe Burger this afternoon, and then the whole gang attended a party at the Drakes.

17, March, 1951:

Left Pearl Harbor at 2030 last night and arrived at Moffet Field at 1015 this morning. Checked in by phone to Dep. Pac. And then on to El Toro where the family had been waiting since 0900.

18, March, 1951:

Dear Don,

Will take a moment to catch you up on the letter I promised you state side. Eve met me at El Toro and we went on to Long Beach to visit the folks. Mother looked better than I have seen her in a long time. Dad, same as usual and seems to be enjoying his work. Then Eve and I went downtown, checked into the Wilton Hotel and had a one night honeymoon, even had coffee in bed the next morning. Since we are not millionaires, we could do this for only one night. It is wonderful to be home.

We are leaving here within the month on our way to Washington, where I will be stationed. We wanted to come to Chicago to visit with you, but understand you are now in Pittsburgh, and we wont' be able to see you anyway. Will visit you when we get settled.

They are assigning me to a temporary job at Headquarters until fall when I will be going to the National War College, here in Washington. The National War College is the top military school in the nation and it is quite an honor to be selected. I wish I had not been selected for another five years, as I'm afraid it might be a little over my head at this time. It is concerned with the principles of mobilization of the country for war and political science throughout the world. I feel like I'm going from high school to post graduate college without having gone to college. After that, I feel I will remain on the Staff at Headquarters, Marine Corps.

The prospect of being here with my family for a time is very welcome.

Say Hi, to everyone.

Ray

7, April, 1951:

Dear Mom and Dad,

Just received a phone call from Los Angeles, asking me to come up and talk with Warner Brothers about a movie they are planning to do about the fight back from the Chosin. And they want me to write the story. I think one day, I might write about the Chosin, but at this moment my hands are tied as we've been told we can't talk about the war while it is still going on. The

THE ASSISTANT TO THE PRESIDENT

MAY 1 4 1951

Dear Colonel Murray:

It certainly is a pleasure to
learn that arrangements have been
completed for your appearance on
the NBC Telecast, Sunday afternoon,
May 20.

As you probably know, the tele-
casts are made from the NBC Studios
in the Wardman Park Hotel. We will
be on the air between 3:00 and 3:30
p.m. I hope you will be able to be
present a few minutes before 2:00
p.m., so there will be ample time
for rehearsal.

Sincerely,

John R. Steelman

Colonel Raymond L. Murray
Commanding Officer
Headquarters Battalion
Marine Corps
Washington 25, D. C.

school in Washington will also be a challenge, but going to Hollywood seems like something Eve would enjoy, so we have accepted the invitation for next Monday,   Ray

10, April, 1951:
Dear Mom and Dad,
It was quite a day. I had lunch with Milton Sperling, Virginia Mayo, Virginia Gibson, Lucille Norman, and Gene Nelson at Warner Brothers Studio. After lunch   Sperling, Gordon West and I discussed the movie they want to make. With what information they have they feel they have enough to do "Retreat Hell." They still want my story and maybe someday I will get around to writing it.

We are still staying at a cottage at the Beverly Hills Hotel, compliments of the Warner Brothers. Very interesting, going through the studios, and how they can reproduce an area looking as a writer describes it. Of course, most of the scenes have props in the back holding up buildings. A great deal of talent at work, but a little out of my element. Will try to see you again before we leave for Washington and I must make reservations for Bill and me to go fishing this weekend. Deep sea fishing is much more expensive than I anticipated but we have done so few things together it will be worth it.
Love you,
Ray

For a month while we were awaiting my orders, we had been visiting family. I became reacquainted with my children. The nine months I had been away they seemed to have grown two sizes. Clothes to buy, shopping to do. Enjoyed home cooked meals. Wonderful meals that helped me gain some of the forty pounds I lost in Korea. There was also sorting of household items and getting the car ready for a long drive across country.

My Thoughts On Korea:

It has been suggested, in addition to the preceding chronology, I give my personal thoughts on Korea. With your indulgence, coming from a person who was there, I will attempt to put into words what was going through my mind in 1950 when we moved into Korea. Some might be repeated, but when I began my story, I said it would be written as it came to me, and not in any direct order. Each hill and battle is a little dim in my memory, but the thoughts and much of the major reasons why we were there are still quite vivid in my mind.

In 1945 the weight of deciding and drawing the line between North

Korea and South Korea, fell to two Army Colonels. It was to be a temporary occupational zone where the United States and the Soviet Union would accept the surrender of the forces. The line was accepted, and soon became the tool of a cold war pawn. By 1948 they became two different countries.(25 June, 1950) the North moved across the 38th Parallel, the dividing line, with a battle cry to unify the country. It took the attackers just three days to enter and capture Seoul, the capital of South Korea. By summer the North Koreans had taken over most of South Korea and the coalition forces had been forced into an area called Pusan Perimeter. If the UN Forces could hold the Pusan Port, supplies could be brought in and remain a lifeline. They could establish a counter offensive. Pusan must be held, or all of Korea would be lost. Walker's Army had taken a beating, needed support, any support, and the best trained Marines at the time were sent in.

Four nights after the Wake Island meeting with the President and General MacArthur, the Chinese, in massive numbers, had crossed the Yalu, the river dividing North Korea from China. The Chinese presence had been denied in Tokyo, MacArthur's Headquarters, even though they had been surfacing in massive numbers. Until then, the Chinese had stayed out, hoping the North Koreans could take care of the UN Forces. The Inchon landing brought another level to the war. The Chinese began to pay attention, and assisted by the Soviets, became a formidable foe.

Lin Piao, a legendary Communist leader, argued strongly against sending troops into Korea, refused to lead them, using for his excuse his poor health. It seemed their manner, even from the top, was their hearts were not in it. Kim Il Sung had played the Soviet Union and Mao against each other, seeking support for the invasion of the South. The solution he came up with was to work with the Chinese Peoples' Volunteer Army. This was supposed to be an untrained, improperly clothed army with very little going for it but numbers. Numbers they had, but the information Almond took for granted was wrong. They were well trained and ready to fight, but Mao still took the position, and cautioned Kim he was not to move into Korea unless the UN crossed the 38th Parallel.

After the success of the Inchon Landing and the completion of the capture of Seoul, General MacArthur made a decision, concurred with the government and the UN to move into North Korea. Now it was his aim to unify the Koreas. I had serious misgivings about going into North Korea. We had not yet destroyed or captured the North Korean units that had been defeated in the South as a result of our landing at Inchon, and I had no knowledge of any plans to do so.

General MacArthur, when visiting my CP, after we crossed the Han River, preparatory to moving on Seoul, had asked me how things were going. I told him, " I'm concerned about all those enemy troops escaping us." He told me, " Young man, those troops will melt into the hills and we'll no longer be bothered with them." I wasn't so sure. But, since a Marine Lieutenant Colonel, of those days, didn't have the clout they have nowadays, no one heeded my concerns. Off we went to the north.

General MacArthur's original plan was for the 8th Army to attack north towards Pyongyang, while the X Corps, of which our Division was a part, would make an amphibious landing at Wonsan and attack west towards Pyongyang and join the 8th Army, after which, both the 8th Army and the X Corps would advance and seize a line across Korea. Anchored on Hungnam in the east and a town called Chongju, in the west, this would result in a straight line across Korea, about fifty to one hundred miles below the Manchurian border.   Only the ROK (Republic of Korea) troops were to advance beyond this line to the boundary of Manchuria. Our landing was delayed because of the heavily mined harbor at Wonsan, and we lost two weeks of weather time. The ROK's 1st Corps advanced up the East Coast and captured Wonsan on 10 October, fifteen days before the division finally landed administratively in the harbor. What had started out to be an assault landing on an enemy shore wound up being an administrative landing on a beach already occupied by the 1st Marine Air Wing, who had been entertained by Bob Hope and his troops, two days earlier.

Meantime, the 8th Army troops captured Pyongang on 21 October and the ROK in central Korea had captured several important towns in that area. This meant it was no longer necessary for the X Corps to cross Korea and link up with the 8th Army. Had we actually carried out the original plan, we might very well have ended up in Hungnam for the winter. However, this is only speculation. In late October it was decided American troops would go all the way to the Manchurian border. Orders were issued for the 1st Division to proceed to the Chosin and Fusen Reservoirs to relieve the ROK forces at those places and be prepared to move north to the Yalu River.

The Division, to carry out X Corps orders, was to advance in a column of regiments: 7th Marines, 5th Marines, and 1st Marines, along a narrow road leading to Hagaru-ri and further on to the Fusen Reservoirs, dropping off units of varying sizes along the way to protect the main supply route. Needless to say, those of us in command were concerned about the orders we received.   All our supplies had to move along a single, and sometimes a one-lane road, for a large portion of its length along sides of steep mountains with sheer drop offs. It was getting further along into winter and we knew the weather would soon become severe. Added to these worries, was the worry of trying to ensure the Marines didn't get frostbitten from the severe cold. Although the division was well disciplined, none of us had ever fought in real cold weather before. A few of us had been in Iceland, but it never really got cold there, and besides, we hadn't fought while we were there. Nevertheless, these were our orders.

I am a very good worrier, and I received information of the very tough battle the 7th Marines had had; I began to really worry about what we were getting into. Making things worse was the fact the 5th Marines in the rear of the 7th, while patrolling widely on the flanks, was not running into any serious opposition. I felt as though I'd rather be fighting the Chinese than hearing about someone else fighting them, sort of like a passenger in a car wishing he could be driving. The Chinese who had fought so hard at Sudong-ni disappeared, and the reason they had disappeared, we learned later, was they had been so soundly defeated by the 7th Marines they were no longer an effective force.

15 November:

The 7th Marines occupied Hagaru-ri while the 5th was scattered twenty-five miles along the main supply route and the 1st Marines were still further to the rear. Various orders had been coming from X Corps in response to directives from General MacArthur's headquarters, but events kept overtaking the last orders.

25, November:

300,000 Chinese entered the war, supporting North Korea. The orders now came through, called for the 7th Marines to capture and hold Yudam-ni and for the 5th Marines to seize a series of towns north of the East side of the Chosin Reservoir, the last of these towns, some forty-five miles north of Hagaru-ri. The 1st Marines were to occupy various points along the main supply route to the rear. General MacArthur's plan at this time was to advance to the Yalu in a series of columns all across North Korea, after which the ROK's Marines would relieve the American troops and we would all go home.

In my mind and, I discovered later, in the mind of General Smith, was the terrible thought: before this was all over the Division was going to be scattered in bits and pieces all along the line from Hamhung to the Yalu River, and if the Chinese didn't get us the weather would. Fortunately this plan was never carried out completely. The 7th captured Yudam-ni and the 5th Marines did begin to move along the eastern side of the Chosin. In a short time orders were received to attack in a different direction. The 5th Marines were to move to the east side, pass through the 7th and continue to attack to the west.

25, November:

The 5th Marines began its movement to Yudam-ni. We had been relieved by an Army Regiment. The Army was to continue to attack the areas where we had been previously assigned.

27, November:

The 5th Marines began the advance, and after running into Chinese opposition all day, the 2/5, who had been leading the attack, decided to dig in for the night and get some rest. I will never understand why the Chinese Commander didn't let 2/5 move out to the west unopposed that first day, since they had planned to attack two regiments that night. Because of the Chinese tactics we had two full strength, reinforced regiments to counter their Chinese attacks. I am not going to recount the actions of all the units during the breakout from Yudam-ni and our return to Masan, but I would like to make a few observations.

First, the Chinese tactics. The survivors are here today because of the unbelievable heroism of the Marines who participated in the operation, but also because the Chinese didn't wait for us to get stretched out into small units, over a long distance, but chose to hit us while we were still in full strength. They chose to disperse their attacks, striking each of our concentrations at Yudam-ni, Hagaru-ri and Koto-ri simultaneously, rather than concentrating their strength where it was needed. They probably thought they had enough strength to overwhelm us in each area, but they forgot or ignored the fact they were lightly armed and we were heavily supported by artillery and air. For whatever reason, I am grateful they chose the line of action they did. As to our own tactics, Colonel Litzenberg and I met the day after the main Chinese attack and agreed to make all our plans jointly and to issue joint orders. We also split our staffs, with some of my staff going to his headquarters and some of his staff coming to mine. This was done so if one of our headquarters was wiped out the other could still function and carry out the joint operation. It was an unusual command setup, but it worked. Mention was made at one point to turn companies loose, for each to try to make it back on its own, but the idea was immediately discarded in favor of moving back in a sort of moving perimeter, keeping our artillery and other supporting units inside a perimeter at all times.

We moved back in that fashion to Hagaru-ri. Once we arrived at Hagaru-ri, there was no longer any doubt we would make it to the coast. We were gaining strength as we joined with the others in Hagaru-ri and later with Koto-ri, while the Chinese were gradually losing strength. There was no system of replacement of supplies. And we successively defeated every attack they launched against us with heavy losses. They became less and less able to affect the outcome of the battle. This is one of the few, if not the only time, a major enemy force was soundly defeated while causing the withdrawal of its foe. I'm still convinced having reached Hamhung-Hungnam area, we could have held against anything the Chinese could have thrown at us. But higher headquarters decided we should go south and try to stabilize the situation. So we returned to the Bean Patch at Masan, from where the 5th had entered the war five and a half months earlier. I would not accept a million dollars to relive the experience of that battle, and I would not accept a million to do it again.

The timing was wrong, had we waited for better weather, reinforced our troops and supplies, held the three vital cities of military value, we would not have paid such a high price in the loss of lives. I never felt we should have crossed the 38th in the first place. But, since we were there, we should have stayed near a seaport for the winter and protected the perimeter, stayed warm. We could have finished the job.

I've always felt it was right for us to come to the aid of South Korea. But also had misgivings about crossing the 38th Parallel.

The Chinese made a mistake of pursuing the UN south. They made the same mistakes we made in North Korea. They overextended their resources and supplies. Now they were facing a reinforced Army and a General who was one of the best in the military at that time. It was now a different ball game. General Ridgeway was to turn the tables about-face and retake Seoul.

Historians have termed Chosin the most savage battle of modern warfare. They compare it with Tarawa, the bloodiest battle of WWII in terms of the ratio of casualties and permanent physical damage from frostbite. President Reagan, in his Inaugural Address, cited Chosin as among the epics of military history. Time Magazine, lauded as unparalleled in U.S. military history, an epic of unspeakable suffering and valiant heroism.

The odds were hopeless, and the battle compared to the Alamo and Custer's last stand. The medals received were: 17 Medals of Honor, and 70 Navy Crosses. The most ever received for a single battle in Military History.

The 15,000 ground troops had been surrounded by 120,000 Chinese in the valley of Yudam-ni. There were also 500,000 Chinese reinforcements immediately across the Yalu River. They had been ordered to annihilate the 1st Marine Division to the last man. Of the 15,000 allies there were 12,000 casualties, 3,000 killed and 6,000 wounded. Plus, thousands had severe frostbite from the 30 degree below zero temperatures.

I'm convinced that our successful return from the Chosin so caught the imagination of the world that it insured the existence of the Marine Corps for an indefinite future. As we all know many attempts had been made to eliminate our Corps from the Armed Forces, but Chosin, combined with the early operations in the perimeter at Incho-Seoul made it certain our Corps will be around for a long time.

Red "Mike" Edson, who had served longer overseas than any other Marine and was the leading officer to becoming commandant, retired so he could devote all his time to getting Public Law 416 through congress. This law made the Corps' Commandant on the level of Chief of Naval Operations, rather than a subordinate to him. The Corps consisted of three combat divisions and three air wings. The Commandant had co-equal status with members of the Chiefs of Staff, in matters of direct concern to the Marine Corps. The Korean War put an end to the political fighting and Red

"Mike" Edson's mission was complete. On June 28, 1952, the 82nd Congress enacted Public Law 416.

A strong military isn't always an effective influence on world's opinion. There seemed to be two different foreign policies. Washington's and MacArthur's. MacArthur did not want to limit the war and Washington did not want an all-out war with China. MacArthur's strategy, so far had been a disaster, betting China lacked the industrial might to wage a modern war. President Truman took it as an open defiance of his orders as commander in chief, and could no longer tolerate the insubordination. The President wrote in his diary: " This is the last straw, I've come to the conclusion, our Big General, in the Far East, must be recalled." It took guts, and Truman had them, to take on someone of this magnitude, the General's star quality, immense personal appeal, the only son of a Medal of Honor recipient, a West Point graduate, the youngest superintendent of the U.S. Military Academy, and Army Chief of Staff; it goes on and on, besides being a five-star general.

Public opinion was not in the President's favor. Truman went on the radio with an address stating if we extended the war through Asia, it would go into Europe and create a third world war. We could not do that. It did allow MacArthur to retire in a blaze of glory, with a ticker-tape parade and a riveting oratory to Congress about "Old Soldiers never die. They just fade away." MacArthur lived well into retirement, and on different occasions would be known to state he had been forced into retirement too early.

General Omar Bradley was correct, when he stated: "extending the war to China. would involve us in the wrong war, at the wrong place, at the wrong time, with the wrong enemy." The idea of an all out war with horrifying results of an atomic war was out of the question.

In William Manchester's biography of MacArthur, he has written: " He believed if the battlefield was the last resort of government, then the struggle must be waged until one side has been vanquished." " He also believed the General should be given the power to make all decisions" This is what went against the grain of the President and brought on the crisis. Truman needed to remind him often that he was, as President, the supreme commander. This had been going on for ten months and finally led to the decision to relieve him of his command. Truman took it as an open defiance of the office of the President and Commander in Chief. (I've tried to reason in my mind MacArthur's obsession for crossing the 38th parallel, especially in the dead of winter, without properly supplying the forces. I cannot come up with any reasonable explanation; either for this or wanting an all out war with China.)

We will leave these evaluations to the historians. There is also a biography by Manchester, going into great detail, MacArthur's personal life, and his years as a general. Manchester writes of MacArthur: In his book " American Caesar"

AGONIZING HEROISM OF MARINES RELATED

Writer describes their retreat Against Overwhelming Odds in Bitter Weather

More than 4000 men of Camp Pendleton's First Marine Division were wounded in the bitter retreat from northeastern Korea to the escape port of Hungnam. Untold hundreds died.

The story of the First's ordeal by fire and ice is told by Tom Lambert, Associated Press correspondent, in the following dispatch from Korea.

Earlier the division's three regiments had fought on the Pusan perimeter in the south and spearheaded the Inchon invasion. In October the division was landed on the east coast. By late November it had pushed more than 70 miles into the interior of Korea.

By TOM LAMBERT, Associated Press Correspondent

On Nov. 25, the Chinese began a series of heavy attacks on the U.S. Eighth Army front. So far as can be determined here, the marines were not ordered to halt their northern movement. They moved on Nov. 25, 26 and 27.

By this time the Fifth Marines, commanded by Lt. Col. Ray Murray, of San Diego were about three miles west of Yudam and the Seventh was strung out between Yudam and Hagaru. The reds cut the road between Hagaru and Koto, where the First Marines were located.

At noon, Nov. 28 the Fifth Marines were ordered to hold at Yudam. Early the next day the Seventh Marines were ordered to withdraw and on Nov. 30 the Fifth Marines received a similar order.

Then began their retreat of agony and death.

Up to six divisions of Chinese were attacking the marine regiments. The Reds were on the high ground behind, in front and on both sides of the marines. The Chinese attacked in waves.

A gray-haired warrant officer who escaped in a personnel carrier, said he looked up once as a hand grenade exploded near him, driving a steel fragment into the roof of his mouth.

:There was a guy about 6 feet away," the warrant officer said, "I got him right in the belly with my rifle. He folded like a wet accordion."

Five others jumped the vehicle. Everyone in our truck was wounded or dead. I grabbed a pistol, and jerked a bowie knife out of my boot top. I shot and cut and slashed and hacked and shot. I don't know how in hell I ever got out of there."

The enemy was not only the Chinese. It was the weather as well.

The temperature dropped far below zero. Rations froze so hard it took an hour to thaw a can of hamburger and who had an hour?

WEAPONS FROZEN

Weapons froze, so did vehicles. The shoe-pack to weather proof shoes proved little protection.

The wind tobogganed down the snow-capped mountains and buffeted the marines with hard driven snow. The wounded suffered immeasurably. Whole blood was frozen into solid red bricks and was not usable. Plasma was frozen in the tube between the bottle and the veins of the wounded.

But weather was as hard on the Chinese. Marines found them frozen dead with their hands still on their rifles. Many surrendered.

Numbed by the cold, the marines fought on. As they fought from Yudam toward Hagaru, the Fifth Marines came across F Co. of the Seventh Marines, which had been surrounded on the main road since the main Chinese attack started. The survivors still held to their high ground and the approaches to their position were covered with Chinese dead.

The marines established "warm-up" points at Hagaru and Koto. The commanders tried to get all their miserably weary,bone-cold fighting men into heated tents for a few moments of warmth.

SOME DEAD BURIED

√At Yudam the marines buried some of their dead. They brought with them to Koto as many as they could and buried them in frozen ground so hard it turned a bulldozer blade. The ground had to be dynamited.

At both Hagaru and Koto the marines built a makeshift airstrip. Marine and Army airmen shuttled great loads of wounded back to safety.

Then the column set forth again and southward. The Chinese sensing that the marines were escaping, stepped up their attacks from the flanks.

As the marines on the ground fought and died on the way south, flying leathernecks and naval carrier pilots struck at the Chinese.

FLEW DAY, NIGHT

Marine fighters lashed rockets and machine gun bullets into Red troops within 35 feet of the marine lines. Day and night load after load of wounded were flown out, more than 4000 in all.

For nine bitter days the retreat south continued. It was a new tactic for many marines whose traditional move is to attack.

"I had to hold school," said Col. Lewis Puller, who commanded the rear guard. "I told my officers we weren't retreating, that we were about-facing. Some Marines, a long time in the corps, cried, they were so damned mad at going back."

FINALLY REACH SAFETY

So they fought the cold and the Chinese through the mountains and the passes and finally came into Hamhung and safety. Many died. But for every marine who fell, regimental officers estimated 10 Chinese died.

They were not defeated. They were tired almost to exhaustion, but they still could laugh and jeer; their weapons were in their hands.

They can stand alongside the men whose exploits never will be forgotten at Guadalcanal in WW II, or Chateau Thierry in WWI, or back to the earliest days of Tripoli.

167

Major General O.P. Smith tells me I am now a
Colonel.

RAYMOND L. MURRAY

T o you who answered the call of your country and served in its Armed Forces to bring about the total defeat of the enemy, I extend the heartfelt thanks of a grateful Nation. As one of the Nation's finest, you undertook the most severe task one can be called upon to perform. Because you demonstrated the fortitude, resourcefulness and calm judgment necessary to carry out that task, we now look to you for leadership and example in further exalting our country in peace.

Harry Truman

THE WHITE HOUSE

Christmas at the Bean Patch. Myself, General
Smith and Chesty Puller.

Correspondent Marguerite "Maggie" Higgins talks with Army
officers. Gen. Craig found her in the thick of things at Miryang.

[United Press Acme Photo]

Col. Raymond L. Murray, 39, of Arlington, who was awarded the Navy Cross for his part in the breakout from the Chosin reservoir in Korea, gets two other awards from his sons, Daniel, 3, and James, 5, after ceremonies at Marine Corps hdq.

The war lasted for three more years and cost over a million lives. An armistice was established, establishing a demilitarized zone. The two Koreas are still at a standstill, the 38th Parallel still the dividing zone. The UN and North Korea signed the Armistice. South Korea has never signed.

The deepest scar on all Korean psyche is the 2.5- mile-wide demilitarized zone, 151 miles long, separating the north and south. Both sides have different ideas of government and the air is tense. North Korea has a military, well equipped, probably one of the best in the world today, but at the sacrifice of their people. They also have the largest commando force in the world today. (NK rules through fear.) South Korea has put their efforts in education, and can be very proud of their universities and contributions to advancing the knowledge of their people.

The Toll
of the "Forgotten War"

- 54,246 US Dead
- 33,651 Killed In Action
- 103,000 US Wounded
- 8,179 US Missing In Action
- 7,000 Prisoners Of War: Only 3,450 returned; 51% Died In Prison Camps
- 389 POWs Unaccounted For
- 22 Different Nations United Into One Powerful Army to Halt Communist Aggression
- The First UN Army Ever Fielded
- This Bloody War Began June 25, 1950, and Ended In An Armistice July 27, 1953.

Chapter Seven

Washington

My next orders were to report to Washington, D.C. Headquarters on May 1, 1951. Allowing ten days traveling time and a few days to find quarters, we started across country on 14, April, at five o'clock in the morning, hoping our three active boys would get a few additional hours sleep before the heat of the desert kicked in. After a long, hot, hard trip we arrived in Tucson at five o'clock, and decided this was far enough for one day. The children made a game of finding a motel with a sign offering air conditioning, and extra points if it promised a swimming pool. This taken care of, we had dinner, a swim and settled down for a comfortable night's rest.

15, April:
Again an early start, putting us into Whites City, New Mexico in the early evening.

16, April:
This early morning departure is working so well, we are hoping to arrive at the Carlsbad Caverns in time for one of their four- hour tours. Know Bill will enjoy it as he is eleven years old. Jim at five will probably remember some of the highlights, the baby we will put in a stroller where it can be used, and carry him the rest of the way. We were hoping the boys would show some interest, and we were happy we made the effort when it was all they could talk about for the next hundred miles.

17, April:
Another early morning; this is to be my day as we are stopping at College Station, Texas. Hadn't been back to Texas A&M since I graduated and wanted to show the family where I had gone to college. It was just a stopover and the time was short, but Eve and the boys were delighted to see where I had played football, also enjoyed the beautiful campus, and the stories I related, as many happy memories when we visited different points of interest.

By now the adventure of our travels is beginning to wear off and the older two are not agreeing on anything, and we dealt with the constant question of "are we there yet?" There would be six more days before we could say "we are here."

Now we needed quarters, getting the family settled before I started my job at Henderson Hall, commanding Headquarters Battalion. This was temporary duty to relieve Wesley Platt, who had put in a request for duty in Korea. I knew it was a temporary assignment, as I was scheduled for National War College in the fall semester. Wesley had wanted to go to Korea for some time, but then a sad thing happened. He was riding in a jeep in Korea when a shell went through his lung and killed him. He was brought home, and I had the sad honor of participating in his funeral before I left the job he assigned to me.

During our travels, had touched base with family with post cards; now I felt we owed them a letter and thought one to Don would bring them up to date.

Dear Don,

I've been assigned to a temporary job at Headquarters until I go to the National War College in Washington. The National War College is the top Military school in the nation and it is quite an honor to be selected. I wish I had not been selected for another five years. I'm afraid it might be a little over my head at this time. It concerns the principles of mobilization of the country for war and the political and economic balance throughout the world. I feel like I'm going from high school to post graduate college without having gone to college. After that, I feel I will remain on the staff at Headquarters Marine Corps. The prospect of being with family during this time is very welcome. Say hello to everyone, Ray

I should not have been so apprehensive about the War College. It turned out to be one of the most pleasant times of my career. It consisted of classes, where we discussed in detail, subjects of military interest, politics and geography. We covered diplomacy and, in a way, we were able to travel and observe Paris, Rome, Naples, Athens, Trieste and Salzburg. Berchestgarten was on the list and some of us spent the night there. We had an eerie feeling of not wanting to spend any more time than was needed or to even linger for awhile.

My next orders were a CO of Basic School in Quantico, Virginia. I was at Quantico for twenty-five months. I relieved Dave Shoup, who had quite a job. It seems everything possible was under the title connected to the school: besides, the OCs. When I was there before, the school had an attendance of several hundred. Now the attendance was into the thousands. It was impossible to know anyone personally They all seem to be looking for role models and were very interested in the decorations of the 5th Marines. I did relate some of my experiences in Korea and this gave them reason for discussions. The schedule was heavy and new courses were added all the time. Housing was short and they lived like sardines in Quonset huts, but I

174

Famed Korean Commander Takes Over Basic School

Maj. and Mrs. James P. Goss are shown being greeted by Col. R. L. Murray, new CO of the Basic School. Shown left to right in the receiving line are Mrs. Murray, Colonel Murray, Mrs. and Col. P. A. Fitzgerald, and 2nd Lt. W. J. Addis. Major Goss is the Executive Officer of the 3rd Training Battalion at Camp Upshur.
Photo By Staff Sgt. J. Shkymba, MCS Photo Services.

Col. Raymond L. Murray

Colonel Raymond L. Murray, former commander of the Fifth Marine Regiment of the First Marine Division in Korea, took over his duties as Commanding Officer of the Basic School last Thursday morning.

A reception was held in his honor on Friday by the staff officers of basic school.

The Colonel who is holder of the Navy Cross and four Silver Star Medals is considered one of the Corps' outstanding tactical leaders.

In July, 1950, when the first Marine Brigade was formed for duty in Korea, Col. Murray, then a Lieutenant Colonel, was chosen to lead the Fifth Marine Regiment which was to be the nucleus for the brigade. The unit participated in the battles at Naktong, Wolmi-Inchon, Seoul and Wonsan. In addition to taking part in the Marine advance north toward the Yalu River.

When the Chinese encircled the First Marine Division at the Chosin Reservoir, the Fifth Regiment participated in the now historic breakout to the seaport of Hamhung.

Shortly afterward, with his regiment committed to guerrilla fighting on the Central Korean front, he was promoted to the rank of Colonel. In the promotion ceremonies, Major General Oliver P. Smith, the Commanding General of the First Marine Division. called him "one of the outstanding regimental commanders in the Marine Corps."

The thirty-nine-year-old Colonel was born in Los Angeles, California, and was commissioned a second lieutenant in the Marine Corps in 1935, following his graduation from Texas A & M College.

During World War II, Col. Murray participated in three major campaigns, Guadalcanal, Tarawa and Saipan and was awarded the Navy Cross for "extraordinary heroism" in the assault on Saipan.

Colonel Murray is married to Mrs. Evelyn Roseman Murray. They have three sons, William F.; James R.; and Daniel W.

never heard anyone complain. I wanted them treated like officers. I felt the better they were treated the better they would treat men assigned to them.

That twenty-five months with family was a very happy time and one I will always cherish in my memories, but not all of them making it a good day. One in particular stands out. Now I laugh about it, but it was a real disaster for Eve. I don't think she ever forgave the aide who was responsible. It was at Quantico when an aide, and for the life of me, I can't remember his name, wanted to put into effect a past practice of lieutenants and their wives calling on the CO on New Year's morning. The only thing wrong with it was he didn't tell us. They started arriving around ten o'clock. Thank God I was dressed and watching a football game. We were not prepared, to say the least. I picked up the phone and called every source on the base that could supply food or drink, and somehow we got through the morning. Years later, one of the comments got back to us. A lieutenant's wife was heard to comment, "Mrs. Murray was very casual, she was in jeans and was going around emptying ash trays." Little did she know. So much for that.

It was during my tour at Quantico, we welcomed twin daughters on 6 September, 1953. Since my first-born I always thought it would be nice to have a little girl in the family. Then after the birth of four boys, we were blessed with twin girls. Of course my ego is inflated, thinking I am the only one on the base with twin girls; I made a few calls, and was informed of eighty other sets on the base. My ego deflated a bit, but decided, although we didn't have the only twins on the base, there were other positive pleasures, comparing progress, weight gains, teething, all part of being a parent. We were allowed to bring home Sherry, who weighed five pounds, but it was five weeks before the hospital would release Terry, who was born weighing just three and a half pounds. It seemed, there must be a tiny body behind the most magnificent brown eyes, and a wisp of dark hair, because that was all we were aware of when we first saw her, but it didn't take long until she gained weight and could hold her own with her sister. When they were nine months old, my orders were to the Marine Corps Base at Camp Pendleton.

1954:   Camp Pendleton

General Selden wanted me to command the 1st Infantry Training Regiment at Camp Pulgas while Ron Vickery was waiting for his next orders. General John Selden was the West Coast chief of staff, and Ron Vickery was his chief of staff and was waiting his promotion to Brigadier General and for his next orders.

I did this for five months. It was a good assignment. The recruits had finished their rifle training but were still under the control of the Recruit Depot. When Ron received his promotion, I moved in as chief of staff. Then

Eve with our first three.
Added twin girls for five

there was a change of command and I became chief of staff for General Frank Good.

We had minor incidents with the city of Oceanside about a water problem, but Oceanside had a good city manager named Frank Lilley, who seemed to get a handle on problems before they became serious. He worked well with the military. One of the major concerns I felt needed to be addressed were the leases to farmers for growing produce. The leases had worked well in the past; they not only produced high quality vegetables but took care of what could be unsightly growth along the highway. It is a good feeling to drive down I-5 any day and see how well cared for the land has become, so well productive and maintained.

The housing was really going downhill because of the riparian rights of the Margarita river. Washington had limited all money going into housing construction on Camp Pendleton. The housing was really bad; in some areas there were problems with plumbing, in other areas roofs leaked; I felt we were never desperate for water, because we did have underground basins supplying our needs, but of course there were no lawns or gardens because of the water alert.

Change of command; General Ed Sneker came in and had a class-mate he wanted as chief of staff. I was moved and became the G-3.

I remained at Camp Pendleton for four years, serving first as commanding officer , 1st Infantry until February 1955, then as chief of staff for the Marine Base until July 1957, During my final year there, I was assigned to First Marine Division, serving as division inspector, chief of staff and assistant chief of staff, respectively.

July 1958:
Jim Riseley wanted me as his chief of staff, and my transfer arrived to Camp Lejeune. It lasted one year. In June 1959, I was promoted to Brigadier General and ordered to Okinawa.

1959-1962   *Camp Pendleton*

July 1959: Moved my family back to San Diego, and in August reported for duty in Okinawa. The division commander was Bob Luckey, a real laid-back person, who, without seeming to work hard, had a handle on everything going on. We trained on the island and he designated me the brigade commander. I made a trip to Korea to consider a landing in the Pohang area of Korea.

Then my life took a turn that is difficult to write about. Letters from home were becoming more and more infrequent, and I received a letter from my sister, Helen, that she was worried about Eve, as she had been ill for some time and Helen felt she needed someone to help care for the children. I was concerned about this letter, but wasn't prepared for the call I received from my good friend, Brute Krulak, telling me to request an emergency leave as soon as possible. Brute met my plane and drove me to the hospital. When I bent over to kiss Eve on the forehead, she opened her eyes and greeted me with "I'm so glad you are home, how long can you stay?" and I answered "as long as you need me, I'm on emergency leave" This seemed to quiet her and she dozed off. I sat by her bed and at intervals she would open her eyes and ask me "to forgive her for being so ill and not being better company." Then she would doze off again. The next time when she awakened, she pulled herself up, almost to a sitting position, and began to talk. "Ray, we must talk about the children. The boys are getting to an age where they can be a handful, and the twins, even though they are almost seven, need a lot of care. I feel I'm handing you the toughest assignment you've had so far, but by now you must know I won't be here to help you, and I can't do anything to change it. Always remember how much I've loved you and our wonderful family." She closed her eyes again, and as I sat by her bed through the night, my mind went back through the years to our early meeting and what had attracted me to this petite, pretty, vivacious young lady. She had a wonderful sense of humor, and I always knew what was on her mind, making every minute with her something special. I saw her joy in being a mother and how happy she was when she had her family together, as she said, "all under the same roof." I knew being away so much had to be tough on her. She had been through so much alone, and had done more for her country than most. She had borne six children, nursed them through illnesses, and lost one to pneumonia. This had all taken a toll on this tiny body, now too tired to fight back the liver condition that was taking her life.

Just before dawn, June 6, 1960, my darling Eve died.

At home I still had twin daughters, just seven years old, and two teen-age boys, with orders to return to Okinawa for three months. Fortunately, I had relatives who provided for the children; no one could take all four, so they were farmed out all over Southern California. My oldest son, Bill, was married and had a home of his own to provide for, and I was anxious to get the rest of my family back together. They had lost their mother and their father was halfway around the world. I asked General Shoup, who was the commandant at the time, if he could place me somewhere where there were stewards. Eve had handled the work all by herself and now, when I was in a position to get her some help, she hadn't lived long enough to enjoy it. He ordered me back to Camp Pendleton as assistant base commander to General Shapley. It wasn't long after, General Shapley was reassigned and I assumed command of the base.

BrigGen R. L. Murray
Takes Reins of MCB

One of the Marine Corps most versatile field tacticians took command of the World's Largest Amphibious Training Base" last Monday.

Brigadier General Raymond L. Murray, double Navy Cross winner and veteran of 26 years service in the Marine Corps, is the new Commanding General of the Marine Corp Base, Camp Pendleton.

He moved into the office vacated by MajGen. Alan Shapley, who has been named to head Fleet Marine Force, Pacific.

In July 1950 the new base commander was serving as Executive Officer of the 5th Marines stationed here.

Brigadier General Raymond L. Murray

When the 1st provisional Marine Brigade was formed for combat duty in Korea, the command was given to the 37-year old lieutenant colonel who had been cited for heroism in three major World War II Pacific Campaigns.

As commander of the 2nd Battalion, 6th Marines on Guadalcanal-Tarawa unit, he was seriously wounded by enemy fire. Determined to see his combat-proven unit through to victory once again, he remained in command during the initial assault and was awarded the Navy Cross for "gallantry above and beyond...."

In Korea the Brigade was shifted almost daily plugging breaks in the cracking United Nations perimeter and regain lost ground. The continuing tactical abilities of the Brigade commander were recognized by the the U.S. Eighth-Army Headquarters and General Murray was awarded his third and fourth Silver Star and the Legion of Merit for the August-September 'pressure valve" action.

After joining the 1st Marine Division during the Inchon landing, General Murray gained command of the 5th Marines and during the Chosin Reservoir action was awarded the Army Distinguished Service Cross for "extraordinary heroism under fire."

Two days later, near Hagaru and Koto-ri, the general won his second Navy Cross for his brilliant organization of defenses for that area. A counter attack under his direct command into the face of near impossible odds was credited with permitting a complete extraction of the encircled 1st Marine Division.

Between combat assignments, the general has attended a wide assortment of technical and tactical schools, including the National War College and the Command and Staff School.

James Harris became my steward, and I will always owe him a debt of gratitude, not only for managing the household, and cooking; on his own time, way beyond the call of duty, he helped the children get ready for school, seeing they were well fed, and worked on behavior. The children grew to love him, and after all these years he is still cherished by the family.

James Harris, our steward, who helped raise the children.

Eve had been gone three months and we are getting ourselves in some order as a family, when friends invited me to go with them to a birthday party. There, a widow, Helen Beihl, gave me her phone number and asked me to call her if I needed help in any way.

About two week later, I was entertaining some young officers, a long standing friend , Pat Hudson, who had been helping with the children, was out of town and I remembered Helen and found her telephone number. I called her and asked if she would be able to come and help serve some of the food. She had gone to bed but if I would pick her up she would be glad to

181

come over. Although she was older than I, she was still quite attractive, and I must say she had a way with those young men. She had them thinking she was terrific in no time at all. We dated and I learned a little about her life. She was born, Louisa Naomi Howard, according to her birth certificate. Her father left when she was a baby so she couldn't tell me much about him. Her mother made her living as a telephone operator, and when Louisa was eight years old her mother married John Longshore, who was an employee of Sears Roebuck. She took the name of Helen Longshore at that time. She shared that her mother had been very protective, almost in an apologetic way, and did everything for her. She never learned to cook or do any menial chores for the home. Her mother took care of all that. She had not considered children in her previous marriages and I wondered if she could take on the responsibility of children, plus the military role of the wife of a general. She was quite upfront that she didn't cook and would not be an early riser, but as long as she had stewards she could handle all the rest. We continued to date, and I knew I needed help with the little girls, so we became engaged , and she set a date. I thought it much too soon after the children had lost their mother. I was concerned since she commented she didn't know how to make oatmeal or jell-o, why she thought she could manage meals for a family We did get married and managed to hold the family together. True to her word, she was adamant about not doing menial chores. (I can't remember her ever cooking a meal, making a bed, or sweeping a floor.)

During my years there, I was chairman for two rodeos. It was an event to raise money for Navy relief. It was successful, to a point, as it brought in hundreds of local residents and some film stars, who had been Marines, and brought additional interest to the event. James Garner, who had been in Korea, Dana Andrews, Glen Ford, and some of their Hollywood friends were always happy to help. It became overwhelming when a carnival was added and the cost became too costly to continue.

Wagon Train Crew Join Navy Relief Rodeo Here

McIntire

Rodeos and stunt riding are nothing new to the stars of "Wagon Train" — John McIntire, Frank McGrath and Terry Wilson — who will take part in the 14th annual Navy Relief Fund Rodeo at Camp Pendleton June 10 and 11.

McIntire, who stars as Wagonmaster Chris Hale in the top NBC-TV series, was reared on a Montana ranch where he grew up thinking that breaking horses was a normal part of boyhood. At the age of 16, after beating all competition in his home state, McIntire won the Teddy Roosevelt trophy for bronc busting at Cheyenne, Wyo., earning the title of National Junior Champion. He still raises horses on his Montana ranch, and is one of the few authentic cowboys in television.

Frank McGrath, who plays the role of the bearded Charley Wooster, has made a living for nearly 40 years by falling off horses. Generally acknowledged as one of Hollywood's top western stuntmen before turning actor for "Wagon Train", McGrath started his career as a jockey.

Terry Wilson, seen as Bill Hawks, the assistant wagonmaster, rose through the ranks of stuntmen to become one of the film industry's top rimrods. After proving himself an outstanding stuntman, Wilson, an ex-Marine, was in top demand for his ability to scientifically plan and carry out unusually dangerous stunts.

The three stars will be present on both days of the Camp Pendleton rodeo.

Wilson ~ McGrath

CLINT EASTWOOD — All dressed up for the Rodeo is Clint Eastwood, who plays the role of Rowdy Yates on the CBS-TV "Rawhide" show. Clint was grabbed for the part when he dropped by to say hello to the receptionist for a network executive producer. Standing six-feet-four, he was a cinch for a tall-in-the-saddle role. Clint and the rest of the "Rawhide" cast will be at Camp Pendleton for the 14th Annual Navy Relief Rodeo and carnival.

You will recognize

some of these cowboys.

183

James Garner, a good Marine, helping with the Camp Pendleton Rodeo.

End of the day and I'm still on the horse.

Governor of Texas giving me "the boot"

Glenn Ford. I'm in the background.

You can see who was the star.

Helen thought it would be nice if we could move into the Ranch House. It had been vacant, so I sent a crew over to the home to clean it. It had been used to entertain when the rodeo party was there, and when the President of Finland visited the base we used the Ranch House to entertain, but those were the only times it had been used. I decided to move in. This was when General Shoup was out here to observe a landing exercise the division was conducting. I told him we were going to move into the Ranch House. He said, " I told you not to move into the Ranch House, and that is what I meant." Again, no explanation. So I guess I'm the only CG who never lived in the Ranch House. He later told me he had other plans for me and didn't want me to move in then have to move out again. He didn't tell me at the time but he had already made up his mind to send me to Parris Island.

July 1962:

My orders came to Parris Island, South Carolina, as commander of the Recruit Depot.

Commanding as Major General.

Helen in her favorite dress.

Parris Island....Quarters One.

Chapter Eight

Parris Island

In July 1962 my orders were to take command of the Recruit Depot at Parris Island. We packed our personal belongings and made arrangements for packers to do the rest. Eve and I had brought back beautiful dishes, Chinese carpets, silver and assorted items for our tour of China. I wanted to keep these for the children, in memory of their mother, and to use one day in their homes.

We were all packed in one automobile, two-teen age boys and twin nine-year-old girls. When we first saw Quarters One, we were overwhelmed with the size, wondering how we would furnish it, and hoped somewhere on the island there would be a warehouse of furniture that would solve the problem. The kids, of course, thought this would be a wonderful place to play hide and seek and find a corner to call each his or her own. They did this along with fishing, making new friends, going to school and enjoyed every minute of the two years we were there. The children and Helen were happy when I requested James Harris, our steward, to be moved with us, and the request was granted. We went about learning more about the quarters that would be our home until further assignment

According to Dr. Stephen Wise, the Parris Island Curator, when the house was completed in 1884, the quarters were very poorly arranged. In 1892 it was moved 500 yards southwest from the bank of the Beaufort River to its present location. This was necessary to make room for a dry dock and expansion of the Port Royal Naval Station. The station name underwent many changes. May 1919, the name officially changed to Parris Island after a previous owner Alexander Parris. In December 1946, the name became the Marine Corps Recruit Depot, Parris Island. Later, Eastern Recruiting Region was added to the Depot title.

The home needed to be split in two to be moved, thus the rumor started that it had been originally two homes. Now we have Quarters One. It has two stories with 6,213 square feet of floor space. There are seven fireplaces, 27 rooms, parquet floors throughout the first floor. The conservatory is a large two storied room with windows into other rooms; this provided the ventilation. Since then, air conditioning, a better system, has been installed. Closets were added later, enormous ones from floor to ceiling. The front porch has a wraparound style, a nice gathering place, as well as an entry to the quarters. We were also aware we were part of the earliest history of our great country and this was hallowed ground.

This is hallowed and historic land. Before it was a colony of Great Britain, there was a struggle between France and Spain for the occupancy of the island. Excerpts below are from a paper read by G.G. Dowling, by permission of his grandson, G.G. Dowling III. The Beaufort Historical Society. Research has gone back 240 years to clarify the history.

Spain had a stronghold from 1520 to 1763 when Spain relinquished all claims to the region. At this point, Spain, France, and England employed every wile of diplomatic intrigue and device of ruthless warfare to take claim to the island. Spain thought it was proper to exploit the area because of Columbus's discovery. The Spanish, in increasing numbers came in for occupation. These men were sent to claim for their King and Church a foothold in the new world. The King's sensitivities were hardened to the sight of human suffering and had given him contempt for human life. In his mind, all science and learning were identified with the Jews or the Saracen (Muslins) at the times of the Crusades. He had divorced morality from religion and felt he had been divinely singled out to be a Christian Crusader fighting against heresy.

France at this time, considered the richest nation in Christendom, was also torn by religious dissension and was aware of the opportunities the new world would bring untold wealth to Spain and make Spain a powerful and dangerous neighbor. Catherine DeMedici and her advisor, Gaspard Decoligney, thought if France had a cornerstone in the new world, it would relieve the religious tension at home.

DeAyllon, was the judge at Santa Domingo and managed through trickery to bring back from Santa Elena 130 natives to work the mines of Santa Domingo. All was not forthright in the development of the land and securing good reasons for religious freedom.

The open hatred between Spain and France and the jealousy of the Spanish influence caused France to disregard all international law to seize lands discovered and claimed by another nation. In 1562 Ribaut landed on Parris Island and planted Charlesfort. What Spain had feared had come to pass, the French could impede passage of the Spanish ships to Bahama Channel. Villafane had quieted Spain's fears and the French had moved in. The French had succeeded in planting a colony in the area that the Spanish had termed unsuitable for colonization.

Coligny, one of the leaders of the Protestant Party in France, developed a colony for his co-religionist in the new world and Catherine DeMedici, the Queen Mother, was relieved of the dangerous religious situation in France.

The French settlement of Charlesfort caused great concern to the Spanish court and King Phillip, in 1563, was seeking advice as the best way or means of expelling the French in order to avoid plunder of the Spanish Fleet. Ribaut left his garrison, expecting to return with re-enforcements, and became involved in the war of the massacre of Vassy. The Protestants were defeated and he fled to England to persuade Queen Elizabeth to follow up on his new discoveries. Queen Elizabeth, fearful the Spanish would complain if she were known to support Ribuat, encouraged him to undertake this himself, promising him half of all he discovered in the new settlement, as this would be an excellent position to prey upon Spanish ships from New Spain to Peru and to Old Spain. She also offered him a pension, a house and other inducements for further discoveries. He was later to deny he had ever accepted a bribe from Queen Elizabeth.

Queen Elizabeth sent a fleet of vessels in May of 1563, bound for Port Royal, when an unexpected development happened. Ribaut and his colleagues planned to escape to France, taking the English as hostages. Ribaut was seized, thrown into prison. His plan has never been made clear, he was either trying to trick Stukeley and Queen Elizabeth or was betraying the French into English hands.

In 1565 King Phillip struck back, acting through the person of Pedro Menendez D'Aviles, and put to death all the captured French, including John Ribaut. Menendez's victory over Ribaut put the French out of the picture and opened the way for complete Spanish domination of the South Atlantic. Menendez then planned a fort on a small island within the leagues of the bar where it would be visible from the sea. It was covered with a dense forest of oak and pines, liquid amber, nut trees and laurel. The fort was traced out on the only elevation the island contained, near the side of a small haven. Historians have pointed out , all the evidence narrows the locations of Port Royal sound and the site of the Presidio to the Southeastern end of Parris Island, Pilot or Means Creek. The fort was completed within fifteen days and mounted with six pieces of artillery, and garrisoned with 106 men under Estaban d'Alas.

We do not know with any degree of certainty the exact location of these French and Spanish, Forts, but it is interesting to note after 350 years, since these forts were abandoned, excavations on Parris Island by Mayor Osterhout of the U.S. Marine Corps revealed the site of the old fort which could be Charlesfort. These excavations also brought forth a number of medieval cannon balls, iron hinges, Indian pottery and stockade logs. Menendez erected a monument to Ribaut that held him in high esteem; it reads:

"I had John Ribaut, with all the rest, put to the knife, understanding this to be expedient for the services of God, over our Lord, and your Majesties. I hold it in good fortune that he should be dead, for the King of France could do more with 50,000 ducats than others could do with 500,000."

It is doubtful any spot in America carries as much historic interest as does old Charlesfort, as this fort marks the first attempt to plant a colony on American shores. It was the first fort constructed in this country, it was also the first point at which the Huguenots, America's first pilgrims, landed and it also was the first place in America to build an ocean sailing ship.

This is indeed hallowed ground. Here began the great history of European's America. We commemorate the daring and valor of the men who explored and settled this region and laid the foundation upon which a later people built a glorious civilization.

It was a fantasy paradise for the children; they never had a boring moment, so much history to explore and vast areas to search for relics. This along with boating and fishing, and just hiding out in some of the unused twenty-seven rooms, where they could pretend not hearing our calls unless it meant for dinner.

James Harris, our steward, with additional help he could muster, kept the home spotless, cooked our meals and always found time for the children. The retiring general's wife took Helen in tow and helped her with the Marine protocol, and responsibilities of a general's wife. Jim, my second son, graduated from high school and was looking forward to going on to college. Danny is an upper classman now and has been speaking about joining the Marines when he graduates. The twins are eleven years old, and starting to be concerned about their appearance; and since we have enough bathrooms for grooming, there are no challenges for the time there.

Exploring Charleston was an adventure in itself. Some of the homes went back two centuries; still had some of the original families living in them, and felt great pride when they could relate that many of the original families had Marines who were born there and became part of the early Corps.

It was a great two years, everyone was busy, including me. Time passed too quickly, and it became time to move on. I've reached the rank of Major General and orders to report to Headquarters, Washington, D.C.

INSPECTOR GENERAL

The children were a bit sad when I announced we would be moving from Parris Island. It had been, put in their own words, " the most fun place we have ever lived." But Washington, D.C. and inspector general seemed to have a ring to it and they approved.

We had enjoyed a fishing boat during our stay here and we were hoping we would use it in Washington. The car packed, towing latch in order, boat attached, we began our journey. Not far into our travels our outdated car started protesting. We got a few more miles and were in the middle of nowhere before it gave up entirely. There was quite a hike to get help and then we made arrangements for a more suitable car, one with enough power to tow a boat to Washington.

We made use of temporary quarters while we began our search for a place to live. Rentals were not plentiful and I was getting discouraged when I ran across a beautiful Georgian home in Alexandria. It was almost walking distance to Mount Vernon in a peaceful, quiet setting. I checked on the schools for the children and everything was just what we wanted. I'd never owned a home; in the service we stayed in an area just long enough for orders telling me where I would be assigned next. Our record this far was for two and a half years. Financing had to be considered and the only way I could see to do it was to use Eve's insurance. She had two policies, one I knew about and another on her own, just in case I was left with the children, (she thought it would help take care of them;) I'm thinking the children needed a home and I was certain she would approve of this one for them. I negotiated, found a price we could be comfortable with, and bought the home. Since Helen didn't cook and we were no longer privileged with stewards, she contacted her friend in Vista, California, Helene Kampe, to see if she would consider coming and living with us and do the cooking. The children said she didn't know much about cooking either and they remember eating a lot of chicken pot pies that could be warmed in the oven. But everything seemed to be in order, so I reported for duty in Washington.

I would be the inspector general for twenty-six months, away from home most of the time. My assignment was to be the eyes of the commandant, not to catch people, but to report the state of affairs on all commands throughout the world, stressing "I'm here to help and if it's something we can take care of, we will find a way."

The G-3s were charged with providing people trained in the areas required, and we needed to make certain the right number of people got there. The Viet Nam War was going on and Brute was getting a little testy about the kind of people we were getting, but a G-3 could not resolve this problem. I was asked in addition to visiting bases, if I could give some attention, much needed attention to recruiting. I started visiting colleges and universities, going back to places where I had taken my training, to get qualified educated men interested in becoming Marines; high school graduations were also considered. (Authors note: These speeches give an insight into his leadership.)

Inspector General
required, traveling,
recruiting and speeches.

As part of the work I was doing as the inspector general I should include the context of what we were doing to recruit. The reason the business I'm in now, is developing in young recruits a feeling they would like to be part of a corps that would serve their country with honor. Seeing they are physically fit and self disciplined, if our country has to call on us we will give full measure of devotion, hoping always, our leaders are right. But right or wrong, carry out our assignment with all the strength we can muster. I will beg indulgence for at least three of the recruit speeches. It seemed I was giving one every month, and since they were somewhat similar, sharing three will be enough. Two of the schools I attended, the other I returned to, was Texas University. Texas A&M had lost a football game to them, but I've recovered, so I'll begin there.

Commissioning Exercises University of Texas
Austin, Texas
4, June 1966:
It is a particular pleasure for me to be here today, under pleasant circumstances, for it is the first time I have been in Austin since Thanksgiving Day, 1932, after Texas University had administered a very humiliating 28-0 defeat against the A&M team. Of which I was a member. I can recall with pleasure, however, in 1931 and 1933 on Kyle Field, our team was able to win both games. I was fortunate to have played in the days when it was still traditional that the Aggies couldn't be beaten on Kyle Field. So much for nostalgia.

You young men are about to embark on an experience you will value for the rest of your lives. For some of you, your military career will be relatively short, and you will resume a civilian occupation, but all of you for the next few years will be officers of one or another of our armed forces. Your assignments will be varied and you will be located from one side of the world to the other. But one thing will be common to all of you. You will command men.

Our weapons, our means of transportation and communication become ever more complex and sophisticated, but the basic element, the most important asset, the heart and soul of our armed forces, will remain and always has been, man. A military commander may conceive the most brilliant plan of battle imaginable, but it is in danger if the men who are to carry it out are poorly led. On the other hand, a weak play is quite likely to succeed if the leadership is exceptional.

While we are concerned primarily with military leadership, I can assure you the experience you gain in dealing with men will be of immeasurable benefit to you in any field of endeavor in which you may engage in the future. I have talked to many Marine reserve officers who have returned to civilian life, and who have stated the most valuable experiences they had while on active duty, were the daily contact with their men. The opportunity to discover what motivates them and particularly to see the difference of which they are capable when well led.

You may be wondering what is so different about leading soldier, sailors, Marines and airmen and leading anyone else. The principal difference is in your relationship with your subordinates. You are the boss, but you are more than this. You will be responsible for every aspect of your men's lives. Not only work performance, but their welfare, their appearance, their entertainment, their morals, their general well being. This gives you tremendous power and whether you exercise this power wisely or foolishly will determine your success as a leader.

Men respond very sensitively to leadership, be it good or bad. I've never in my career seen an indifferent command. It is either proud of itself and competent in the performance of its duty, or it has low morale and performs poorly. While the circumstances under which a command operates will either hinder or assist in the maintenance of high morale and effectiveness, it will not finally determine it. Many people have the idea USO shows, extensive recreation programs and fancy lounges are required for morale. Let me assure you these things, by themselves, will not make a happy and efficient command. The greatest boon to morale in any organization, is belief in itself. The unit that knows what it is doing is worthwhile and will do the job better than any other like unit in the world, is the unit with good morale. The way to generate these feelings is through dynamic, aggressive leadership.

Don't misunderstand me, the recreation, entertainment and other comforts are all necessary when they can be provided, but they are not the things alone that produce morale. Factors today, which will affect your problems of leadership, did not exist when I began my career. Young men today are far more independent than they used to be, they generally have traveled more and because of the improvements in mass communication, they know more about the world. Generally speaking, they want to know more about why things are done the way they are than the way they used to be. There are very vocal young men who employ various widely published methods to dramatize their opinions, which of course, they have a perfect right to hold. All these things can, and do, affect the thoughts and feelings of the men you lead and present a particular challenge to your skill and dedication as a leader.

You, too, are thinking persons, and you have your own opinions about things, but your job as an officer is to inspire the enthusiastic and competent attainment of the objectives of your command regardless of personal opinion. Once the civilian heads of our government have made a decision to employ armed forces, our job is to carry out our orders faithfully and expertly and to inspire all whom we command to the same dedication.

I believe the most important aspect of this job is example. Your men will overlook many of your shortcomings, but they will not overlook a poor example. On the other hand, enthusiasm, professionalism and integrity displayed by you will be reflected in everything done by your unit. You must be sincerely interested in your men. It is not enough to know their names, and birthdays, you must get to know them, so well you know their hopes, their fears and their problems. You must establish such a rapport they will want to discuss any problem or question bothering them with you. In other words, the relationship you establish must be one in which your men have complete trust and confidence in you. Never forget what to you may be a simple thing, to a man who relies on you, it may be the biggest problem in the world, and one which in his eyes is unsolvable. If you can establish this relationship, I can guarantee your men will follow you anywhere and will never quit until the job is done.

The next suggestion I will make is, go out of your way to make every man in your organization feel if it weren't for him, the whole outfit would fall apart. This isn't as hard as it might seem either. You know, all of us have to feel our work is appreciated and the only way we know whether it is or not is to be told by our leaders. A word dropped here, complimenting a man on his work, or an indication in some way you are aware of his contribution and appreciate it, will pay tremendous dividends in quality of performance.

What I have said about leadership applies on the battlefield or in a bureau office in Washington. I personally think the rewards of combat leadership are greater than any other a man might receive. But I admit I am prejudiced. I can say, when a man tells you, if you go to war again he wants to be in your outfit, it gives you a sense of personal satisfaction and pride no amount of money in the world can equal. But whether in combat or not, the respect of your men for your character and qualities of leadership rather than for what your social or economic position might be, is something you will treasure the rest of your life.

Before closing, I would like to say a few words to the wives and soon to be wives, who are here today. Your husband or fiance has chosen a career, even though only for a short while for some, that requires dedication. He may from time to time have to leave you for longer or shorter periods of time (I left for China nine days after I married and it was a year before my bride would join me.) He will have to move with disruptions to a normal life. His rewards will be great, however. The respect of the men he commands, the knowledge he has been of significant help to men who have problems, and the feeling of satisfaction at having been in the service of his country. You ladies will share in all of this. In fact, much of the success he enjoys will be determined by your attitude and actions. There will be rough times for you ahead, but you, too will have rewards. You will know you have contributed significantly to his success in an honorable profession and his pride in being an officer of the armed services. I salute you.

To all of you, good luck and God Bless you.

I was asked to speak to military schools, and high schools, as so many of these young people were looking forward to a career, and of course, my love for the Marine Corps, would direct me to a Marine Academy, one where I had graduated.

Marine Military Academy, Harlingen, Texas
28, May 1966:

You young men have completed the first phase of your education. I'm sure there have been times during the past twelve years when you thought that your education process was never going to end. For as long as you can remember you have been going to school for nine months of every year and it must have become very wearisome. But I repeat, you have completed just the first phase. The process of your education will continue throughout your lifetime. So far, you have been more concerned with acquiring the tools with which to secure a real education. You have been learning facts, formulae and methods, but possession of these tools does not make a person educated. You must now begin to use the tools, discover meanings and relationships as they apply to your life and society. Only when you do this effectively can you claim to be educated.

I don't know, of course, what the future holds for you individually. Some of you will continue with schooling in colleges and universities. Some may attend technical schools and still others may interrupt or conclude your schooling at this time. All of you will soon have to take your place as citizens and assume the responsibilities of citizenship. It is of this I would like to speak this morning.

As you move into adulthood you face what must appear to be an uncertain future. The world is seething with unrest. While we fight a war on one side of the world, we are troubled with differences with our allies on the other side. We are concerned with the fear of inflation or recession here at home. Our people seem to speak with many voices and we are not always certain of the motives of the various groups which loudly proclaim their point of view. We are concerned with the convulsions brought about by changes in our social order and many, many other problems and concerns. In short, it may seem to you as you stand on the threshold of your adult life that everything is really goofed up and that the generations which will have preceded yours have made a thorough going mess of things.

While I will not for a moment try to tell you nothing is wrong with the world, I would like to point out your generation is not the first that has been confronted where problems seem insurmountable. When I graduated from Harlingen High School in 1930, the country was in a midst of the Great Depression. To me it seemed inconceivable a country as rich as ours could have been so terribly mismanaged where a person couldn't find any kind of a job, even though he was willing to work at anything. Just a few years later the high school graduating classes were faced with the fact Europe was at war, and there was a great uncertainty as to whether or not we could be involved. Then the graduates of 1941 took their places in a world at war.

We could go back in the other direction and find our country has been facing periodic crises ever since we declared our independence. Before, the graduates of other lands were facing the same kind of crisis. While there seems to be more problems today than can ever be solved, we should not despair. We will never solve all our problems, for as fast as we solve some, others will arise to take their place. In fact, a world without problems would be a rather dull place indeed. Boredom is bred where there is an absence of challenge.

The challenge for you today is a progressive, intelligent, and patriotic citizenship. Rome fell, not because it was overwhelmed by barbarians. Rome was finished before the enemy attacked; it was finished because citizenry who should have cared about the integrity of their civilization were more concerned with the pursuit of pleasure.

Any great nation can fall if its citizenry fails to take interest in it. If they lose their pride in the values it represents, if they become lazy and adopt a "Let George do it" pose with respect to their responsibilities as citizens.

Let me give you some guidelines or rules, if you will, in my opinion, that make the difference between a responsible citizen and one who is merely a parasite on the body politic. First, the foremost among the characteristics which must be possessed by one who claims the title of good citizen, is a willingness to accept responsibility for himself and his own actions.

In this day and age, with our affluent society, and the popularized versions of psychiatry and psychology which tell us there is always a reason in our past life for our present derelictions, some use it to escape responsibility. Tendency to look for someone else or something else to blame for one's derelictions and shortcomings must be guarded against at all times. An example of what I am talking about is the Marine who is absent over leave because he has missed a train, and then feels he is being treated unfairly when he is punished for not returning on time. He wants to blame the train which left him, rather than himself for not allowing enough time to be sure he could catch it. In civilian life, the boy who had broken a law and whose father arranged for him to escape responsibility, will develop a habit

CHAMBERS OF
JUSTICE BYRON R. WHITE

November 1, 1966

Dear General:

    You were very thoughtful to arrange the visit to Quantico and to commit your own time and energies to providing a most interesting time for me. I did appreciate it, I learned a great deal and, most of all, I was impressed with the people I met and the procedures employed in the training program. And this is to say nothing of the fun it was to meet and chat with some of your new second lieutenants in the Corps.

    It was a privilege to be with you and I hope that we shall meet again sometime soon.

                       Sincerely yours,

                       Byron

Maj. Gen. Raymond L. Murray
Assistant Chief of Staff, G-3
G-3 Division
Headquarters, Marine Corps
Washington, D.C. 20380

of not accepting responsibility.

Accept responsibility, seek responsibility. It is a sign of maturity and the prime characteristic of a good citizen. We have many rights granted to us by our Constitution, the right to vote for our representatives, the right to express our ideas, the right to print news and opinions, the right to equal justice under the law and many others. Some people tend to forget these rights are conferred on all of us equally and not just certain individuals and groups, so I would say another important rule for the good citizen is to respect the rights of others. We are free to express our own opinions, let's respect the right of another to his. I am not trying to say we shouldn't change his opinion if we think he is wrong, but we should do it by proof rather than insulting or belittling him.

There are many activities perfectly legal, but which we don't show some restraint, will infringe on the rights of others. A simple example is the use of a public facility such as a campground, a library, or public streets. We are all free to use facilities but if we litter or deface them we are infringing on the rights of others to enjoy these facilities. Many times people are merely thoughtless when they commit these acts, but it is a sign they have not learned to be good citizens.

It goes without saying a good citizen needs to be well informed. I realize how difficult this is. With the vast increase of knowledge, the complexity of our system of doing things, and the proliferation of the means of mass communications it seems almost impossible sometimes to master the facts of our existence. We hear many conflicting voices, some of them quite shrill, and have a most difficult time sifting facts from the amount of information and misinformation with which we are bombarded. Yet we must continually try to get at the truth of the questions facing us. For only by knowing the truth can we act intelligently. Your training here at the Marine Academy has been directed at teaching you to seek the truth. In your activities as a citizen you must demand proof in the arguments of those who urge you to think the way they do. An unthinking electorate which accepts whatever a flowery talker tries to sell, without demanding proof, may soon find itself controlled by such a talker. History affords some sad illustrations.

It is not enough to inform yourselves solely in matters of local or national domestic issues. The citizen today must be informed in world affairs. We face many dangers and there are nations in the world who would give us a problem if they could. This can only happen if we permit it through ignorance or inattention. It is not only necessary to know and understand the objectives of our enemies, but also know and understand our friends and allies. We often become impatient with our friends when they don't see things the way we do. We must try to understand their interest and the pressure under which their leaders operate which cause them to think the way they do.

Then finally, we must participate in the affairs of our community and our nation. Too often, I feel, we have the tendency to consider service to our country as meaning only military service, or service in time of war. In my judgment, service to one's country is the responsibility of every citizen all the time. The problems that face us deserve the most intelligent thought and action of every member of our nation. The most basic way in which you can participate is by voting for the candidates which, in your opinion, are best qualified to handle the reins of government. There are many ways in which to participate, however, and you can make your views known through various forms. You can serve on boards in your communities, showing you care deeply for the community and your nation. And find ways to participate.

Lastly, I would urge you to support your government wholeheartedly. I don't argue you must always agree with what is done or you should not support practical alternatives to what is being done, but there is a big difference between supporting practical alternatives and merely opposing a present course of action. As an example of what I am talking about, one may not agree we should have become involved in Viet Nam. But we are there and will be there until some practical way is found to conclude the participation. There are many characteristics of a good citizen, but I believe these have been discussed and are fundamental. If everyone in our nation possessed these characteristics we would never need fear we would be overcome by anyone.

I congratulate you on your achievement this graduation represents. You have set a standard, as the first graduating class of the Marine Military Academy, others will be proud to follow. As I leave, I think it will be quite fitting if you take as your motto for the future the same motto of the Corps which serves as the inspiration of your school: (Semper Fidelis, Always Faithful) Faithful to your standards, faithful to the things your academy stands for and faithful to the ideals of your country.

Visiting the bases, my report most often was: Everyone here is trying to do a good job. In my visits, I was hoping to impress them enough so they wouldn't regret seeing an inspector general in the future. Most of the units I inspected were in fairly good shape. Now and then there would be an imperfection, but nothing insurmountable. I was very thorough and did run across problems in the record taking. Sometimes it was putting a new recruit, not qualified, who put something in the records in the wrong area, or simply made a mistake. Most of the equipment inspection turned out well. They seemed to have very well qualified mechanics who were keeping the motorized vehicles going.

Other than being away from home at rather long intervals, my job was very enjoyable. We seemed to be running into a lot of minutia, not with the inspections but with work coming from Washington. I was convinced there was a tremendous amount of work in Washington making work, rather than necessary work. Then there was, also, some speculation I was being considered being ordered to Viet Nam.

Had wanted for some time to visit my alma mater at Texas A&M, in appreciation for the education I had received there. And with the rumbling going on about Viet Nam I felt this must be taken care of sooner than later. I had received an invitation to speak to the university, and we came up with a date of **April 21, 1967:**

Texas A&M University
College Station, Texas

This is a proud moment for me. Thirty two years ago I left this campus and became a second lieutenant in the United States Marine Corps. Because our installations are located principally on the Atlantic and Pacific Coasts, it is not convenient for me to return to the campus except at occasional times as I was en route from coast to coast. In spite of the long periods between my visits, however, I have felt close to the school because of the many A&M men I have met and been associated with through the years. In fact, of the eight Aggies who entered the Marine Corps in 1935 and 1936, four are major generals and still in active duty. Two others have retired within the last three years.

A&M, as you are aware, has provided leadership in our armed forces for all the years of its existence, and the point I wish to make to you today is now and into the future, the need will continue to exist for the leadership our school so ably provides.

When I was five years old, American doughboys, among whom were many Aggies, helped bring to the end the terrible war devastating Europe. The armistice of 1918 ended the war being fought, " To make the world safe for Democracy." It was hailed as the "war to end all wars." For insurance, good men established the League of Nations. I grew up during the peaceful years of America in the 1920s and 1930s. There were a few minor disturbances in the world during those years of "Peace." The Graeco-Turkish war of the 20s left us the present bitter legacy of Cyprus.

While I was an Aggie like you, fighting the battle of the books here at College Station; Ruhr Valley, annexed Czechoslovakia's Sudetenland and then swept Poland. Twenty years after the armistice, a second world war, which was to end all wars and make it safe for democracy, had begun. It proved to be more widespread and more devastating than the first world war, or any other war in history of mankind.

The equivalent of a Division of Aggies sacrificed personal comfort and desire for duty and country and led the American G.I., soldiers and Marines to victory. Many of those we honor today made the supreme sacrifice in that war.

In the aftermath of Hiroshima and Nagasaki, the awesome weapons created by the technology of our modern civilization caused reasonable men to be certain war had to become too horrible for any civilized nation to contemplate waging again. These reasonable men established the War-Crimes Tribunals and the United Nations Peace-Keeping Organization to prevent the dreaded Horseman of the Apocalypse from ever riding forth to scourge our civilization. But the echoes still reverberated from the bells that heralded the "dawn of peace." The formal treaties ending World War II, had not been signed by civilized men, when armed conflict raged in Greece, the cradle of western civilization, and in Jerusalem, where the Prince of Peace walked.

Shortly thereafter, Aggies once again led, and bled, when violence shattered calm in Korea. More names were added to our memorial muster. Even today, Korea knows not peace, only an uneasy truce.

Since the truce was enacted. in Indo-China, Egypt, Indonesia, Pakistan, Malaysia, Lebanon, Tibet, Iraq, West Iran, the Congo and South Vietnam, the hounds of war have been unleashed. From East to West, back and forth across the earth, they have ravaged the land, and people have died defending their homes, their freedoms, and their families. Even today, as we honor our fallen heroes, who gave theirs so we might live in freedom, war boils in Vietnam and simmers in a dozen other places. I hope I have made it clear, in my lifetime, although reasonable men and powerful nations have earnestly sought peace and the means for preserving it, even the most Christian nations, with the most advanced technology of our modern civilization, have become embroiled in war. And it seems fairly certain, with the strains and pressures now existing in the world in our lifetime and the foreseeable future, although we dream of the hope for peace, war will be a sober reality.

You, and your sons after you, will be called upon to lead your fellow Americans as warriors. More than two thousand years ago, Aristotle observed all that's necessary for evil to triumph, was for good men to do nothing. One may also logically assume until the millennium, when strong warriors are good men, it behooves all good men to be strong warriors. The holding of this muster is overwhelming evidence of the immeasurable contribution which the Texas Aggies have made as good men and as strong warriors, so you and I could continue to enjoy the freedom and the way of life they have known. And their mantle of responsibility and leadership has now descended upon your shoulders. I therefore urge you to accept the challenge eagerly and to prepare for it to the utmost of your ability. For the task of the leader is becoming increasingly harder and more complex. When I took the oath of second lieutenant of Marines in 1935, our recruiters could be highly selective in the few recruits they accepted. Most were high school graduates and many had attended college. The private first class was an experienced, tested and proven veteran, relatively mature in age and skilled in the profession of arms. Usually he was the product of a stable home where God and Country were synonymous with virtue. The weapons and tactics we employed were relatively simple. Our rifles were single shot, bolt action, Springfield 03s. We could direct air strikes and naval gunfire by semaphore flags if our radios failed. Our enemies in World War II and Korea were readily identifiable. They wore uniforms and deployed on the battlefield in the conventional manner.

Those of you who will become lieutenants in these times must cope with leadership problems which my generation of lieutenants never imagined. It has been predicted the Vietnam War may last for several more years, and many of you will see duty there. Many of our troops may be high school dropouts, from broken homes, who have grown up in an atmosphere where patriotism is embarrassing, authority is resented and ridiculed, and the draft is something to dodge.

It will be incumbent upon you to lead these men so they can operate computer-directed missiles, maintain the radars which drop bombs from supersonic jets on unseen targets, or simply shoot automatic M-16s with fire discipline so your ammunition re-supply does not become an insurmountable logistics burden at a critical moment. You will have to engage and destroy an enemy who fires from ambush and then disappears in the jungle, while you avoid accidentally destroying the lives and property of innocent people, whom this enemy hides among and uses as a shield.

You must not only fight in this environment but you must also help to rescue a primitive illiterate from economic, social and political chaos, literally building them into a nation. The French were there a hundred years and failed. Indeed the task sometimes seems impossible, but we must try. There is no alternative if you wish your children to enjoy the free air and precious rights we have taken for granted. If we fail, how long can our nation endure? Where can we find liberty if we are surrounded by totalitarian enslavement?

Already, it is only a rowboat ride away from Key West, and there are mighty efforts to spread it. Nearly a billion Communists are being indoctrinated and committed to bring about our downfall Perhaps among our own people, too, some manifestations of Mao Tse Tung should be required reading for he has written down the plan and the strategy; his lieutenants or minions must slavishly obey his divine precepts.

The U.S. Marines fought skirmishes and rebuilt a couple of nations in the Caribbean, the year I graduated and was commissioned. Mussolini's legions invaded Ethiopia with guns, tanks and planes. Japan was persuading China to become a member of "The Greater East Asia Co-prosperity Sphere" while the Russians and Finland fought in ice and snow of the Arctic

203

Circle. Nazi storm troopers occupied most of Europe.

No one has dictated to you, and no one will, what your course of action will be. Your privilege, your responsibility, your sacred trust as free men is to devise, judge, invent, accept or reject, build upon the wisdom, the contributions of all those good men who have gone on before you. It is now your task to perpetuate and make work the noble experiment of mankind begun in our land in 1775. It will be your obligation to extend the fruits of your experience to those who need and seek them.

As far as mind's eye can peer into the future, your country, and the world, will need the courage, the skill and the dedicated leadership of good men who are strong warriors. The need has never before been more critical nor the challenge more demanding.

I have every confidence you will prove equal to any compelling task. God Speed. And Thank you.

The rumblings were soon correct and I left headquarters in September 1967. My orders were as deputy commander of the 3rd Marine amphibious force, Viet Nam.

Korea taught us we may have wars in far off places where it may be difficult for the fighting troops to understand why we are there. The only way we can win under these circumstances is to have a force of finely disciplined troops, who are proud of themselves and their outfit. Who feel their job is to fight for their country and if necessary die for their country. Korea made very evident a few basic things Marines have always felt. First, our nation must have a force in readiness, highly trained and ready to go on a moment's notice. This is what our Marine Corp provides. Since Korea we have three divisions strong, we are not only ready, we are ready from a deployment standpoint, and with our division wing in Japan and Okinawa ready to join the amphibious force of the seventh fleet, we can be anywhere in the western pacific on very short notice. From the third division in Okinawa there is a battalion landing team of helicopters constantly afloat, ready to be moved to any area of Southeast Asia. Our first division on the west coast can move in either direction and our second division and wing on the east coast has a floating BLT in the Mediterranean at all times, and another BLT in the Caribbean. This is the reason for the business I'm in now, developing in young Marines a feeling they can never let their Corps or their country down. Developing a pride in themselves and in their Corps. Seeing they are physically fit and self disciplined, so when our country calls on us, we are ready in full measure and hoping our leaders are right, because we are there with all the strength we can muster, only then will most of us come back alive. I have spoken so often, these words. Now they will be put to the test, in a war I couldn't understand….Viet Nam.

JACK VALENTI
PRESIDENT

May 17, 1967

My dear Tiger

Although it's not my alma mater, most Texans are
well aware of the annual muster of Texas A. & M.
It is a unique and moving program to honor those
graduates who have given their lives for their country,
as you so well stated it. I read General Murray's
speech that you placed in the Congressional Record
and I want to compliment you for doing so and General
Murray for making a most inspiring address.

With warmest personal regards,

Sincerely,

Jack

Honorable Olin E. Teague
House of Representatives
Washington, D.C. 20515

205

HEADQUARTERS MARINE CORPS ROUTING SHEET
NAVMC HQ.335-CMC (REV. 9-84)

μ 5-1028

DATE
2 5 MAY 1967

RTG.	OPR. CODE	DATE IN	DATE OUT	INITIAL	ADDRESSEES
		5/25			COMMANDANT
					ASSISTANT COMMANDANT
					MILITARY SECY TO CMC
					CHIEF OF STAFF
					DC/S (PLANS & PROGRAMS)
					DC/S (RD&S)
					DC/S (AIR)
I	A	5/25	5/26	R	SECY OF GEN STAFF
					G-1
					G-2
					G-3
					G-4
					ADMINISTRATIVE
					DATA PROCESSING
					MCCC
					FISCAL
					INFORMATION
					INSPECTION
					PERSONNEL
					POLICY ANALYSIS
					RESERVE
					SUPPLY
					WOMEN MARINES
					LEGISLATIVE
					COUNSEL
					STAFF DENTAL
					STAFF MEDICAL
					STAFF CHAPLAIN
					OP-09M

FROM
Assistant Chief of Staff, G-3

TO
Commandant of the Marine Corps

SUBJECT
Letter from Motion Picture Assn of America, Inc.

REMARKS (Entries to be dated and signed)

1. Submitted as possible interest.

2. I believe I'm "over the hill" from Hollywood.

R.P. Murray
R. L. MURRAY

206

Chapter Nine

Viet Nam

September, 1967:
Ordered to Viet Nam as a deputy commanding general, with Headquarters at Phu-Bai. I was assigned to guarding the so-called Rocket Belt and patrol of the area. We were on a hill out some distance from Da Nang, and the 1st Division stayed there the entire time I was in Viet Nam. The 3rd Division was placed further north. By the time I arrived there were doubts being raised from several of the generals about the feasibility and the unreality of the war. Also the people were beginning to ask why we were caught up in a civil war.

Problems had been going on for some time. Ho Chi Minh, president of Viet Nam, was born in French Indochina in 1890 and lived in central Viet Nam as a communist, and led attacks against the French. By 1934, he was successful in driving the French from Viet Nam. In 1958, his guerrilla army began their fight to bring the entire country under communist rule, and by 1966 had rallied the country by telling them it would be a long war, and would not negotiate until he could liberate the south and achieve unification.

Unrest began at home, Defense Secretary McNamara left his post and rumors concerning domestic controversy were circulating. It was felt McNamara was not in favor of escalating the war and Johnson was not coming up with a solution. Criticism was also coming from professional military people. General Norstad, former NATO commander, General Mathew Ridgeway and General James Gavise were questioning the policies. The public was growing weary and the opinion polls were not in favor of the war, and congressional sentiment was also lagging. We were told we were protecting our domestic way of life. President Johnson commented, "A different kind of war, there are no matching armies or solemn decoration."

There was a sense of unreality about this war. The Marines were not tuned in to the amenities, The war was operated from very comfortable quarters, with hi-fi sets and many comforts of home. Conventional wars always had a fixed enemy; you fought, and were either killed or your enemy was defeated. I was out of my element to be assigned the job of overseeing the MacNamara line 1 Corps. This was a bulldozed, wide strip that ran to the mountains in directions of Dong Ha but stayed along the flatlands. General Westmorland kept pressuring to get it finished. The line was to be equipped with barbed wire and sensors. It was like putting an Erector Set together, with missing pieces. The attacks took a toll on the material, some probably, in battle, used against us. It troubled me and everyone else when we had to fight and then go back to building it.

The materials coming in, designated especially for the line, had been used in local defenses. These materials, as in an Erector Set, were shipped according to a place, right size and length specifically for each purpose. Everyone was confused about where the materials had gone. We came to the conclusion , when we were being attacked, some of the material was used for defenses. We could never get a handle on it. In my opinion it should have been engineered with a separate staff, a technical one where I could have been an inspector or supervisor. It was not a workable setup and was terribly frustrating. Who was going behind the barbed wire and resetting sensors? It did get done in a haphazard way, and was abandoned after the TET offensive.

Learned later, the initial order for the line came from the Department of Defense, the logistical, engineering and technical should have been done by the same people, not farmed out. They were building something no one believed in and it should not have interfered with whatever else was going on in the war. It would have been worthwhile in a sense that it might have helped to keep people informed.

The TET offensive began on January 28, 1968, and was to be a week long truce celebrating the Vietnamese New Year. The rules of war were ignored and we were ambushed. We are questioning again our purpose of being there. The war had now lasted through four presidents, Eisenhower and Kennedy sending in military advisors, and Johnson and Nixon presidents during a limited war. Where and when will it end?

I had the feeling I was out of the mainstream of things, the feeling I wasn't advised on everything going on. I was used to running the show, and it was difficult not to have any responsibility. My ideas might have interfered with General Cushman's and this couldn't happen, as it was his show. We were all working for him. I was ADC 3rd Division in Okinawa and it was frustrating being a deputy commander, not a comfortable position for someone who has spent years as a commander. It was a strange war, unlike conventional warfare. With civil affairs and battleground coincided, we would fight over villages back and forth, behind lines we established. The pressure the commander was under must have been tremendous, deciding who deserved the closest attention, civic or tactical action. Your sole concern should be your actual combat. To try to defeat the enemy and keep him from defeating you.

I was assigned to community action platoons, which I liked, going to the villages and trying to help them. We hoped this would make a difference. There was always a chance some were Viet Cong and might come back at night and kill us. Our objective was to prevent the Communists from taking over South Viet Nam, not to win a war. I felt the better way to have fought the war would have been to defend major population centers, do only enough patrolling to accomplish the mission, and equip and train South Viet Nam armies to do their own fighting. Troops at Khe Sanh? There were no people there. We should have worked on infrastructures that could support themselves.

This type of war is not the Marine Corps forte. We charge, wipe out opposition. We are not an occupation force. We do not do best with this type of warfare. What we learned was: we should not get involved in a military war such as that. We were there, General Westmorland said we should be there. Once the attack started on the Khe Sanh, there was nothing else we could do. There was a constant stream of visitors through headquarters, and at times it seemed everyone from Washington and the White House took their turn. They wanted to know what was going on but it took a hell of a lot of our time. Everyone had an opinion and many thought we should sweep the area, get it over with. This would have taken twice the troops we had.

Then a health problem kicked in, and my balance didn't seem right. Viet Nam is hot, humid and run over with the biggest mosquitoes ever recorded. Whether I caught something from them or another bout with malaria, or a gall bladder acting up, something was wrong. I thought it would go away , as it had in the past, but it didn't. It just got worse. I was coping with that, when a dear close friend, General Hochmuth, was killed when his helicopter was shot down. Then, a second tragedy, when a Marine attached to our security compound was senselessly and deliberately shot and killed by a fellow Marine; feeling the way I did, there seemed to be a hopelessness creeping in, about this war.

My balance became worse. I was actually afraid to drive a car. Then I began worrying, if something happened to Bob Cushman, and I had to take command, with this health condition and my feelings about the hopelessness of this war, I wondered if I could do it. I managed to drive to the command post. I knew I had to level with Bob about my health problem. My first sentence was, " Bob, I need to be relieved. Something is wrong with me. My balance is off, to a point I don't trust myself driving a car. I feel like hell and if I don't get some medical attention soon I will not be of any use to the Corps or my family." I didn't get any further with my problem. Bob looked at me and said "I've noticed you haven't been up to par and I was going to ask you what was wrong. But I didn't know how serious it was. I'm not going to relieve you. There isn't anything to relieve you for. I'm putting you on the

Vietnam.
Standing Tall.

210

With Senator Bush in Viet Nam

Congress of the United States
House of Representatives
Washington, D.C. 20515

WASHINGTON OFFICE:
LONGWORTH
HOUSE OFFICE BUILDING

DISTRICT OFFICE:
FEDERAL OFFICE BUILDING
HOUSTON, TEXAS 77002

January 12, 1968

Dear Mrs. Murray:

I am just back from Vietnam. Last week I had breakfast
with your husband and then he took me on a tour of some
hamlets.

I thought you might like to have these pictures. They
are pretty good of him. My feelings will not be hurt
if you clip me out. They were taken at Swinwa Village.

The General looked well and game me a great time. The
respect his men have for him was evident. I particularly
noted his warmth and affection for those beguiling Vietnamese children in the hamlets.

Don't bother to acknowledge. I simply wanted to give you
this first hand report on your far away husband. Let's
hope he will be home soon.

Very truly yours,

George Bush, M.C.

Mrs. R. L. Murray
1100 Emerald Drive
Alexandria, Virginia   22308

GB/vj

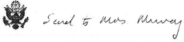

Send to Mrs. Murray

GEORGE BUSH

212

Illness of Gen. Murray Forces Return to U.S.

EVENING TRIBUNE News Report

Maj. Gen. Raymond L. Murray, deputy commander of the 80,000 Marines in Vietnam, was flown from the combat zone today after being stricken ill suddenly, an official said.

The Marine Corps declined to reveal the nature of the illness but said medical treatment in the United States is necessary. Nor would the Marines say where he was being taken.

Murray, 55, one of the corps' most colorful combat leaders and former Camp Pendleton base commander in 1961-62, became deputy commander of the 3rd Marine Amphibious Force last October.

Popular Figure

The Los Angeles-born general, a popular North County figure, was first awarded the nation's second highest combat decoration — the Navy Cross — during World War II when he led a battalion in the Saipan campaign.

He later received a second navy Cross during the Marines march to the sea from Chosin as commander of the 5th Marine Regiment during the Korean war in 1950.

Served In Washington

Before being assigned to Vietnam, Murray was Marine Corps inspector general and chief of personnel in Washington.

Murray was promoted to his two-star rank in 1963 while commander of the Marine Corps Recruit Depot at Parris Island, S.C.

Murray is one of the most highly decorated Marines currently on active duty. Besides the Navy Cross, he was awarded four Silver Star Medals for heroism at Guadalcanal, Tarawa and in Korea.

He also holds the Army's Distinguished Service Cross and two Legion of Merit awards.

GEN. RAYMOND L. MURRAY
Flown to states

General Named

WASHINGTON, Sept. 2 (UPI) — Maj. Gen. Raymond L. Murray is the new deputy commanding general of the 76,000 Marines in Vietnam. Murray, a much decorated World War II and Korean War veteran, was named yesterday as second in command of the Third Marine Amphibious Force.

MARINE GENERAL IS ILL

Maj. Gen. Ray Murray Flown Back to United States

Da Nang, South Vietnam (AP) —Maj. Gen. Ray Murray, deputy commander of the 80,000 U. S. Marines in Vietnam, was stricken with a sudden illness and was flown to the United States today.

The Marine Corps declined to reveal the nature of the illness but said medical treatment in the United States was necessary.

The 55-year-old general arrived in Vietnam last October.

Appeasement...Helen's Cadillac and mink.

Our home in Alexandria, Virginia

sick list and calling the doctor right now." This he did.

The doctor's recommendation was, " The first thing you do is to get the hell out of here. Preferably on the next plane and get to a hospital, stateside."

My letters to Helen alerting her about my health had been very difficult to write but I thought I should prepare her:

12 February: I wrote:

For the past several weeks I've had a problem, and I decided today I must go to Bob and tell him about the trouble I'm having with my balance, and the dizziness coming with it. He and the doctor are going to figure out what to do. In any case I will be home soon, possibly to Philadelphia for treatment.

I know this is a great blow to you, but I simply felt the Marines here deserved to have someone in my position who was not about to fly apart. I don't know how soon this will take place, but it will be soon. I'll let you know real fast just as soon as I know.. Ray

My letter February 13:

The decision has been made . I will turn in to the hospital here sometime today and within two or three days will be evacuated to the states. I don't know if it will be Philadelphia or Bethesda, but I'm sure it will be one of the two.

I hope you will forgive me, God knows, I've gone through hell with this thing, and I still feel, under the circumstances, I did the only thing I could honorably do. I'll try and get word to you in advance of my time and place of arrival. Ray.

I was flown home and put in Bethesda Hospital, and my condition worsened . A feeling of hopelessness took over as the doctors didn't come up with a reason for my illness. I began to believe they thought I was goldbricking, because the tests they were taking were never conclusive. I wondered if goldbricking meant I was afraid of being in a war, but I was carrying enough lead in me, battle scars, and medals to prove that wasn't so. I asked to be evaluated.

I was put into a holding area with young troops who had lost arms, legs, body parts and more of them coming in every day. If I wasn't depressed before, it was on its way to doing the job now. Finally two doctors came in for the evaluation. We went through the usual examination: blood test, blood pressure, listening to my heart, asking me about current news events. They picked up the crossword puzzle I was working on, asked about the Pacific wars and Viet Nam… remember chatting for about an hour, then they left.

Said they would see me the next day, and they returned the next day.

They showed me their report, most of it I already knew. Male 6 foot 3 at 185 pounds, all vital signs in order, very alert, a wiz at crossword puzzles, aware and up to date on current affairs. Seems well adjusted for the trauma he has just been through. There is a fever, and something is still wrong. They asked me to walk across the room. I was a little wobbly but I did, then they put a cloth from one of their kits over my eyes and told me to walk across the room. When I was free from support I fell. They helped me up and immediately they were M.D.s They tell me " We think we know what is wrong with you, but it is advanced to a serious condition. We need more tests but it appears to be a viral infection of the inner ear; all symptoms are leaning that way, your loss of balance, the nausea, vomiting and an indication of vertigo. If it is what we think it is you will need to be in the hospital for some time. It has advanced beyond being something simple to take care of. You might have dizziness and imbalance for a number of months and a chance of vertigo for some time to come. We will do all the tests but we feel this is a possibility." That was what it turned out to be and I was months in the hospital, and the ugly head of vertigo , throughout the years, often made its appearance.

I was opposed to our intervention in Viet Nam in the early sixties. We didn't win the war, and it was a tough war to fight, because we never knew who we were fighting. I don't know if we ever accomplished anything or not. Maybe it was wrong to go there, but when a decision is made to go and at the time of the decision, if you don't go, you won't have a military organization. Much, I would have done differently, but that too is hindsight.

The retired generals began to speak out. Had time on my hands to read newspapers, and the opinions of these seasoned combat generals. One in particular caught my eye as I had known General David Shoup for years and he was now retired as the Marine Corps commandant, submitted his thoughts to the Senate.

"The United States cannot defeat North Viet Nam, in South Viet Nam, because they (the Northerners) don't have to send the bulk of their forces down there. We can continue these murderous methods and the North Vietnamese will finally have enough of it. But I don't think the gains, no matter how greatly they are embellished, will ever equal one thousandth of the cost."

This seemed to be the thought he was trying to get across to the Senate, and although he spoke for some time I'm certain the newspapers didn't carry his entire outlook on the war.

Other questions were beginning to surface about the physical evidence of two attacks on our destroyers in the Tonkin. The first assault was on 2 August, and didn't get a response from Washington. The second incident was doubtful. When it was reconstructed, it seemed it was a created incident and a report was written before the 4 August attack, and was most likely referring to the first attack on 2 August, when the North Vietnamese were salvaging boats damaged two days earlier. Was the intelligence manipulated? Or, a massive intelligence failure.?

We also know the communists lied about the U.S.S. Pueblo, at the time of its 1968 capture. We asserted the Pueblo was in international waters and gave data to prove it. Captain Lloyd Bucher was following orders and was in international waters at all times. The North Koreans had no evidence to the contrary. To save 82 crewmen we signed lies we knew were false in advance. This undermines the morale of our military. If we are going to continue to be a world power we should learn something from each incident where we ourselves have not come through with the highest honor.

I was sounding like a Monday morning quarterback, or someone with too much time to read the papers. I began to feel better but, not knowing how long it would take to clear the problem and thirty-three years as a Marine in service, it seemed time for me to step aside and allow these energetic young officers an opening to fill. I retired, 1, August, 1968. Helen was not happy, she enjoyed the social life and the amenities that came with being a Marine general's wife. I don't think she ever quite got over it. Thinking of ways to make her happy, I gave her a Cadillac, a new mink coat, and promised her we would take two months driving across the U.S. back to California. I think she was happy we would be going back to the west coast. Our next project was to sell the home in Alexandria.

I was not in Viet Nam very long, four or five months would have covered it. Most of what I've said is my impression of the war. Some things I know for a fact, some I don't. My health, and these feelings were what I had, when I asked to be relieved and flew back to Washington.

For the first few days, out of habit and under orders for thirty three years, I thought every phone call coming in was or could be new orders. In time I did settle in and began to look forward.

Retirement is something everyone anticipates, but for me it was time to think about the future and the pragmatic possibilities in the real world. I was still young enough for another career and had twins to educate.

Our first objective was to decide where we wanted to relocate, find a home and get the girls in school. After a very democratic gathering of the family the discussions all turned to the west coast. All other decisions could be taken care of later with the exception of a good golf course; that was a must.

These were the thoughts I was dealing with when we started packing for our trip to the west coast and our new life

Chapter Ten

Retirement

Our beautiful Georgian home in Alexandria, Virginia was difficult to give up. First, because of the location; just a stones' throw from Mount Vernon, and because of the way it was financed. But we needed a home where we were going. Driving across the miles, my mind often reflected on Eve's thoughtfulness and the consideration she had for her children. She often spoke of the kind of home she wanted for them, and she would have loved that one. The home was put up for sale, and, because of the location, brought twice the price I paid for it.

We decided to take our time driving across country, making it a geography lesson for the girls, and stopping, of course in Alamosa, Colorado, where Helen was born. We couldn't relax too long; we needed to find a place to settle as we still had two sixteen-year-old twin girls at home, and the school year was rapidly approaching. The boys had been on their own for some time. Bill was married before Helen and I married, Jim had graduated from high school, was working and continuing his education. Danny was in the Marine Corps.

By summer, we were in Oceanside, combing the area for a home to buy. We considered ourselves lucky having relatives who offered bed and breakfast, while we searched. Finally, a home in the Fire Mountain area met our needs. It seemed ideal. It had four bedrooms and three baths, divided into two wings. One side gave the girls privacy and the other side was the master suite. Helen had a fourth bathroom added and practically an additional new room she called her dressing room and closet. It was now a large family home, adequate for the family.

The girls soon graduated from high school. It had been easier for Sherry, but Terry had been battling dyslexia all her life and was working her little heart out trying to maintain grades that would get her into college. She wanted to be a nurse; she knew her dyslexia would keep her from getting an RN so she was striving for an Associate of Arts Degree and a license as a Vocational Nurse. She made it and the entire family went to her graduation. She was a happy young lady; she would be doing the work she loved in geriatrics. She loved the elderly patients and they loved her.

During this time, Helen began having trouble with her digestion, and checked into the Base Hospital. Her trouble turned out to be in the colon; she was scheduled for and given a colostomy. She did remarkably well, bounced back from the surgery with a positive outlook, and often took time to counsel others, who would be facing the same surgery. She spent time at the hospital working as a volunteer and served on the Board at Tri-City Hospital. She was in her element, happy with her social activities; in fact, she was on the telephone so often, I threatened to get her a headphone she could carry along with her.

Sherry did a semester at Santa Barbara, came home and went to work for an attorney. During this time she met a young doctor she eventually married. Helen and I enjoyed vacations, cruises and a return to Korea. Terry was always coming up with surprises, and, for Father's Day, 1974, she brought in a Guinness Book of Records, so proud, it was she who discovered Chesty Puller and I had both been listed for our medals.

We settled in. I played golf three times a week. Tried my hand at real estate; the only knowledge I gained there was respect for the agents who could follow through and make a living. Long hours and waiting at open houses takes a special kind of person. It wasn't for me. I was also asked to run for a political office. Being a general and having the last word on decisions, I felt, would not be what a council could cope with. So I decided I would keep my thoughts and ideas on how to run a city to myself. I preferred to work with the youth in the community, the veterans, and once a month get with my buddies, the survivors of the Chosin Few. I joined and became president of the Rotary. This was nice as, the year I was president, the convention was in Canada.

The children were all married and we had grandchildren who came to visit. Of course they were the brightest and the best looking children around, and we often joined in with the other grandparents comparing these little miracles. Retirement years are rolling by quickly and life was going almost too well.

My vertigo kicked in again, and the only good thing about its resurfacing, was it finally had a name to the problem I had been battling for so many years. Labyrinthitis. Once you've had it, it never goes away, and you are prone to recurrences, again and again. Vertigo always accompanies it; any time I've been above the second floor, and happened to be near a window, the dizziness and the imbalance kicks in. This time it brought an additional hearing loss, worse than any in the past. Then, Terry became ill. She seemed tired all the time, so we had her move in with us so she could get some rest. Her checkup diagnosed: Non-Hodgkin Lymphoma. She put up a brave fight, this little girl who came into the world weighing just three and a half pounds. She had overcome so many obstacles in her short life. Had

Being groomed by my favorite hairdresser.

worked so hard to qualify for the work of her dreams. We had so hoped she could have enjoyed this happiness longer, and in better health. It wasn't to be. Terry died July 9, 1997, at forty-three years old, the same age her young mother, Eve, died.

Our steps got slower. I managed my golf dates, trying to break my age. The advantage of getting older is the score goes up. Helen and domestic chores have never been compatible, and she suggested we find a facility where we could retire, have our meals prepared and the cleaning taken care of. We started looking around our area and as far north as Laguna Beach. After several months of checking, we decided to stay in our own area and chose La Costa Glen.

There was a big problem, the unit we wanted wouldn't be available for two and a half years. It did give us time to start down sizing and getting rid of what we were not going to use. It was overwhelming, a forty-foot attic of castoffs. Friends had given Helen everything they didn't know what to do with, and she saved every cork, broken rubber band, pencil, belts, broken pens. She never threw anything away. She had been raised during the depression and always thought we might need it. This seemed to be something she had difficulty dealing with and her old problem surfaced. She could not keep anything in her stomach and checked into the hospital. She was diagnosed with a protrusion in the colon, scheduled for surgery, and the surgery went well. For two days she seemed to be improving and we talked about her coming home the next day. I stayed and visited until nine o'clock and went home to get some rest. About two AM the hospital called and said her blood pressure had dropped and was continuing to drop. I rushed back to the hospital and she didn't rally. She died early March 23, 2000.

I was alone for a year and a half and my condo at La Costa Glen was still not ready. During the year, I visited the children in different areas of the mid-west. Each of them had been busy checking facilities where they thought I would be comfortable, but my heart was in the west, preferably on the west coast. During the last thirty years this had been my home and my friends were all here. My military service had been in climates either freezing cold or steaming hot, I didn't want to live anywhere where there would be drastic climate changes. So, back to Oceanside, and settled in waiting for my condo to be finished.

In February, a friend called. Zona had known Helen better than she knew me and seemed to be a little hesitant in asking if I would judge a youth forum. She had been working with juniors and seniors from high schools for over twenty years, doing forums on problems facing society. She mentioned I would enjoy the day, as these young people were well informed and ready to deal with current problems facing society. Our job was to initiate a subject, then facilitate, but not enter into the discussion. There would be a table scoring for each student and our judging would determine if we had candidates to send on to the next level of debate at Whittier Law School. From there they would select three students to go to Japan for the same kind of forum with other countries. I was asked to continue to the Law School, but I declined. The additional three selected came from other areas of the United States, two from Hawaii and one from Northern California. Zona would accompany them to Japan and they were to leave August 2.

After the forum, I called her home several times to tell her how much I enjoyed the day with the students, and I also wanted to add what a good program I thought it was. Through March and April there never was an answer, then one day in early May she answered her phone. She said she had been at Pine Mountain Lake, helping her daughter move to a smaller home. Her son-in-law had died of small cell lung cancer, and her daughter needed family there for support. She had written me a note thanking me for judging the forum , but thought since I was alone, I might like a home cooked meal. Would I like to come to dinner? And would May 29th be a suitable date? Of course I answered "yes and may I bring a bottle of wine?" She answered ," if you have a favorite." (Author's note: Held up finishing this book for a year, wrestling whether to include this diary. Decided I would delete parts that are sacred to us and write the rest in its entirety)

Ray: "I've never kept a diary, but from the minute I walked into her home I didn't want a minute of the time I would know this lady to get away, so I could savor every memory."

These are my entries:

The minute I walked in the front door, a feeling came over me, not easy to explain. It seemed I had seen this home a hundred times before. From foxholes halfway around the world, from the frontlines in the middle of a battle when I was wishing I would again feel the warmth of a home. You could tell this was someone who loved her home. She had taken a hundred year old home, about ready to fall in, and made it into one of the most charming farmhouses I had ever been in. I commented on how charming it was and she mentioned most of the furniture had been in the family forever. She thanked me for noticing.

She apologized for setting a table in the kitchen. It had been a rough day at work and she thought a fire in the small kitchen fireplace would lend its own charm.

It didn't take long to know she was a good cook. She had a roast going on the rotisserie, and I could see a dessert on a sideboard. I can't remember any time in my life when I felt more comfortable. It was a delightful evening and when I left I thanked her and kissed her. Believe me, she didn't know it then, but I knew somehow I was going to marry this girl.

30 May:

I called and asked her if she would go to the Arts Museum Ball on July 26. (I thought she would remind me it was two months away, but she didn't) She answered she would be leaving August 2 for Japan, and this would be a lovely event to look forward to before she leaves.

I had a little time to reflect where and how often I had seen her through the years. She traveled a lot with her work, as she was a master restorer of porcelains, and worked from time to time in England and France. When real estate was good she would switch to selling real estate and had been working on four hundred acres she wanted reserved as a wildlife reserve. This was completed; she found the money for the financing through the state, and mentioned this was one of her proudest accomplishments (I'm writing this all down.) She tells me she doesn't have much time for social functions, and has always thought it would be nice to have all her work caught up so she could. From time to time I would see her at charity events, but it was the only time I remember seeing her, and a time or two when she would stop by and pick up Helen to take her to Hollywood to another charity event. Now I'm observing this person, there is something about her very different. She is tiny, and I have been known to like tiny women. She can be in a pair of jeans, or a formal gown, and comfortable with who she is. I think beautiful, nice, but not gushy. She must have forty awards for her work and charities. She seems to be without ego, but anxious to be working on the next project.

Now she tells me she has bought property near her daughter who lost her husband. It was just a statement, I don't know whether she is moving or has bought for an investment. She didn't say. I am beginning to think I'd better see how deeply my feelings are or maybe she won't be here when I find out.

All through June I'm thinking of ways we can get together and I called and asked her out for dinner on July 2. She seemed surprised and asked me how I knew it was her birthday, (I'm not about to tell her); she answered "sounds wonderful, I'm certain it will be the best offer I'll have, thank you." Again it was a lovely evening, we could talk for hours, I talked she listened. My son Danny came to visit, and I wanted her to meet him, so I asked her to dinner. After dinner we were sitting in the living room and I thought I would test the water. When I said, "Danny you must come back when Zona and I get married," she smiled but she didn't say a word. I'm beginning to think, now I've had it.

She didn't say much on the way home, but when we stopped at her door she said, " I didn't say anything, Ray, because you are such a nice person and I didn't know how to answer, because asking me in front of Danny, I

She said...Yes.

didn't know if you wanted Danny to come back and visit or if it really meant you wanted to marry me. If you really mean it, it would be nice to be asked. Then I asked her and she said, yes.

The next day I called the office where she worked and asked Shirley Demory what size ring Zona would wear. She said she didn't know but would call back in a few minutes. I understand she asked Zona to walk down to the jewelry store with her. While they were there they tried on rings and came up with a size. I took care of the rest.

I tried to condition her to some of the crazy comments people would be making about our ages. But I can tell you, with me, the older this happens the deeper the love and commitment. I had loved twice before, but this time I am in love, head over heels in love and there is a difference. It was a turning point in my life and certainly the happiest. I knew my real friends would be delighted; they were, and kept expressing how lucky we were to find each other. I wanted to show her every place I've been, bases, schools, vacation areas, any place where we could tie our lives together.

This decision wasn't reached overnight. I had been wined and dined by several nice families. Many times to round out their table there was an eligible lady. All of them lovely, interesting ladies and I enjoyed their company, and I would have hoped they found me to be an interesting dinner partner, but I'm sure they were as anxious to get on with their lives as I was with mine.

With Zona, I was never so sure of anything in my life. As we were deciding on our future, there was only one thing we didn't agree on. She wanted a small wedding, just family. I wanted the whole world to know the happiness is still there in the "golden years." So I promised her ten wonderful years and apologized it couldn't be fifty. She agreed to a big wedding and we set the date for September 29.

We decided on Quebec, Canada for our honeymoon, and it was to be in the walled city at the Chateau Frontenac. We did everything honeymooners do and found time for sightseeing and shopping. I bought her some Channel No. 5 and an ornament to add to her Christmas collection. We either walked or buggy-rode within the entire area of the walled city. Knowing the French history was also outside the walls, we took available tours to the islands where the permanent residents live. Stopped by the little stands and the little cafes for homegrown treats. Bought some of their local honey and some wonderful French pastries. The tour brought us by the beautiful churches; one special visit to the cathedral Pavarotti chose to do his Christmas special. We were in Quebec five days, every day was special, but we had scheduled a reservation in New York and it was time to leave.

In New York, we had a beautiful room at the Palace Hotel, looking down on St. Patrick's Cathedral; from this elevated area she watched

226

cardinals come and go, I did not go near the window, afraid my vertigo might kick in. We did venture down to attend a mass.

Zona doesn't like to shop for herself, so I slipped out to Saks Fifth Avenue. I wanted her to have something we purchased on our honeymoon. I bought her the most beautiful dress, and she loved it. Also thought she should have a necklace to go with it and I took care of that.

The only negative in the honeymoon was the recent devastation of 9/11 and we both agreed we didn't want to go near the area. We didn't.

We flew to St. Louis and were met by Sherry. Had a nice visit and played some golf. Decided it was time to go home. We had much to get in order there.

We put away wedding presents. Zona wrote thank you notes and we settled down to everyday living. We always wonder, if and when the butterflies settle, if the glow will still be there. I should not have been concerned. She was everything I had ever hoped for. I'm happy with her in the morning. She wakes with a smile, goes to the kitchen and makes coffee, brings it back, where we sit in bed and discuss our plans for the day. I'm happy with her at night; after a nice dinner, and she can cook; we enjoy time together, read books, watch a special or just enjoy a quiet evening. I'm reminded of a phrase from Shakespeare, I've remembered from an English class. "If this be error and upon me proved, I never writ, nor no man ever loved." By now I've gotten to know the girl I married. We have travels to plan, parties to attend and a whole lot of living to do.

November:

Was our first military engagement was in the Bay Area. I was booked to speak in Walnut Creek and in Danville. We flew to San Francisco, and we were met by Don Monson, who would be our driver. They sent us a winner. Don had been a Marine, was there for every engagement and extended a courtesy to driving us around the areas familiar to Zona. She pointed out a home she referred to as 517. A home on Florence Avenue, in Piedmont. A special family home of beautiful holiday memories. Also a tour of the Claremont Country Club, where her brother-in-law had been the professional for thirty-five years.

Thanksgiving:

We decided to invite family to our first Thanksgiving dinner, and were well on the way to planning it when we had a desperate call from grandson Eric. He had just returned from a vacation in Europe, had been home two weeks. When he was there he had met some nice people and commented if they were in the States be sure to give him a call. Well, they were here; what was he to do with them for Thanksgiving? Two of them could speak English, somewhat, and they would interpret for the others. We decided this was what Thanksgiving was about, so bring them along. I decided I would help with the dinner. My job was to peel potatoes. Everything went well and the potatoes were peeled nicely and clean; than I put too many peelings in the disposal and clogged the drain. Really clogged. Where do we get a plumber on Thanksgiving? We decided there were two ways to go. Our guest, were arriving in three hours. If we could get a plumber in an hour and a half, we could go on with our plans, if we can't we will meet them at the door, invite them in for a drink and start calling restaurants for reservations for nine people. The problem was solved when a plumber decided he would help us and still get home in time to watch a football game.

The quests arrived and the fun began. After they settled in, we were asked why we celebrated Thanksgiving. We seemed to get through about the Indians, but when it came to the Pilgrims, we were in trouble. The interpretation wasn't getting through, we could see by the puzzled expressions on their faces. Finally one of the girls came right out and asked when would they get to meet the Pilgrims, and were they expected for dinner. We muddled through somehow and they seem to understand the party would be the guests who were already there. It was an enjoyable day, especially for my wife, when the guests who were staying at the Hilton, said our dinner was better than any they had had at the hotel.

The next hurdle to cross was to get my furniture off to Missouri,

Time out for the hospital ball.

where Sherry would decide where it was to go from there. Her brothers had put in their request and she was building a new home and could use some of the pieces. Zona said she had more furniture than she would ever need, as she had been in the antique business, had family pieces and had sent home pieces from her travels. Now she needed a place to put them. And we wanted to get the home in order for Christmas. I called "Sullivan's Moving and Storage" and with some of their best packers it took us two days to get everything ready to be stored in their warehouse. It would be there until Sherry gave the signal to send it to Missouri.

I don't know how we did it, but we were reasonably settled in by Christmas and the home was beautiful. Our first Christmas was one to remember.

Christmas behind us we started looking towards a busy 2002. On April 25th we flew to Quantico, Virginia to attend an SBC reunion. We toured the area, visited the school where I had taught basic training, walked through the area where the president's helicopter was based and were told not to take pictures while it was on the ground. My ego reached out a bit and wanted my wife to see where my picture was hung in one of the school buildings. She was impressed.

We were quartered in unit 109, a comfortable three bedroom, two bath cottage, equipped with anything one would need, from a well equipped kitchen to an office with computer, a living room with fireplace and a television. We watched television and waited out a projected tornado. It was a scary and exciting experience for us. I had weathered through typhoons, and we both were veterans of California earthquakes. This was different. No one else seemed concerned, but we didn't go to bed, expecting any minute to hear where and when it was going to hit. Well, it jumped over us, shifted and bypassed Quantico and devastated an area in Maryland. When the weather subsided, we were able to go on with our plans to visit Washington D.C.

The weather was again beautiful and we were able to visit most of the places of interest. As a history student, it was exciting to Zona as she was seeing so many things firsthand, but it also brought a desire for more information, and since our time was short , she put it on a to-do list. Had another surprise I hadn't told her about. It was tickets to a Jacqueline Kennedy dress exhibit. A beautiful exhibit of over one hundred dresses Jackie had worn during her tenure as first lady. She said it didn't take long to appreciate the exquisite taste of this first lady. No glitter, Just fantastic materials, workmanship and design. The design, Zona said, was classic. The dresses would be appropriate today or any time in the future. It was a wonderful day in D.C. and this was one of the highlights I had planned.

We returned to Quantico to have dinner at Quarters One with General and Mrs. Hanlon. A lovely evening and a very memorable one.

Driving around the base, we passed by the home where Eve and I had lived and where we brought home our twin girls. A surprise was in store for us as the name on the sign was: Colonel Murray. For a fleeting moment, I thought we should stop and introduce ourselves, but had second thoughts when I remembered other times when unexpected guests arrived, and it wasn't always the best time.

Now it was time to leave and we were doing it reluctantly. Our visit there had been one to remember. But we had another important event to attend in Missouri. Granddaughter Jessica's wedding in June. From there we flew to Atlanta, Georgia to visit with Bill and his family. I also promised Jim and Bette we would drive to So. Carolina and go from there to Parris Island. Jim and Bette agreed to accompany us to Charleston, Beaufort, and Parris Island. As I've said before, I wanted to show Zona all the places I've been and this one was tops on the list. She couldn't get over the size of Quarters One and was so impressed with the history of the area, she put it on her list to research. It is nice traveling with someone who loves history, who is nice, asks questions we could answer; many brought back stories Jim and I told when we lived there.

August 2002:

Flew to San Antonio Texas to attend a Chosin Few Reunion. The Marriott, where we were staying, was on the banks of the " River Walk." It was also the choice of the survivors of the reservoir. Some of them remembered me and we had some nice visits. There was a breather and a free afternoon and I wanted to visit my alma mater; we rented a car as it would be sometime before we would be this close again. We drove to College Station, walked around all the familiar places. I pointed out the points of interest and when my memory allowed me to zero in would relate memories there. The stadium where I played football, was still something I could remember in detail. The museum where, in a cabinet, they had a letter I had written, and a picture of myself with MacArthur. When I attended it was an all male college, now it was co-ed, no longer a college but a university.

We called grandson, Brad, and his wife Alison to meet us for dinner. They did and brought along little Mackenzie, who was seven months old. Alison related most of her family had graduated from Texas A&M, back as far as a grandfather who was ninety-eight. So the college was very familiar to her. She had gone on to get a masters in ecology, at Denton, where Brad had done his student teaching. That is where their romance began. She was a Texan.

Now it was time to get back to San Antonio, and the reason why we were here. Vice President Dick Cheney was to be the keynote speaker. Everyone was interested to hear where we stood on Iraq and any advanced decisions being made. He had been held up somewhere and was two hours late. He didn't lose his audience. They were still waiting. He began, of course with 9/11 and how important it was to get a handle on the terrorists. They had intelligent information, Iraq, weapons of destruction, and Saddam was a terrible man that needed to be dealt with.

Our information was different: Osama bin Laden was the culprit and we were certain he was the cause of 9/11. The inspectors so far had not come up with any evidence of weapons. And the concept is: we are going to send troops into Iraq before the inspectors finish their job.

He lost me there. I found myself not listening and getting into my own thoughts on what was being taught in officers basic school. War should be the last resort not the first objective. There have been many generals in our history, some great and some we have doubts about. Some stands out in my mind and I carry a small notebook of some of their quotes. Those who had been in the frontlines and probably knew more about war than anyone in the room. So it was natural for me, being a veteran of three wars, to think of Eisenhower, a former president, almost forgotten by the Republicans, but was most in tune with the teachings of Theodore Roosevelt. We had been without war during his administration and taxes were spent on jobs and the building of the freeway system across the United States.

Eisenhower had a long career, reaching, in 1944, the rank of a five-star general, and serving as supreme commander of the invasion of Europe. He resigned in 1948 from the army and in 1952 ran for, and became president of the United States. He often quoted:

"The U.S. never lost a soldier or a foot of ground in my administration. We kept the peace. People have asked how it happened. By God, it didn't just happen, I'll tell you that." "I hate war as only a soldier who has lived it can, only as one who has seen its brutality, its futility, and stupidity." another one, "I have no patience with extreme rightness, who says anyone who disagrees with them is un-American." And another, after he left office, he worried about the military industrial complex and was not quiet about this quote, " 'In the councils of government, we must guard against the acquisition of unwarranted influence, whether sought or unsought, by the military complex. The potential for misplaced power exists."

One of his first introductions to the army was serving as an aide to General MacArthur. And he was constantly being told to manipulate information when MacArthur would say to him "we will tell them, what I want them to know." His objection was: when you manipulate intelligence, it could set up a principle for manipulating intelligence in the future. (Now my memory returns to Korea. And no Chinese in the war.)

Now I turned to another page and the quotes of another savvy warrior, Theodore Roosevelt. He welcomed criticism, and he often remarked, "To announce there is to be no criticism of the president, or we stand by him right or wrong, is unpatriotic and servile." He was willing to listen, and welcomed differences of opinions.

Another quote, "A man who has never gone to school may steal from a freight train, but if he has a university education, he may steal the whole railroad." and another, "Our aim is not to do away with corporations. We draw a line against misconduct. Not against wealth." Both men had been excellent military men; both had been presidents. We should pay attention.

My thoughts are now back in the present. Now: How far can a retired officer offer an opinion or would anyone be interested.? So I'll just sit here, be polite, and let my thoughts go back to what I taught in basic school. War is a sober reality and before we are embroiled; if we are going to play war games, we should have plans in place, they should be analytical and not reactive, ego's set aside, highly trained force in readiness, and be able to uphold the reason for being there. There should also be a definite exit plan. If it lasts as long as the Vietnam war, Osama bin Laden's threat to break us financially, .might be something we should not overlook. Going in without an exit plan, would keep us there for years an obligate us to restore the devastation we help cause. We should keep this in mind. Above all, loss of lives should be the top priority considered. Why aren't we after him instead of Saddam.? You can see I'm a worrier and it may not be necessary. There must be more to this than we know, but I can't help having the feeling we are heading for Iraq, without knowing enough of why. Two religions had been fighting in Iraq forever. It quieted down during Saddam's reign of power, but how will we deal with it, if it becomes a civil war and we are caught in the middle.? History affords some sad illustrations. I am also worried about the economy as I have survived one depression. Also, the main responsibility of any government are their borders, why are we ignoring, closer to home, what is happening in Mexico? Speaking of terrorist, the drug cartel seems to be taking over Mexico. We should be concerned not about if but when it will be crossing the border. (Note: These were Ray's worries before we entered the war…August 2002)

We've been invited out for dinner, a welcome reprieve from the seriousness of that convention, and I can put my worried mind to rest.

Back home to take care of speaking engagements, also an invitation from the Globe and Anchor Salute that I am being honored, in San Diego, hosted by the Marine Museum. We are keeping busy, just everyday chores and getting ready for the holidays. We really enjoy Christmas and this year we will have something special to look forward to, Brad and Alison are coming in from Texas, bringing MacKenzie here for her first Christmas.

2003:

The holidays over, in April, we joined Fred and Sherry in Hawaii. Fred was there for a doctor's convention, and the three of us enjoyed the beautiful island.   Kauai is one of the quietest of the islands, the only noise coming from the clucking of the bantam hens calling their chicks, and an occasional crow from a rooster, letting us know who is in charge here.

The story is: Captain Cook went aground with a shipload of bantam chickens. Some were rescued and do what chickens do and populated the island; now the island belongs to them. No one pays any attention to them, just be careful not to step on the chicks or back up a chair on a family.

We are now into a quiet summer when a call comes in from Ollie North, about an interview for "War Stories." It was to be about Korea. It kept me busy for a few days going over notes as I didn't trust my memory on everything. The meeting was scheduled at Camp Pendleton. Found Ollie North to be very knowledgeable, and certainly well qualified to do "War Stories." His homework had been done and his questions were in such a manner making it easy and comfortable to answer.

September 29:

We had reservations for a weekend in Catalina for our anniversary. Neither of us had been on the island since we were teenagers, and we were surprised at the changes. The beautiful ballroom had been changed to a museum. It really brought home to us that the big bands were a thing of the past, and younger groups were now in charge. We decided to also leave the snorkeling to them and take a few tours.   Our reservation was at a bed and breakfast with a beautiful view of the bay, with a fireplace in the room. A television was a must, and a highlight of the visit was sitting in this lovely room and watching the release of "War Stories." My part had been cut a bit as there were other stories to work in the time slot.

October 2003:

We were invited to San Francisco for a Korean reunion. Koreans sent dignitaries and several notables from Washington attended, among them George Schultz. We stayed at the Marine Memorial Club, in the heart of the business area of San Francisco. It is a club the Marines can be very proud of, open to all Marines, regardless of rank. We had dinner with James Brady, still very much a Marine, a successful author, who has written several best sellers about Marines.   He gifted me with his latest book "The Marines" and autographed it with a very flattering note. " For the great Ray Murray, from the author who got there three years later. With much admiration. Jim Brady."

Home again for the holidays: Thanksgiving went well and two days later, kept an appointment with my doctor. It was to be a routine checkup. The doctor suggested I have additional tests made at Tri-City hospital. Called Zona, and told her not to worry, it was for checkups. But she would need to come and pick up the car. This she did with the help of a good neighbor. We visited for several hours until it was my turn for them to start the checkups. She was with me every time I was awake, hoping every day they would say all was well and I could go home. Three days later, I've been told, I contacted a staph infection, I've been told this often happens in the hospital. I don't remember much of anything, for two weeks, then one day I recognize Zona, and asked what day it was , she answered "December 15." She was just told, if I continued to get better, I would be going home for Christmas.

December 19:

Fred Williamson put me in his SUV, Joe McMonagle was waiting at home to help him get me into the house and I was home. How good it was. Home always looks good but when it is decorated for Christmas, it brought back thoughts of how many years I had dreamed and been promised, when I was in the service, to be home for Christmas.

I was so weakened by the staph infection, I did not have the strength to stand. The doctor had told me not to be too impatient, as even athletes needed weeks to recover after being hospitalized for several days. I'm home again, but we needed to figure how we were going to manage. For three weeks we were assisted, 24 hours a day, by a local in-home care facility. Then it was the two of us.

I really appreciated the girl I married. I don't know how this tiny girl stood up to the work she took on. But she did. She never seemed to sleep; each time I moved she was awake, if I couldn't sleep she would massage my back and legs. Give me a bed bath, sometimes at two in the morning, warm the towels in the microwave, wrap me in them so I wouldn't get a chill, change the bed, by this time I'm relaxed and ready to go to sleep.

There is some romance in me and I've read a few such novels in my lifetime, but I've never read of this type of devotion. At two in the morning when she is worn out and beyond tired, I look at her and remembered when I thought she was beautiful, now I think she is "gorgeous."

By February I walked with a cane. In March, into therapy at Tri-City Hospital. April 19, after an hour's session on a treadmill, drove home, walked into the house , and felt my ankle break and I fell to the floor. This was the only time I've ever seen Zona panic. The look on her face said it all: We've come so far, dear God, help us through this. An ambulance was called, there was no room for me at Tri-City hospital and I was taken to Palomar in Escondido. It was a good choice. The ankle was set, surgery done steel support added, and now we are facing another long recovery. I was transferred to Carlsbad by the Sea, a rehab facility in Carlsbad, until my strength returned and could go home, June 3, I remembered the day, home again with my favorite nurse. My sister, Helen, pitched in when Zona needed time off, and we were very proud of ourselves.

(Authors note: this is where Ray's diary ends; and I continue with my own thoughts.)

Everything was going well until the end of October. He was dropping his food at dinner and I helped him into his chair. A few minutes later, I decided to call his dear friend, Doctor Jerry Colling. He came by and suggested we call an ambulance. Back to Tri-City Hospital for four days, then transferred back to Carlsbad By the Sea. The facility provided a way for him to vote in the election, and he had a twinkle in his eye as he held the ballot close, and voted so the rest of us couldn't see. The next morning, Carlsbad by the Sea called me and said he had been transferred to Scripps Hospital in Encinitas. My daughter, Pam and I were there within minutes. He was waiting for tests and joking with the technicians, again, assuring us it was just for tests. Three days later, his medical records from Scripps said: he had contacted another staph infection at Tri-City but they had it under control He was getting better and would be home in a few days.

Pat Murray, Ray's son Bill's wife, arrives, from Atlanta Georgia and, we are both visiting the hospital. She insisted I go home and get some rest. I was apprehensive as I had never left him with anyone but his sister, Helen. And Helen was so devoted to her brother, it was as though I were there with him. He was her hero, and he knew it.

He hadn't slept well the night before and they said they had a private room where he could get some rest. Sometimes he tried to get out of bed and we were afraid he would fall, so I said I would stay with him. We needed to be careful how he ate his food because he had trouble swallowing and his water needed to be thickened. Pat kept insisting I needed some rest and I should go home and get ready for him to come home from the hospital. Again, I cautioned Pat about being careful about the instructions. Reluctantly, I left the hospital. Stayed up until about midnight, and took the advice that I should get some rest. I could not rest, but almost dozed off when bolted up in bed with the same reaction from feeling an earthquake. Something was wrong.!

I don't remember the exact minute, but I know it was after midnight when I called the hospital, They called me back, informing me, Ray had gone into a coma and I was to get there as soon as possible. I called Frank Whitton, his aide when the General was at Camp Pendleton. He was there within minutes, and we were on our way to the hospital. Pat was standing in the hall, and she told Frank and me she had no idea this was going to happen. This was about the only conversation among the three of us that took place. We stayed there until morning waiting to hear of any progress. The doctor assured us he would keep us informed so please try to get some rest. Frank took us home.

The hospital report reads: " He was getting better every day, until he choked on food. When they resuscitated him, he was injured internally, and they couldn't stop the bleeding." The vigil was excruciating, praying every minute some miracle would happen and his beautiful smile would tell us he

had been through some tough times before. They gave him eight units of blood during the remaining days he was in a coma, but his blood pressure kept dropping. I was told again to get some rest , and I was called, after midnight, November 10, to come back to the hospital. I saw them wheel him into the hall, on his way to X-ray, heard the dreaded Code Blue.
Highpockets is gone.

My hero, our hero is gone. This wonderful man, whom, we will not soon see his equal again, died early morning, Veteran's Day, November 11, 2004.

17, November 2004:

The Navy Hymn was used as the processional, and eight hundred friends, members of family and mourners from everywhere were seated in the Serra Center of the Mission San Luis Rey, when I was escorted in by General Donovan. They were all waiting to say goodbye to their hero. I've heard silence could be deafening.   I was suddenly aware of the meaning. There wasn't a whisper in the crowd. Had a feeling, their thoughts, were as mine, how this man had played such a part in their lives. The short time we had had together and all the beautiful hours we enjoyed, just doing ordinary daily chores. Everything had a special meaning, gardening was more fun, fixing dinner was fun while he sat with me in the kitchen and enjoyed his one drink for the day, traveling to all the places he had lived and served in the military and the excitement he brought into even a small gift or occasion. When he tried to impress me by being a handyman and put the equipment back in the bathroom backwards and we needed to flush up instead of down. How proud he was when he could peel a nice shiny , clean potato. How mischievous he was when he voted at Carlsbad by the Sea, His presence brought life into anything or anyone he touched and the best in everyone around him.

I'm thankful for the few, but wonderful years we had together. Happiness I never thought possible. I can now say, I've been to the mountain top. How lonely it will be without him.

I must pay attention: General McMonagle is reading from the old testament.

Wisdom: 6:1-11

Next, Sherry, one of Ray's cherished twins, is reading:

Ephesians: 3:14-21

And Father Michel Gagnon the Gospel:

John 3, 5-17

An eulogy by Father Michel:

He describes Ray Murray as a "Man's Man, who stood head and shoulders above us all, but never used his position for himself. It was his humility that was paramount to his ability to lead. He was a man of deep faith, that is why we are here. That is why we loved him. He acknowledged us whether we were big or small. It didn't matter to Ray. He loved people."

The Choir is singing "Ave Maria" and my thoughts are wandering again. Often he spoke of times when he thought all was lost on the frontlines, he would hear the Catholic Marines saying "Hail Marys," and he found comfort from and hope listening to their prayers. Now I'm looking at the children and my heart breaks when I think of all the years he was away from them and how much they must have missed him.

The eulogies are continuing. This time it is his dear friend and golfing buddy' General Kenneth McLennan.

Highpockets is gone: But Ray Murray will always stand in the forefront of the pantheon of heroes. Whenever our country was involved in a conflict, Ray Murray was given a combat command. He never claimed credit for his outstanding performances. He always gave credit to the Marines who would do more than they were asked. He was not only an officer, but a gentleman. A legendary Marine, a hero, father, devoted husband,. How pleased his friends were when he related he had found such happiness with Zona. A public spirited citizen and friend. Having known him we are all better. He will always, always be with us. I'm a four star general and I look up to this man. He saw bitter fighting in several Korean campaigns and the Vietnam War. But he was best known for leading the 5th Marines Regiment out of the Chosin Reservoir, in 1950, in sub-zero weather. A feat never excelled in military history. He was a Lieutenant Colonel, filling the command of a Colonel; for this service General Douglas MacArthur personally presented him with the Army Distinguished Service Cross. An award rarely given to a person not in the U.S. Army.

Lt. Col. Frank Whitton, a long time friend and his former military aide: Highpockets is gone, but we will always remember the late general as a man whose leadership saved lives and who was always concerned about the well being of those whom he served, as well as his friends. While, a commanding general at Marine Corps Base, Camp Pendleton, he devoted efforts to improve the safety of the river crossing, on what is now College Blvd. By bringing this to the public's attention the bridge at College Blvd. and North River Road was built. It was named in his honor, on his birthday, January 30th, 2003. (The City of Oceanside and the Marine Division Association arranged jointly to dedicate the flagpole one year later).

His son, Jim Murray: I've always known his character would be his legacy. He was a man of loyalty, unselfishness and integrity, who knew, loyalty and truth are bound to come to the surface. He loved the Marine Corps and he loved you.

He often spoke of his golf buddy group and different organizations he enjoyed, and I would like to thank Father Michel for providing the spiritual guidance to Dad in the last five years.

The great turning point of his life was his marriage with his beloved Zona. On that I have testimony of a loving and grateful husband. "Zona came along and saved my soul." We share her grief today, but we also share her pride and the grief and pride of my brothers and sister.

Zona, none of us can take away the sadness you feel. I hope it is a comfort to know how much he means to us, and how much you mean as well. Your honor, your grace, your courage and above all the great love you gave my father. When these days of ceremony are completed and when he is laid to rest in a few minutes, under his beloved California Mission sky, we will be thinking of you as we commend to the Almighty the soul of his faithful servant, Raymond Leroy Murray. So in the presence of his beloved and indispensable, Zona, my family, friends and the Marines he so deeply loved, we say goodbye to a gifted leader and a gracious human being.

The choir is singing " Let there be peace on earth" and the Recessional The Marine Corps Hymn.

We have now said goodbye to a distinguished warrior, an honored citizen , a friend, a buddy, father and a devoted husband.

(Author: A First Lieutenant who had served with him, said, "You couldn't let him down, he made you think you could do the impossible, and you did, because you adored the man. His posture, his voice, his actions, he was an inspiration.)

"His leadership by example was superb" McDonald said. There wasn't a job in the regiment he couldn't do himself. He inspired people to do their best, no one wanted to let him down, whatever the cost, and there was a large cost in combat," he added.

"Everyone was proud to be in his outfit. They felt comfortable being under him because he never made a mistake. Nothing he asked of us was a chore; we respected and obeyed him with no fear of punishment, because we trusted his leadership."

During the campaign, Murray was assigned as commander of the 5th Marines, the junior officer among commanders of three regimental combat teams.

His regiment which served the longest time in the fight credited with ratings highest in combat effectiveness according to: "Frozen Chosin, U.S. Marines at the Changjin Reservoir," a retrospective prepared by the Corps for the Campaign's 50th Anniversary.

"Our main priority was to get up on the ridgelines and keep the Chinese from firing at our convoy that made a column through the mountains," McDonald said. "We attacked them and drove them away from the ridgeline. If they were there we fought them."

"(Murray) was an aggressive fighter and we were aggressive. The mindset was we would die before we would be taken prisoner. His organization and tactics made it possible for us to get out alive." McDonald credits Murray's command with saving countless Marines.

"We lost a lot of people from the Chinese and the cold, but it would have been a lot more if his tactics weren't so effective," he said. "We wouldn't have been able to control the road and would have lost all our wounded."

Murray, never inclined to comment extensively on his own accomplishments, offered some advice to Marine Corps leaders:

"Know your job thoroughly and make all your training as realistic as possible," he said. "Be serious about it, because the harder you train, the less lives you lose in combat

"Highpockets is gone, but his history is well known, and has been recorded many times. It will be sung for centuries, if the universe has any order at all. But, keep this in mind,:

Murray was the hero of the Chosin Reservoir in Korea, where he saved thousands of lives, by leading a fearful, bloody trek to safety."
John Van Doorn

Major General Raymond L. Murray, USMC (Ret.)
January 30, 1913 – November 11, 2004

A BRIEF SUMMARY OF
MAJ. GEN. RAYMOND MURRAY'S MARINE CORPS CAREER:

1935:   Entered Marine Corps from Texas A&M.
        Attended Basic School in Philadelphia for nine months.

1936:   Assigned to San Diego.

1937:   August 20: Married Evelyn Roseman.
        August 29: Sailed for Shanghai, China.

1940:   Stationed in Peiping as a Platoon leader.
        Eve joined him in 1938.
        Promoted from 2nd Lt. to 1st Lt.

1940:   July, Returned to San Diego for six months.

1941:   Promoted to Captain. Sailed to Iceland as Company
        Commander. Pearl Harbor occurred.

1942:   Returned to San Diego for six months.
        Promoted to Major. Became a Battalion
        Executive Officer.

1942:   New Zealand - Trained for combat.

1943:   Battalion Commander, Guadalcanal. (Two Months)

1943:   New Zealand, for additional training.
        Promoted to Lieutenant Colonel.

1943:   November. Landed at Tarawa.
        Battalion Commander.

1944:   Hawaii, Heavy training until June.

1944:   June, Saipan. Wounded, Evacuated to Hawaii.
         Returned to San Diego, Ordered to Quantico, Virginia.
        Instructor in Marine Corps School.
        Formed a Brigade for use in Caribbean.

1945:   G-3 Brigade sent to Camp LeJuene. N.C.

1946:   Ordered to China. Stopped in Hawaii. Orders changed to stay

In Hawaii.
Served as Deputy Chief of Staff to Garrison Forces in the
Pacific. Traveled a lot.

1948: Ordered to Camp Pendleton, Division G-4 Logistics.
Executive Officer of the 5th Marines.

1950: Commanding Officer of the 5th Marines.

1950: July... Korea.
Pusan Perimeter, Inchon Landing, Seoul,
Wonsan, Chosin Reservoir, back to Bean Patch (Pusan)

1951: Promoted to Colonel. Returned to Washington D.C.
Attended National War College.

1952-54: Commanding Officer, Basic School, Quantico Virginia.

1954-58: Stationed Camp Pendleton. Base Chief of Staff.
G-3 of 1st Division, one year, in charge of operations
and training.

1958-59: Stationed at Camp LeJuene, N.C. Base Chief of Staff.
Promoted to Brig. General.

1959: Stationed at Okinawa.

1960 6, June, ...Eve died.
Married Helen.

1960-62: Assistant Base Commander, then Commander.

1962-64: Recruit Depot Commander, Parris Island.
Promoted to Major General.

1964-66: Washington D.C. Inspector General, Marine Corps.

1966-67: G-3 Operations and Training Director of Marine Corps.

1967 : Stationed in Vietnam for three months.

1968: Returned to U.S. Hospitalized.

1968: August 1, 1968. Retired from Marine Corps.

TEXAS A&M UNIVERSITY

College Station, Texas 77843-1256
(409) 845-4728
FAX (409) 845-3320

J. Malon Southerland
Vice President for Student Affairs

July 9, 1999

MG Raymond L. Murray, USMC (Ret.)
1504 Laurel Road
Oceanside, CA 92054

Dear General Murray:

Congratulations on your selection for the Corps Hall of Honor.

I would like to add an invitation for you and your guests to join in a post-game reception at my campus residence after the Kansas game.

Best wishes.

Respectfully,

Malon '65

J. Malon Southerland
Vice President for Student Affairs

Murray, Maj. Gen. Raymond L.
"Ray" "1935"

All Southwest Conference football, and 1933, football letters,
1931, 32,-33
Most valuable player 1933. Assistant football coach 1934. Freshman
football coach 1934.

As a student, Murray was a Lt. Col. Commanding the infantry
regiment in ROTC and member of the T. Association.

Upon graduation, he was one of the first three Texas Aggies ever
to receive a direct commission in the United States Marines. (Lt. Gen.
Bruno Hockmuth and Col. Joe McHaney were the other two.) and went on
active duty immediately.

He received his BA degree in Liberal Arts with an English Major.
He served in the U.S. Marines continuously and has been decorated in
WWII, Korea, and Viet Nam. He retired from service July 31, 1968 and
made his home in California.

His medal decorations include:
(2) Navy Crosses, Distinguished Service Cross,
(4) Silver Crosses
(2) Legions of Merit
(2) Purple Hearts, Presidential Unit Citation
(4) Korean ULCHI medal with Gold Star
Korean Presidential unit citation, and several campaign and
theatre of war medals with battle stars.

During his 34 years of service in the Marines he has
commanded a platoon, company battalion, a regiment, been a
Commanding General of the Marine Corps Base, Camp Pendleton, Calif.,
Commanding General Recruit Depot, Parris Island, S.C. G-3
Headquarters Marine Corps, Inspector General USMC, and Deputy
Commander General Amphibious Force, Viet Nam.

He was the speaker for the Muster on campus, April 21,1966.

In the G. Rollie White Coliseum
1968

You are cordially invited to attend the

Globe & Anchor Salute 2003
Legends of the Corps

Honoring
Lieutenant General Victor H. Krulak, USMC (Retired)
and
Major General Raymond L. Murray, USMC (Retired)

Saturday, September 20, 2003
6:00 pm   Cocktails and Silent Auction
8:00 pm   Dinner & Live Dance Band

San Diego Marriott Mission Valley
Pavilion
8757 Rio San Diego Drive
San Diego, CA 92108

Civilian: Cocktail Attire
Military: Service "A"

RSVP by September 15, 2003
For more information call
MCRD Museum Historical Society at 619-524-4426
Tickets will be held in the name of the Host at the reception entrance

Room Reservations at the San Diego Marriott Mission Valley
619-692-3800

244

President's Welcome 2003

Welcome to the MCRD Museum Historical Society's annual Globe and Anchor Salute Dinner. The Board of Directors, Council of Advisors, staff & volunteers of the MCRD Museum Historical Society thank you for your support.

Tonight we honor two legends of the Corps, Lieutenant General Victor H. Krulak and Major General Raymond L. Murray, with a total combined service of sixty-seven years involving three wars. It is fitting that we, a society dedicated to preserving our Corps' history and presenting it to our Marines, the recruits and to the public, should honor these two who have been so involved in creating that history.

Within the next few months the Museum, with the support of the Museum Historical Society, will commence the long awaited expansion project which will include additional exhibits and displays. We hope that each of you will take the opportunity to participate in this exciting project.

Again, we thank you for your continued support and for sharing this wonderful evening with us.

Semper Fidelis

Don Fulham
President

FORMAL DEDICATION

of the

MURRAY BRIDGE

IN HONOR OF:

RAYMOND L. MURRAY

MAJOR GENERAL, U.S. MARINE CORPS (RET.)

30 JANUARY 2003
9:00 am

at the
INTERSECTION OF NORTH RIVER ROAD
AND COLLEGE BLVD.
OCEANSIDE, CALIFORNIA

General Donovan and Zona Murray

James Murray
Zona Murray

The 1st Marine Division Association Honors
The Memory of a Great American Hero

Major General Raymond L. Murray USMC (Ret)
1913 – 2004

Dedicated January 31, 2005

Family and sibling support.

Major General Raymond Murray

Vista Unified School District
Board of Trustees
and
Joyce Bales, Ed.D.
Superintendent of Schools

Invite you to attend the

Dedication Ceremony
for
Major General Raymond Murray
High School

2 p.m., Thursday, October 18, 2007

215 North Melrose Drive, Vista

RSVP to Raylene Veloz (760) 726-2170 ext. 2219

The school has been a success. The students are very serious about completing their courses and graduating from High School.

2008:   43 Seniors received their diploma's and all 43 are continuing their education. One scholarship was given to a student who will be going into law enforcement.

2009:   72 Seniors graduated.
         Scholarships are increasing..... This year 10 were presented.

As the school is getting better known in the community, more Service Clubs and individuals are becoming interested in seeing those students continue their education.

There can be no greater legacy to an outstanding man than:

The Major General Raymond Murray High School.

The End